Inside the Information Superhighway

Inside the Information Superhighway

Nicholas Baran

Publisher *Keith Weiskamp*
Copy Editor *Diane Green Cook*
Proofreader *Jenni Aloi*
Interior/Cover Design *Bradley Grannis*
Cover Photo *Richard Wahlstrom*
Layout Production *Bradley Grannis*
Publicist *Shannon Bounds*

Distributed to the book trade by IDG Books Worldwide, Inc.

Library of Congress Cataloging-in-Publication Data

Baran, Nicholas
Inside the Information Superhighway/ Nicholas Baran
p. cm.
Includes Index
ISBN 1-883577-10-1 : $19.95

Printed in the United States of America

10 9 8 7 6 5 4 3 2 1

Contents

Chapter 5 The Highway on the Move 107

Chapter 6 A Matter of Policy 129

Preface

This book about the information highway covers one of the fastest evolving and most widely talked about technologies of our time. But in spite of the outpouring of articles, talk shows, and books covering the subject, the information highway remains a mystery to most people. We are confronted with a deluge of new terminology and buzzwords such as "cyberspace" and "bandwidth," and in the end, most people read or hear these terms with only a foggy notion of what they mean. This book attempts to dispel the mystery. While readers with technical backgrounds will find useful information in this book, the book is also aimed at those who have had little or no exposure to the basic ideas and issues that form this amorphous concept called the information highway.

The information highway doesn't really exist as yet. Some people think that the now-famous and insanely popular Internet is in fact the information highway. This book covers the Internet in the context of a much broader information highway of the future—one that is in the very early stages of construction, with the Internet as one of its primary foundations.

This book tries to present the big picture. It contains what I believe is a very useful resource guide, but it is not a catalog of services. It is not a "how to" book, nor is it a highly technical book. If you're looking for in-depth technical discussions of the difference between TCP/IP and FDDI, you may be disappointed. But if you're looking for some simple, straightforward explanations of both the technology and the legal and social issues surrounding the information highway, hopefully you will find this book useful and informative. At least you'll be able to talk bandwidth and e-mail at your next cocktail party.

The technology and issues that are shaping the information highway are changing with breathtaking speed. It is therefore a tremendous challenge to write a book on this subject that will remain timely and current and not become outdated before it appears in the bookstore. I have tried to focus on the issues and technical topics in a general way, so that they will remain relevant over the next few years. For example, I avoid getting into specific business mergers and regulatory decisions, because, as anyone who follows the daily business pages would have noticed, these kinds of things are totally unpredictable. In early 1994, when I started the research for this book, I could have easily devoted a chapter to the pending merger of Bell Atlantic and Tele-Communications, Inc. (TCI). That chapter would now be outdated because the merger fell through. Instead, I discuss potential mergers of telephone and cable companies in more general terms so that the insights apply to *any* such merger.

After finishing this book, you should have a pretty good idea of what the information highway is all about. You'll know enough to discuss the topic intelligently, and you'll have enough resources to find out more and to get more directly involved, if that's your intention.

Before plunging into the subject, I would like to acknowledge a number of people who have contributed to the writing of this book. First of all, I would like to thank my editors at The Coriolis Group, Keith Weiskamp and Jeff Duntemann, for their patience, support, and excellent suggestions throughout the project. Thanks are also due to Shannon Bounds of The Coriolis Group for her cheerful and timely assistance; to my long-standing colleague Jonathan Erickson of *Dr. Dobbs' Journal*; and to Andy Reinhardt of *BYTE Magazine*. Thanks to Professor John Donnelly, John Webb, and Geoff Allen, all three of Washington State University; to Dr. Patrick Mantey of the University of California at Santa Cruz; to Clifford Friedman of Bear Stearns; and to Rory McGreal of TeleEducation New Brunswick. Thanks also to Vince Emery; Ron Mahan of KPBX Public Radio in Spokane; and Joe Wiencko of the Blacksburg Electronic Village. Above all, I would like to thank my wife, Esther, for her unswerving support and encouragement during those tough times that all writers endure. I never would have finished this book without her.

Finally, I would like to acknowledge four publications and one online news service, whose excellent articles and coverage of information highway related topics were real life-savers: *The Wall Street Journal*, *BYTE*, *Scientific American*, *The New Yorker*, and *Newsbytes*, which I was able to read on the Byte Information Exchange (BIX) online service.

Nicholas Baran
Sandpoint, Idaho
Fall, 1994

For Esther

Foreword

Scenes from the Highway

By Jeff Duntemann

> *"Is it kind of like billions and billions of tiny little Bac-O bits of valuable information strewn in every direction across that great salad bar in cyberspace?"*
>
> Lily Tomlin's alter ego Ernestine,
> Superhighway Summit at UCLA, January 11, 1994

1996: Human Resource Director

At the home office of Zircon Corporation, a New York manufacturer of office equipment, human resource specialist Carmela Lizzo carefully encodes a job candidate description into a special computer program. The program is dedicated to seeking out job prospects using the National Information Infrastructure (NII). Carmela creates a profile by specifying things like education, years of experience, nature of experience, and so on.

Behind the scenes, the program produces a specialized e-mail message which most people who surf the highway for a living refer to informally as a "ghost." After Carmela has finished filling out the form, the ghost is ready to mail in less than a second.

The ghost message is mailed to several hundred professional and community-run electronic resume centers, which are called "servers," around the country. The resume servers recognize the message and process it so that it is transformed into an actual computer program itself ready to go to work with a vengeance.

The program sifts through tens of millions of posted resumes, looking for candidates for Zircon Corporation's newly created Director of Technology position.

Resume servers charge a modest annual subscription fee to maintain a person's resume on file. The resume contains a detailed profile of its author, along with information that indicates one of several current statuses, such as, "I'm actively looking for work," or "I'm not actively looking but I'd jump if something good came along."

Most professional resume servers specialize in certain professions, such as Law, Medicine, or Electrical Engineering. Most community resume servers represent geographic areas, such as Midwestern Rural or New England Small Town. Some defy categorization, such as one resume server calling itself Coastal Creative Crazymen. A person may post a resume in as many servers as he or she might wish to pay for, though an occasional server may offer a reduced subscription rate for an exclusive posting.

When a ghost finds a resume that meets its criteria, it sends that resume to Carmela. She scans the returned resumes, tosses a few that match names in Zircon's "no rehire" file, or that simply "look bad," and then she electronically submits the remainder to a screening agency retained by Zircon. The agency uses a "screening server" to look at each resume and consult an enormous database of police and court records, looking for drug or other felony convictions, bad debts, lawsuits, and other negative public records. The screening agency returns each resume to Carmela with an attached summary of public information found in the nation's databases. The screening agency can also verify things like degrees and coursework taken at universities, publications claimed on resumes, and other matters of public record.

Carmela discards resumes that do not meet Zircon's standards for things like felony convictions, and then forwards the surviving resumes to the hiring manager. She does this several times a day, every working day of the year. The system works very efficiently in many ways. Sending several hundred or even a few thousand ghosts out over the network takes far less time and resources than attempting to have thousands of resumes (many not even relevant) sent individually to Zircon for examination.

This system is especially valued by the resume holders themselves, who (if they have good records) often find themselves with several requests for interviews coming in every week. It is the closest thing to a perfect employment marketplace that the world has ever seen. Along the information highway, people don't go looking for jobs. *Jobs go looking for people.*

1997: The Virtual Universal Encyclopedia

The problem with the age-old dream of summarizing all human knowledge is the sheer *quantity* of it all. No single computer would seem large enough to hold everything—but that matters less than simply devising some means for people to find what they're looking for and bring it home in a reasonable amount of time.

By the mid-1990s, so much information had been made available through the sprawling Internet that a special project emerged to systematize searches in the manner of an encyclopedia. The result of this project, called WorldVUE (Worldwide Virtual Universal Encyclopedia), was first made available at the end of 1996.

WorldVUE's rather ambitious goal was to provide indexed access to short (approximately 2,000 word or less) articles describing every important person, place, or thing, with hypertext links leading away from a particular "encyclopedia page" to more detailed discussions in other files and documents and even multimedia presentations in the form of music, sound, and video. WorldVUE was considered *virtual* because its information was left scattered among the quarter-billion networked computers around the world in 1996; only the *index* to the first-level encyclopedia pages was maintained in a single place.

To create WorldVUE, a major university published the specs for the encyclopedia pages, and invited contributors to mail back index lines describing what topic was described and where its page was stored—with a hopeful promise that the address of the stored page would be updated if it were ever moved to another location on the network.

No one would have anticipated the response. In its first six months, WorldVUE merged twenty-five *million* index lines to pages stored around the world. The pages were multimedia in nature and contained images, sounds, and animated diagrams. Everything that could be described was deemed important enough to be included. No person was too obscure, no house too humble that its image and story would not be indexed, assuming its page was maintained somewhere along the far-flung connections of the information highway.

Being "in" WorldVUE was soon seen as a "status thing," and local committees around the world worked hard to create pages for local celebrities, architecture, recipes, folk music, dances, animals, and anything else with a describable identity. WorldVUE didn't attempt to discriminate—although there were some decisions to be made when five different descriptions of the chemical compound boron nitride arrived in a single day.

By 1997, WorldVUE had outgrown the Internet, and was incorporated as a nonprofit public utility accessed through the nascent National Information Infrastructure. Access was now on a fee basis—with the fee being one cent per item read through the central index. As painless as that seemed to WorldVUE's enthusiastic users, the "penny candy" fee structure provided the nonprofit utility with 1997 income of 1.4 million dollars—enough to support a full-time staff of five and the lease of a local network of three powerful computers to handle indexing requests.

WorldVUE identified "bad address" entries and either corrected them or removed them. An average of ten thousand new index messages arrive at WorldVUE every day, automatically verified and merged into the central index database. A volunteer governing board handles complaints that a WorldVUE item isn't "true" for some reason. Most complaints are easily dealt with but significant errors are discovered regularly and corrected.

A forward-looking design allowed WorldVUE to replicate its central index site to several different locations around the network, so that world traffic could be dispersed a little. By the end of 1997 there were four WorldVUE index sites, all automatically keeping one another current with a small but furious traffic in messages. The replication also provided incidental backup: If one WorldVUE site had a data-loss crash, the data could quickly be replenished from one or all of the other sites.

More than any other single entity, WorldVUE provided the impetus for the international expansion of the United States' National Information Infrastructure. By the close of the millennium, fiber optic cable had linked all the major western nations, and the dream of a day when all human knowledge—whatever *that* might mean—would be at the fingertips of any human being with a network connection was within sight.

1998: Netgamer

Homework could wait until Sunday night—that was the way it was with Jim Vavrik. This was Friday afternoon, and it only took him five minutes to race across his home town from middle school on his bike to the games arcade center. Jim had a three-thirty appointment with a game called SuperDoom—a date that would cost him the greater part of his allowance.

He got there in time to watch his close friend Charlie Sokolowski getting very frantic. Charlie was in trouble; the game was beating him again. His health was down to 60 percent and his ammo was almost gone. He still had a few weapons but they were no match for the two former humans bearing down on him fast and furious.

Jim recognized one of the attacking former humans as Metal Warrior, an extraordinarily talented "netgamer" known only to be male, 12 years old, and living in Erie, Pennsylvania. Metal Warrior had done him in a few times, and Jim was a whole year older. In SuperDoom, age didn't matter. Reflexes, instincts, and *practice* did.

Then, out of nowhere, Metal Warrior got Charlie with his secret weapon, a siren howled, and the screen went deep blue. Charlie's time was up. He had played well for his precious twenty minutes and racked up an impressive score—especially for a novice. Charlie pulled off the bulky helmet and wobbled out of the little playing booth. Jim squeezed in almost before the poor kid had gotten out. He plunged his playcard into the slot, validating his appointment, and debiting his play account. He pulled down the helmet (which was suspended on springs), stuck his head into the hole, and hit the *Play* button.

The blue screen displayed his net name, score, age, and hometown of Chandler, Arizona. Jim tensed as the scene cleared in the dual active-matrix displays inside the helmet. He opened the door from the transport booth, stalked down the hall a few steps, and looked around. Fractal-rendered 3-D stone walls, a few doors in the distance, and a larger space off down a passage to one side with some flashing lights. Jim was in no danger yet. Known in the maze only as Ungoliant, he clomped down the stone passageway, looking for treasure, ammo, and prey.

A planet held multiple bases, and each base could host up to fifty players. The system was always full on Friday afternoons and all day Saturday. Around the world, 49 other kids were stalking the halls of Gamma Base, weapons in hand, all having paid ten dollars for each ten-minute stint.

Only eight months after the first SuperDoom booths were installed, ten thousand booths were in operation around the world, connected to one another at the highest communication speeds possible through a new world-wide telecommunications network jointly owned by several major entertainment conglomerates. Here and there, fiber optic links acted as backbones connecting heavy concentrations of machines in California, New York, Boston, Washington DC, and in major cities in Canada, Germany, England, and Japan. New booths were being installed as quickly as they could be manufactured, and local phone carriers were only too happy to bring in the network lines to connect them.

The super-arcades in the bigger cities sometimes had twenty or thirty booths in clusters, working into multiple optical links.

SuperDoom was being called the amazing application of the newborn information highway, and you could take that any way you chose. No one was denying the assumption that the dream of SuperDoom would accelerate the installation of fast digital lines direct to the home, and few were complaining that the information highway was being born amidst shambling monsters and violence.

Certainly Jim Vavrik wasn't complaining. He cared nothing for an information highway, or for much in the line of information. He was drawing a bead on a former human from Calgary, Alberta and letting fly with his awesome gun. The player fell, and Jim's score ratcheted up furiously.

Another villain came from the left—Jim whirled, watching the scenery jerkily revolve with him. The creature was coming fast, taking big, staccato steps that indicated the system was running at capacity. For *smooth* you had to play on a schoolday morning—and he would catch more than *this* kind of hell for cutting school to do that.

1999: Bookworm

Corinna Wolczewski (Corey to those who know her) doesn't care that much for e-mail. She's always been a loner, preferring the company of books. She has not had to work since 1988, when her father's death left her several million dollars and a brownstone townhouse in Baltimore very near the Amtrak station. In those 11 years, she has filled her townhouse with books, so that now every wall is a bookcase, and every spare room is another branch of her personal library.

Her days have settled into a routine of sorts: She wakes at six, jogs to the park and back, showers, breakfasts, and then reads nonstop until noon. Paper books still dominate—after all, she has hundreds of years of publishing to catch up on—but after a light lunch she begins patrolling a newly created world-wide network called Fibernet for the new, odd, and interesting.

With money nothing more to her than a means to acquire food and books, Corey was first in line when Amtrak began selling personal fiber hookups to anyone close enough to the right of way of the Amtrak tracks to afford to run the link from the main fiber optic cable. Three blocks was expensive, but Corey had the money, and simply didn't care if it got cheaper over time.

Corey keeps her control room in the master bedroom of her house. Piles of books waiting to be processed, logged, or sold, are everywhere. Sitting in front of her personal computer, she hammers in data on newly acquired paper books, while listening to voice messages left by her compatriots on the fiber, most of whom she has never met and has no serious desire to. The TV is on, Corey's portal to the cable, though there is nothing but a soft blue-grey pattern on its screen.

"Corey! Sarah here. You still got that first edition of *Fail Safe*? My brother told me he'd pay at least a hundred for it if you still had it . . . ."

Corey pauses at the keyboard, thinks momentarily, then begins speaking to the mike taped haphazardly to the top of her PC screen. "Sarah dear! Tell him he's a month late and at *least* $200 short. It had water stains so I sold it for $300. Byeee! *Send Message. Next*"

A man's voice with a hint of an accent: "Miss Wolczewski, I was given your name by Michael Warren in Chicago. He said you were looking for a mint copy of Colin Wilson's *The Outsider*. I have one and it's been bagged for twenty years. One minor fold on the right side of the dust jacket, but apart from that it's flawless."

The TV screen cleared to show a man's hands holding a book, turning it right and left so that all parts could be closely seen. Corey turned toward the TV, leaned on a pillow, and peered at the presentation. "Well, now. Book looks good; that fold is a problem. I have one here, mint but minus dust jacket, so I think I'll pass. Those jackets *are* a problem, aren't they? Thanks. Byeee! *Send Message. Next*!"

"Corey? Nance here. Hey, I just got the *coolest* romance off the glass. New author I never heard of but she's *great*, set in Boston 1820s and I *knew* you'd want it! First chapter attached, whole thing four bucks. Interested?"

Corey giggled. "Your word is law, dear; no need for the sample. Thanks. Hugs! Byeee! *Fetch. Pay. ID. Seven-oh-oh-six-queue-zee-nine-tee. Go. Bind.*"

Corey's system sent a money ghost to the publisher owning the "free sample" chapter in Nance's message. Two seconds later, the book itself came down the fiber, scarcely three megabytes of Postscript. Beneath the TV set, a laser binder chugged to life, quickly feeding and printing paper into signatures, folding the signatures, and finally hot-gluing a spine and printed cover over the pages. In five minutes a pale paperback lay in the tray. Not as classy or as colorful as a true paperback, but fast, cheap, and something you could read while sunbathing up on the roof.

Later that day Corey spent a few hours scanning Publisher's Row on "the glass," as fiber people had come to call it. She rolled her eyes watching two authors debate the merits of their very similar books on the same topic, took in some eye-catching animations for a new book on the internal workings of nuclear power plants, and downloaded any number of sample chapters, few of which she would ever actually read. One sample chapter she *did* read with considerable excitement—new research on the origins of the Old Church in Glastonbury from the University of Glasgow—and then sent for the book itself. But rather than having it returned to her electronically, she had it mailed to a bindery, where it would be professionally printed in high-resolution four-color, then bound in the fancy embossed red leather she favored for books on "those special subjects," and finally shipped to her door by UPS. Sure it was expensive—but you could always get more money, and there was only *one* Glastonbury!

With the new information highway, books had indeed gone electronic, but they could only go so far. Paper really *was* forever.

2000: Security Hacker

Danny Simon wiggled the connectors again on his makeshift wiretap, and sat back in front of his high-powered PC. He was using an illegal wiretap where the Clipper/SKIPJACK voice security system kept the voice stream over the line to a raucous series of apparently random bits. For several years now the unassuming University of Arizona math student had played around with the Clipper board in his phone, watching this line and that, modeling different bit sequences, just looking for something that was dancing around the edges of conscious perception. He was trying to crack the Clipper security system adopted by the government some years ago to find solutions for security on the greatly expanding information superhighway. For Danny, this was a math problem; a challenge and an obsession.

There were trapdoor functions involved, he knew that, and he even had some strong hunches what *kinds* of trapdoor functions were being used. He had tried what seemed like thousands of different approaches, searching for something that probably wasn't there.

Danny fooled with some parameters in one of the programs that he had created to probe the SKIPJACK software and through it the Clipper security hardware. After it ran for a few minutes, he stopped cold. There were voices coming out of his PC's speakers. That was a secure line, wasn't it? He was using his own private keys! There was no way he could be hearing any intelligence on that line.

Unless, of course, everybody who had been condemning the top-secret SKIPJACK/Clipper technology from its beginnings in the early '90s was in fact correct. It was the first cryptography system every seriously proposed in which its inner workings, that is its algorithms, were kept secret. Pundits claimed that the National Security Agency had built a wide-open back door into Clipper that would allow them to listen to any phone conversation encrypted with Clipper. Otherwise, why all the secrecy about how Clipper worked? The details of cryptographic systems were *always* published, so that the best minds in the world could test them and make sure they were in fact as secure as their inventors believed.

No one had ever been really sure about how good Clipper actually was. Now luck or skill or perseverance had allowed Danny Simon to stumble onto the NSA's dirty little secret—there was a back door. Part of Danny's mind wanted to shout in triumph—but another part was deeply saddened.

Danny spent another day making sure that his special little trapdoor function really worked, and a second day making sure he understood how he had done it. Then he began to write a multimedia e-mail message describing the research that led up to his discovery of the function, and how he had used the function to force his Clipper-equipped telephone to decrypt any line hooked to it.

Finally he brought up the Newswire mailing list, containing the e-mail addresses of virtually every newspaper, electronic or otherwise, still being published in the United States. Who needs a wire service when just about everybody is already on the wire?

His finger paused over the command to send. As soon as this got out, billions of dollars in Clipper encryption hardware would be worthless. His message would be passed from mailbox to mailbox, replicated endlessly, perhaps hundreds of millions of times. In another hour, the name Danny Simon would pretty much be a household word. He shivered.

There would be Congressional committees, independent prosecutors, and loads of unpleasantness on every level. He'd draw a lot of attention to himself—and his school would probably tell him to graduate (it had been six years, already!) or hit the road.

Forget it! Danny pressed the Send key savagely. Clipper was about to sink, and Danny was more than happy to let it take down with it anyone who had shared in its preposterous fiction.

2001: Cableton

In the wild, flat lands of western New Mexico, there had been a cement plant, which in its time had made cement, concrete blocks, and poured drainage piping. It had its own two-mile siding from the nearby Santa Fe tracks, and 2,000 acres of land. The plant closed in 1973 and simply lay in the sun decaying, until a developer bought the entire parcel in 1995.

The idea was to make a new small town for people who wanted to escape the pace of America's big cities. The developer intended to build the best possible communications right into the ground, before the first brick was laid. A deal was cut with the local telephone company, which was anxious to bring people and premium connectivity to this sparsely populated region. The developer paid for the fiber optic cable within the town itself, and the phone company would install the fiber from there to their main fiber trunk. The railroad was interested in its "fiber rights" along its right of way, and gave the operating company favorable terms—if they would continue the fiber all the way to the Arizona border. In this way, that fiber was weaving its way all through the American continent.

Every lot platted had water, sewer, electricity—and fiber optics. The developer brought in restoration experts to rehab and modify the main factory building—dating back to 1925—into Town Hall. Around the square he began building storefront buildings with apartments above them, all in red brick and gray stone shipped in on the Santa Fe, down the siding and right to the center of town. Outside of town he built an airstrip.

It was, many said, a totally insane project—until a month after the first lots went up for sale. Half the town was sold as lots within a year. In another year, the half that was sold was built. The town's success was almost accidental: Millionaire pilots from Dallas, Houston, Phoenix, and San Diego bought lots to build hideaways for escaping the crush of city life on weekends—with good aircraft tie-downs an easy walking distance from anywhere in town. The new residents brought with them all the fiber-ready workstations that were rapidly taking over the big cities. Many who had escaped there only on weekends found themselves spending three, four, or even five days "away," working over the cable as easily as they could work from their offices. Only here, there was clean air, low crime, and mountain views in nearly every direction. The developer had intended to call the town Corazon but in the minds of those who lived there, the *cable* was the thing and the town took on the name *Cableton.*

Cableton was the first settlement in the world where *every* habitable structure had a fiber optic connection. Early buyers of the residential lots were the lone-wolf creatives in the electronic world: programmers, graphics artists, writers, musicians. The storefronts were bought largely by high-end "e-mail-order" companies, who placed their multimedia catalogs on the networks and packed their orders in the storefront back. The mail-order companies filled the storefronts themselves with elaborate showrooms for their products, knowing full well that the retail traffic on Cableton's town square would always be light. They had the storefronts—and they were re-creating an American legend.

Cable service in and out of Cableton was the same as what was available in the hearts of the nation's largest cities: voice/video mail, network gaming, feeds from the Internet, and ordinary TV and cable stations. But within Cableton itself, the universal nature of the service led to a completely paperless local government, with a virtual bank as well, housed in machines in the basement of Town Hall, but extending into every home in town, into windows on the HDTV or personal computer screens.

At any time of the day or night, spontaneous "bull sessions" were happening on the many conferencing channels. Flip the channels, and on your HDTV screens would be three, seven, or even twenty windows, each containing a Cableton citizen, speaking animatedly, or listening to those who were speaking. Some conferences were of course private—local companies working with employees both in and out of town—but most happened simply because they *could* happen, and like conversation at a cocktail party, simply continued whatever way the "wind" was blowing.

At build-out (planned to happen by 2004) Cableton will have about 2,500 residents. Such small towns rarely seem "lively," but with a culturally diverse citizenship, and without countless hours every day lost to grinding commutes, Cableton seems much larger, livelier, and energetic than it has any right to be. In a very real sense, it is the electronic re-birth, with the new millennium, of the American Dream.

2002: Lasersats

In 2001, space suddenly got cheap. Early that year, McDonnell-Douglas began mass production of their DC-1, the first generation of inexpensive single-stage-to-orbit spacecraft that was initially demonstrated in prototype form in 1993. A crew of three could loft as much as fifteen tons to low Earth orbit for as little as $40/pound. The squat, finless cone-shaped rockets were only 80 feet high, and could take off and land from any flat, solid surface 100 feet square that would not catch fire.

Best of all, they were cheap—barely three times the cost of a typical jumbo jet. All around the world, nations best known for exporting tropical fruit were suddenly planning space programs.

The Lasersat program had begun as a civilian outgrowth of the American SDI (Strategic Defense Initiative, a.k.a. "Star Wars") project, and had sat idle on a shelf for five years for lack of a vehicle to loft it into space economically. The DC-1 made it not only practical but profitable in its first year.

Over that year's time, an international consortium of communications companies orbited three hundred satellites the size of large garbage drums to low Earth orbit. Each lasersat had at its core a modulated laser capable of being steered in any direction, not as a weapon but as a continuously reconfigurable network link with enormous bandwidth—the equivalent of fiber optics in the sky.

From their scramble-oriented low Earth orbits, the lasersats could not remain in any predictable position with respect to Earth, as did the fabulously expensive satellites in scarce geosynchronous slots. Instead, as the lasersats swept over the Earth, they handed off duty as links to ground stations from one to another, and changed their positions dynamically in the orbiting constellation such that the *shape* of the lasersat network remained the same—even thought its component satellites changed identities every fifteen minutes or so.

Any given lasersat's orbit would decay in about five years, at which time the satellite would burn up in Earth's atmosphere. No matter; by that time the aged satellite would have been fully written off, as well as obsolete and ripe for replacement by a newer, more powerful, more precise successor implementation of the technology.

The lasersat network added badly needed capacity to the world data superhighway, now increasingly dubbed Worldfiber, and allowed inexpensive high-bandwidth links to reach remote portions of the world where it would be far too expensive to lay fiber optic cable over mountains or on the seabed.

The lasersats extended Worldfiber to places like Mauritius, far from any land mass, and Tannu Tuva, a splitoff Siberian republic near northwest Mongolia that gained its independence in 2000 against the wishes of all of its neighbors.

More than any other single technological development, the lasersats made high-bandwidth connectivity a worldwide phenomenon—and simultaneously made space travel a profit center rather than an expensive research money-sink.

2003: Dance Student

Cora McCarron is the daughter of a Montana cattle rancher, and she lives almost forty miles from the nearest significant town. She loves dance, however, and takes dance lessons three times a week from a prestigious studio in New York.

At eight o'clock sharp on Monday, Wednesday, and Friday mornings, Cora towels down after her shower and enters her dance studio in one of the sprawling ranch house's spare bedrooms.

She pulls on an exotic leotard that covers her completely down to her toes and fingertips, and includes a hood that fits snugly around her head like part of an arctic diver's wetsuit. Over her eyes she places sleekly designed goggles that connect to a square lump attached to a belt at her waist. She pushes a button on the lump, and instantly she is somewhere else.

The walls of her smallish studio in Montana remain in view; somehow less than important in this new way of seeing. But around her she now sees seventeen other figures as sleek, almost detail-less human forms sketched in bright light, stretching and practicing certain sequences. From general body contours, she can identify them as male or female, but from the unique color patterns of their virtual presence she knows them to be her friends and fellow students.

Then, a voice appears, that of Roger Kreunitz, their teacher for the term's course in ballet. Suddenly the channel is open to all, and the chatter of seventeen students gradually quiets, somehow impressed upon the sense of empty space that exists acoustically in Roger's cavernous New York studio, where none of the students have ever been. "'Morning, gang. I was rerunning last Wednesday, and you know, I'm not real happy with coordination on 'Appalachian Spring.' Some of you may have to turn your walls down a little. Let's go through it again before we get into the new number. Frieda tweaked the costumes a little, so they won't look quite like they did last time."

In New York, Roger works at his own keyboard. All at once the appearance of the dancers changes. While before they were merely sketched in broad geometrical patterns in bright colors, now they "wear" a far more realistic costume. The costume suggests the spare, simple clothing of the Shaker people, whose hymns inspired Copeland's masterpiece.

Whereas now the costume is simply rendered to hint at the collective vision of the performance, (and coincidentally to minimize the bandwidth required to coordinate the virtual studio) when Roger is satisfied with the students' performance he will have Frieda fully render the costumes onto their moving forms with photorealistic quality. Although some students may pay the studio an additional fee for Frieda to create a cloth version of the costume to wear for their own pleasure, for most of the students the costume will simply exist as a design impressed electronically upon their animated forms in the performance recording.

Cora moves to her position in the middle of her small studio in Montana. Scattered around the world, the other students do the same. Seemingly from everywhere around them, the majestic music of Aaron Copeland rises, and in the guise of a Shaker woman from the nineteenth century, Cora dances.

In New York, Roger Kreunitz watches the screen in front of him intently, showing a stage that does not exist, upon which dance seventeen teenagers living in six nations. Each student wears a leotard containing loops of magnetic thread, and in the floor and ceiling of their studios are sensors that scan and locate the position and orientation of the leotard within the studio's space. That information is sent in real-time to Roger's studio, where his computer integrates the data from all the students into the single animated image on Roger's screen.

From Roger's computer the image is re-rendered individually and sent to seventeen diverse destinations across the cable, so that each student may see the scene from his or her own viewpoint through the virtual reality system goggles.

There are practical difficulties with the system. The lesson happens at 10:30 AM New York time; students in other parts of the world must be motivated enough to connect in their studios whenever that might be in their local time. Each student dances within a space that may be large or small. Roger's choreography takes each student's situation into account. Those who have room to leap and run do so; those with little space emphasize grace and expression.

When it all works as it should, it can be breathtaking. Roger slaps on his goggles and moves around the nonexistent perimeter of the virtual stage, speaking privately to each dancer, making suggestions, reminding them of areas to which they must give extra attention.

This time the performance is better. No one runs into their "realworld" walls, as happened the previous Wednesday. Roger nods to himself. These kids are *good*—and this dance could be his next shot at the national virtual choreography awards.

2004: Citizen of the World

Meet Phil Sydney, a quiet, intense man of 40 living alone in a ramshackle farmhouse in the backwoods near Greensboro, North Carolina. Locals know him as the author of numerous country-western songs who sometimes performs at local bars. Nationally, he has a reputation for his technical seminars on fast connectivity. A peeling bumper sticker on his 1958 Chevy pickup puzzles his neighbors: "T-3 is a *T*rillion *T*imes *T*oo Slow!"

For his seminars he asks $2,000 per day plus expenses—and he's booked months in advance. Each year he gives seminars until he's made about as much money as a man with his education might be expected to make. Then he stops.

Phil winters in George Town, Grand Cayman, where he owns a small building. Downstairs is a souvenir shop. Upstairs is Phil's apartment and a small office. In the office Phil employs two young men to monitor the operation of his Worldfiber server, which connects to the fiber-optic communications system he helped the Caymans' governor implement in the small island nation.

Phil's Worldfiber node supports several businesses, including Litigation Research, Inc., which maintains a database of lawsuits filed in the United States. A freely distributable, query-generator front-end allows subscribers to retrieve whatever information they desire. Subscribers can earn "free" time on the system by submitting data on newly filed suits, which keeps the cost of maintaining the database quite manageable. Phil does not do much marketing of the system anymore since he pays a referral fee (also in "free" system time) to people who refer new subscribers. He is, however, pleased to see that 80 percent of his business comes from corporations running background checks on job applicants. His goal, never stated, is to make it impossible for people who sue employers to find work. Having the desired effect may take a few years. But he's in no hurry.

Phil understands electronic funds transfer and international markets, and he plays those markets like an expert; he makes his stock and currency trades anonymously from his node in George Town (controlling the node from Greensboro in the summer), where he does all his banking. He has a head for money and spends almost nothing, and his income is well over one million dollars per year, almost all of it outside the United States, and almost none of it explicitly in his own name. Much of his income is earned by shell corporations in half a dozen small nations around the world who opened shop with the new millennium selling *privacy*—basically, encrypted bank accounts—for a minuscule slice of each transaction.

Phil Sydney was never one to be seduced by fast cars, easy women, drugs, or elaborate houses. Since he already has a pickup truck and a winter place, as well as all the computers he can use, Phil spends his money, as he thinks of it, on "changing the world."

He subscribes to numerous electronic polling services, and he watches carefully for close elections. By providing anonymous cash, he tries to tip elections toward candidates who support an unfettered global economy, limited government, and personal liberty. He gathers political dirt through a pair of e-mail accounts maintained through a "privacy exporter" physically located in Brunei: one account for conservative pols, and another for liberal pols. Occasionally planted fictitious messages maintain the facade that the two accounts are owned by warring electronic factions when in fact they both simply feed his gargantuan optical disk in George Town. Political activists do his legwork for him, mailing the two accounts all sorts of information, gathered legally or illegally: lists of campaign contributors, stolen "private" e-mail, and encrypted phone conversations recorded years back during that delicious period between the time young hackers had discovered the NSA's "back door" into the Clipper phone encryption system to the time when the government finally tore Clipper out of its systems by the roots.

He uses the damning information to plant rumors against any politician who opposes his agenda, regardless of party. The recipients of his information never know where it comes from—nor do they care. Rumors pass from mailbox to mailbox, inflaming passions as they go. Phil can't be sure, but he believes that negative campaigns based on his research removed six Democratic congressmen and two Republicans from office in 2002, cutting the already razor-thin Democratic majority in the House to only five votes, and increasing the Republican majority in the Senate to seven. Back then, he was only warming up. Now, in 2004, scandal-tarred incumbent Gore retires, and Phil already has megabytes of dirt gathered on every Democratic hopeful.

Phil Sydney is not necessarily a nice guy. He's a blandly amoral "citizen of the world," and surfs the international data superhighway furthering his own mission. He is never quite who, what, or especially *where* he appears to be. He sends plain brown envelopes full of $100 bills to people who unwittingly augment that mission, with a short unsigned note indicating that the money will continue to come as long as they persevere.

Is Phil Sydney possible? Yes. By 2004, he will be *inevitable.* Does he exist? Hard to tell. If he did exist, Phil would be the last person on earth to admit it.

Road Construction Ahead

The Challenge to Build the Highway

> *"The information highway is something that people talk about, but the applications that will be used and the people who will win are still uncertain."*
>
> **Bill Gates, chairman and CEO of Microsoft Corporation**
> **Commonwealth Club speech, October 21, 1993**

In the Foreword to this book, we saw some "scenes from the information highway." We imagined people in different walks of life and how they might be affected by a communications medium that is as common as the telephone today, but has the power to not only transmit the human voice, but also text, sounds, and video images from a wide variety of sources at great speed. Before we consider this communications medium in detail, let's first consider how you might be affected in the year 2000. Then, we'll explore how the computer and communications industries are converging to create the information highway of the future—the highway that could have the power to transform the way you work, play, and live.

The Year 2000

In the year 2000, your home, neighborhood schools and colleges, local, state, and federal governments, and your workplace will probably all be connected by two cables—a coaxial cable similar to the one that currently plugs into your TV set, and a fiber optic cable that replaces the current copper telephone cable with hundreds of times the transmission capacity of that copper cable. The signals passing through these cables will be digital—zeros and ones that represent all forms of information—text, sound, and video—the same signals that today are exchanged between computers. These cables will enable two-way communications, allowing you to both send and receive all forms of information.

The fiber optic cable will connect to your personal computer and to your telephone. Your television set will connect to the coaxial cable and will have a little box on top of it (a *set-top box* in current jargon) that has the power of a desktop computer. The fiber optic cable will allow full two-way communications. You'll be able to send as well as receive video clips, music, and illustrated text through this fiber optic cable. The coaxial cable to your television set will be biased towards receiving information (and that will be primarily video) but will also allow you to respond and make selections and choices from a menu or a graphical display that appears on your TV set.

The New TV

Let's first consider your TV set with its set-top box. (All of this technology is explained in full detail in Chapter 4.) You control your TV with an infrared pointing device that looks a lot like the TV remote controller of today. But it has only one button. Pressing that button activates a pointer on the screen. When the pointer highlights the desired icon or menu choice on the screen, pressing it again executes the action represented by that icon or menu item.

When you first turn on your TV, you will see a list of choices. A sampling of these choices might include:

- Network TV
- News
- Movies
- Interactive Entertainment (Games)
- Shopping
- Travel
- Sports

- Restaurants
- Education
- Community Services
- Medical Hotline

You select one of these choices by moving the pointer on the screen to the item you want (simply by moving your hand) and then pressing the button. For starters, let's say you pick movies. Another menu appears on the screen with a variety of movie categories such as Westerns, Mysteries, Comedies, Science Fiction, Classics, and Foreign Films. You can select the type of movie you want to watch, or you can request a search based on the first few letters of the movie title. If you search, you use a small keypad attached to the remote control to type the title. If the movie is available, the screen responds that the movie will begin showing in, say, two minutes. An option allows you to schedule the showing, say, an hour from now, if you so desire.

Once you're watching your movie, you can pause or rewind. Perhaps you would like to order some food while you watch. (If you thought ahead, you may have done this before the movie started.) First, you pause the movie and return to the main menu. Next, you select the Restaurants option and a choice of restaurant types appears on the screen, such as Fast Food, Mexican, Pizza, Italian, Japanese, Thai, Chinese, and so forth. You select a type of restaurant and then a specific restaurant in your neighborhood. You select from a menu of appetizers, entrees, desserts, beverages, and so on. The order is automatically charged to your credit card and the time required for delivery is posted on your screen. (You can cancel your order at any time during this process.)

After watching the movie, you remember that it's time to renew the vehicle registration for your car. You select Community Services and a menu of services appears on the screen. You select Motor Vehicle Services. You select Vehicle Registration and a box appears askng you to type your license number. After checking if there are any outstanding parking ticket fees and some other statistics, the screen reports that your vehicle has been registered for thc next year, and that the registration sticker will be mailed on the following business day. The fees are charged to your credit card.

After closing the Vehicle Registration option, you're back to the Community Services menu and you notice an icon at the bottom of the screen with the title "Election 2000." You select this icon and a list of candidates for city mayor with their photographs appears on the screen. You select the candidate representing the Democratic party. He appears on the screen and delivers his pre-recorded campaign speech. You can do the same with the other candidates. There is also a bulletin announcing a debate between the candidates to be televised the following week. Viewers will be able to ask questions after the debate, directly from their TV sets.

It's getting late, but you have been considering making the leap to an electric car. You would like to get some up-to-date information on what's available. You select the Shopping option. Using your pointer, you scroll through product categories until you come to automobiles. You select the Product Information option and are presented with an array of icons for different car manufacturers such as GM, Ford, Chrysler, Mitsubishi, and a new company called ElectroCar, which has been getting rave reviews. The information linked to these icons is in the form of paid advertisements by the car makers. You select the model you're interested in and a full-video demonstration follows with all the important specifications of the car. A list of dealers in your area is also included. There's also an option in the Automobiles section for Consumer Reports and Other Reviews. You select from a list of current makes and models, and browse a variety of articles reviewing the car.

Finally, you investigate some possibilities for the family vacation coming up. You select Travel and are presented with a menu of different possibilities, such as vacations on the beach, in the mountains, overseas, and so forth. A list of local travel agents also appears on the screen. When you select a particular vacation category, a list of icons appears representing trips and vacation packages. Again, these are paid advertisements showing full-video clips of the area, the hotels, sightseeing features, and so forth. You can also book reservations directly from your television.

While you've been busily engaged with your television, your wife has been taking a "distance learning class" on child psychology, using the family personal computer. She needs just a few more credits to get a Master's Degree in Education from a university located several hundred miles away. Since she works during the day, the distance learning class has been a Godsend. The child psychology class meets two evenings a week for two hours. The professor appears on the computer screen. Graphics and other "instructional aids" also appear on the screen. A multiple choice mid-term exam is given directly on the computer—your wife clicks on her choice for each answer using the computer's mouse, and the answers are transmitted to the school administering the exam. The results of the exam are transmitted back to her computer at the end of the class.

Your kids also use the computer not only to write papers, but to do research. The other day, your son retrieved some summaries of research done at the University of Sydney on the behavior of kangaroos and how it differs from that of other, non-Australian animals.

Your family uses the computer to send and receive electronic mail. Yesterday, you sent your parents a home movie of your son's recent birthday party. You communicate regularly via electronic mail with relatives and friends around the country. Your son has established an electronic "pen pal" relationship with a boy in Russia. The Russian boy writes surprisingly good English—certainly better English than your son writes Russian!

The next day you go to your office. You don't always go, since it is very easy to work at home, but it's important to maintain "face-to-face" contact with your colleagues on a regular basis. The other day, however, your son was sick, so you conducted the weekly staff meeting from your office at home, with members of your staff at your satellite offices all participating. Using a scanner attached to your computer, you were able to display a new organizational chart resulting from the retirement of one your employees. Video conferencing has become an indispensable tool, saving thousands of dollars in travel expenses and time.

The Great Convergence

This book is about a technology that represents the convergence of two formerly distinct technologies: telecommunications and computers, and, in particular, *personal* computers. This convergence is by no means a sudden breakthrough, but rather the culmination of a process that has being going on for many years. It wasn't that long ago that operators sitting at a switchboard connected telephone circuits by hand. Today, circuit switching is done by powerful high-performance computers. And, of course there are high-speed networks in existence that have already demonstrated the convergence of telecommunications and computers, as we shall soon see.

But this convergence is taking on new dimensions. PCs, televisions, and telephones have, up to now, coexisted in most homes and offices in relative isolation from one another. Today, they are in the process of merging into a single device. It is the convergence of the telephone network, the cable network, and the computer that makes possible the so-called information highway.

The PC Parallel

There is a strong analogy between the development of the information highway and the place of the personal computer in the history of computing. The personal computer was not a sudden technical breakthrough, but the culmination of major advances in microprocessor technology. Just as high-speed networks existed before anybody heard of the information highway, computers with impressive capabilities existed years before the personal computer. What changed was the accessibility and affordability of these technologies. The personal computer brought the power of the computer out of the air-conditioned corporate computer lab into people's offices and living rooms. The information highway will bring the high-speed networks of NASA and well-funded research laboratories into people's homes and into their schools and offices.

The information highway is still in its early stages and full of uncertainties and technical challenges. It was only a decade ago that connecting a modem to a PC and dialing up another computer system or a bulletin board was a task relegated to serious computer enthusiasts. Most of the time, the two computers that tried to connect couldn't communicate because they used different protocols. And when they did connect, communications speeds topped out at 1200 bits per second at best, and for most users only 300 bits per second. At those speeds, it was only practical to exchange short text messages.

Today, connecting to another computer system, usually an online service, is quite a bit easier than it was ten years ago. Most personal computers are equipped with modems running at speeds from twice to more than ten times as fast as the modems of ten years ago, and most systems today use the same communications protocols. Nevertheless, telecommunications from a computer is still relatively difficult. This is largely because of the different communications signals used by the local telephone system and those used by the computer. Telephone and television signals, originating as they did at the dawn of electronics (television was developed by engineer Philo Pharnsworth in the 1920s although it didn't become widely available until the 1950s) are entirely analog in nature. *Analog* here means that information is communicated via electrically transmitted waveforms, with the shape of the waveform and its amplitude (size) changing constantly in the process of carrying that information. The development of digital logic after World War II radically changed this picture, with digital circuits passing information solely as a pattern of "on" and "off" states—with the amplitude, frequency, and shape of the data pattern not carrying information at all. We'll discuss these technical issues in detail in Chapter 4. If all goes according to plan, within a decade both television and telephone signals will all be digital and communications between computers (and computerized televisions) will become as effortless as picking up the phone and making a call.

While there have been astonishing changes and improvements in computer and telecommunications technologies over the last decade, truly intuitive ease of use has been an elusive target. Improvements in ease of use have been accompanied by increased complexity and a deluge of "features." A few years ago, you were faced with a terse command line (unless you used a Macintosh); today you are faced with a bewildering array of icons and other twists on the original Xerox PARC user-interface concepts. Ease of use is a major challenge for the information highway. We're on the threshold of much easier and faster interfaces and communications tools than are available today. Much has to be learned and much has to be done before the information highway lives up to its promise.

One Hot Topic

But aside from these sober thoughts, the information highway has become one of the hottest topics of the 1990s. It's been called the "information superhighway," the "national data superhighway," the "digital superhighway," and in the official jargon of the Clinton Administration, the "National Information Infrastructure" usually (and mercifully) abbreviated to NII. Whatever you call it, the information highway as it's presented in the press can mean just about anything. Newspapers and magazines gush forth a deluge of articles on this topic. Some articles call the present Internet the information highway. Others refer to cellular telephone networks as the information highway. A few more skeptical ones claim that no information highway is in sight.

Companies ranging from long distance telephone carriers to software developers to radio stations are advertising themselves as pioneers of the information highway. One radio station, in fact, calls itself "your key to the information highway." (Modesty seems not to be a hallmark of this emerging industry.)

And if you believe everything you read, by the beginning of the next century, you'll never have to leave your house. Movie theaters will be obsolete, books will head the way of the dodo bird, and you won't need printed newspapers or magazines. In fact, you'll never have to see other human beings. You'll just do everything electronically. You'll order movies that will appear on your 40-inch big screen TV instantaneously with the push of a button. You'll download newspapers and books from electronic information services and read them on electronic tablets. You'll have intelligent electronic assistants that know what kind of information interests you and what information should be screened out. You'll be able to monitor the activities of your children or subordinates even though they are miles away. You'll be able to order food electronically so you can forget about cooking and going to restaurants! If you believe all the hype, that's where we're heading—into a sterile, electronic world that is the grist of science fiction writers and "futurists."

In the real future, the information highway will bring us a world nothing at all like this. What futurists tend to forget is that human nature changes much more slowly than technology. Technology always has its impact on human nature and human behavior, but the force pulls in both directions. A technology that no one wants will never dominate an industry. (Remember video discs?) In any case, the information highway is going to develop far more slowly than some of its advocates would have us believe. A myriad of technical, social, commercial, and legal issues still have to be worked out before the information highway becomes a reality.

We've already mentioned ease of use as one of the technical challenges. The conversion to digital communications and increased communications capacity, going from one-way to two-way communications systems, the enormous complexity of the software required, and the computational and storage capabilities required, are other technical challenges. We'll discuss them in Chapter 4.

Social and legal issues abound, as we'll see in Chapter 6. How will copyrighted material be protected? Recording companies, movie producers, software developers, and book and magazine publishers all have a tremendous amount to lose on the information highway if copyrights are not rigorously protected. Is universal access possible? If so, how will universal access be guaranteed? What will be the government's role, if any, in regulating the information highway? How much competition will be allowed?

But while the shape of the information highway of the future is still uncertain, smaller scale models of the information highway exist today—the Internet, corporate electronic mail systems, and satellite and cable entertainment systems. So, if we can understand how these current systems work and what they're good for, we'll be ready to take advantage of the information highway of the future.

A Moving Target

One of the prime characteristics of technology is that it changes so fast that it's impossible to keep up with. The fast pace of technology doesn't hold a candle, however, to the frenetic and unpredictable pace of business. At least you have a few months or maybe even a year between technological advances. But business deals and collapses seem to come and go on almost a daily basis. And so far, development of the information highway has been more in the realm of business and government regulation than in the realm of technology. (We'll discuss the government in a moment.) During the months that this book was written, Bell Atlantic and Tele-Communications, Inc. (TCI) announced their merger and then the merger collapsed. Ditto for Southwestern Bell and Cox Cable. Electronic Data Systems (EDS) and Sprint announced a merger to big headlines in *The Wall Street Journal*. The deal was off within days! CBS and QVC announced merger talks, which also fell apart within a few days.

One has to wonder what causes such volatility in the business world. TCI and Bell Atlantic blamed their falling out on the FCC's cable television rate cuts. Surely, the vagaries of regulatory agencies must have been considered before announcing a merger worth billions of dollars. Perhaps it's a cheap way to get a lot of publicity. Much like software companies announcing grandiose products years before their release, big businesses like to dangle big merger plans in front of the noses of "industry analysts" and journalists, who then scurry off to write lengthy reports and analyses of what the merger could mean. In fact, *The New Yorker* ran a feature article on the CBS/QVC merger appearing in the July 18, 1994 issue, which hit the newsstands after the merger had already been scuttled.

Microsoft is a case in point in the software business. Windows 95 (code-named "Chicago") was announced years ago, and you'll be lucky if it's available as you read this book. Bill Gates has announced a multi-billion dollar venture with cellular phone magnate Craig McCaw to build a global low-orbit satellite system by the turn of the century; a plan that most scientists think is totally unrealistic. But perhaps it's a good marketing ploy. Microsoft has further announced an ambitious operating system for managing the information highway, which will handle everything from video on demand to ordering pizza, using a "rate-guaranteed kernel design, which guarantees the fastest possible network response time, delivering all consumer requests for time-sensitive data with no disruption in service." [1] We can only hope that this project moves faster than "Chicago," which, considering its enormous complexity seems highly unlikely.

In spite of the various hiccups and stumbles of the business world, it is indeed business that will build the information highway. We'll discuss further the players and the applications for the information highway in Chapter 5. However, we would be foolish to try to predict the next merger.

A Very Slooooww Moooooving Taaarrget

We mentioned that the information highway has so far been dominated more by business and government than by technology. While business is characterized by its volatility and unpredictability, the government is characterized by inertia. It was September, 1993 when the Clinton Administration, under the leadership of Vice President Al Gore, announced its Agenda for Action for the National Information Infrastructure (see Chapter 6). As this book gets ready to go to press more than one year later, one would have to characterize the government's policy as an agenda for *in*action. There have been "field hearings," according to a government source, a Task Force Advisory Council has been convened, and a "20/20 Vision Statement" has been released, as well as the text of a speech that Gore delivered in March at an international conference. Meanwhile, when we logged into the government's National

Telecommunications and Information Agency (NTIA) bulletin board in mid-July, it hadn't been updated since mid-May.

In addition, endless hearings about the fate of competition among the long distance telephone companies, the cable companies, and the regional Bell operating companies, drag on with no end in sight. See Chapter 6 for a discussion of federal policy.

Blacksburg, Virginia: A Model for the Future?

Although there's a lot of hype and grandiose talk about the information highway, there are also real projects going on that serve as models for the future. We discuss a variety of these projects throughout the book, and many more are being launched as of this writing. One of the earliest "information highway" projects is the "Blacksburg Electronic Village" of Blacksburg, Virginia, which was formally initiated in 1991.

Sponsored by a partnership consisting of the town of Blacksburg, Bell Atlantic (the regional Bell operating company), and Virginia Tech (Virginia Polytechnic Institute located in Blacksburg), the town of Blacksburg is being linked "with a 21st century telecommunications infrastructure." [2] The basic idea of the project is to establish a communications network in the town, providing local information, connections to Virginia Tech, to public schools and libraries, and a connection to the global Internet "network of networks."

The project is gradually growing in scope. Bell Atlantic wired apartment buildings in Blacksburg with coaxial Ethernet cable (although not free of charge), allowing residents of these buildings to communicate on the network at transmission speeds of up to 10 megabits per second, which is fast enough to support delivery of video and audio information. The town's main library has seven computers connected to the network, available to all citizens of the town, which has a population of about 34,000.

Any citizen in Blacksburg can have an electronic mail address and an Internet host name, allowing citizens to gain direct access to the Internet and its search and retrieval tools such as Mosaic,

Gopher, and ftp (all of which are described in Chapter 3). The project also includes training classes for citizens to learn how to use the Internet, which for the average person is no easy task.

The public schools in Blacksburg also have network connections. One example that shows the educational power of information networks is an elementary school geography class in Blacksburg, whose students learned about longitude and latitude by tracking the locations of wolves in Canada. These wolves wear radio collars that transmit their geographical coordinates. The radio tracking information is stored on an Internet server (a computer that is part of the Internet network). Students download the information from the Internet and plot the travels of the wolves. We'll discuss education and the information highway in Chapter 7.

Local businesses and companies are participating in the Blacksburg Electronic Village. One grocery store posts "electronic discount coupons," which customers can print and bring to the store. A flower shop provides online pictures of flower arrangements. Listings of restaurants are available, and one of the goals of the project is to make ordering take-out meals and other commercial services available on the network. We take a look at many of the services available "online" in Chapters 2, 3, and 5.

Community information is available in the Blacksburg Electronic Village. Bus schedules and maps of the town bus lines, entertainment listings, amusement park activities, and a *Town User's Manual* are all available online.

As summarized in a document from the Blacksburg Electronic Village:

"a unique feature of this project is to invest sufficiently in the prototype to achieve a critical mass of users of an information service suite, and then to tune these services to cost effectively meet the needs of people and businesses in town. Once this is done, replications of the commercially proven parts of the project can be implemented in other locations." [2]

The Blacksburg Electronic Village is indeed a microcosm of the information highway of the future. It deals with many of the same issues. How will it be funded over the long term? Who will control the network and the information that travels over the network? How will it be integrated into classrooms? How will businesses and commercial services operate on the information highway? What will be the role of government? How will privacy and security be protected? These are many of the questions and issues raised later in this book.

And so we begin our investigation of the information highway. We start with what is available today in the way of information networks and services, followed by a separate chapter on the Internet. These currently available services are the stepping stones into the next century. We then pause to get a basic grasp of the technology behind the information highway, presented in Chapter 4. Chapter 5 looks at the emerging applications emerging and at some of the business alliances we can expect to see (but remember, no merger predictions). Chapter 6 covers the role of the federal government and examines the difficult legal, social, and political issues. Chapter 7 assesses the impact of the information highway on education, particularly in public schools and libraries. Chapter 8 looks at the messy issues of security and invasion of privacy; how criminal and unethical activities can be kept in check.Chapter 9 covers wireless communications—such as cellular, microwave, and satellite—and their role. We'll also take a look at federal regulatory policy with regard to wireless communications. Chapter 10 examines the role of CD-ROM as a multimedia delivery vehicle and its role. We'll finish with a look at doing business on the information highway in Chapter 11.

Foundations and On-Ramps

What's Available Today

> *"Online services turn that blank home computer screen into a library, a bulletin board, a mailbox, and a town meeting"*
>
> Michael Wofsey, *The Wall Street Journal*, November 15, 1993

In Chicago, the John Kennedy Expressway follows a northwest route out of the city. Along the way it plays tag with Milwaukee Avenue, a major city artery that dates back to the earliest days of the metropolis. Unlike most streets in rectilinear Chicago, Milwaukee Avenue runs at a diagonal, and if you dig into the historical archives that chronicle the city's origins, you'll find that Milwaukee Avenue evolved from a dirt trail used by the Illinois Indians to travel from their settlements near Chicago up to what is now called Wisconsin. The trail was there before the avenue, and the avenue was there before the expressway.

Human needs dictate the paths taken from one point to another. The newer paths are built upon and grow out of the older paths. Understanding the way the information highway will be created starts with knowing what paths we have today. Where do they go? How did they come about? Construction on the highway has barely begun. Much of it is barely in blueprints, and some of its most intriguing aspects are still unsolved problems. But many of the paths that the highway will take are already in place. They may resemble the eventual highway no more than a dirt trail resembles the Kennedy Expressway—but the route will be the same, serving the same human needs. Many paths exist for communicating and exchanging information. Let's look at a few, to get a glimpse of where the information highway will go.

Right now, you can get an electronic mail (e-mail) address and exchange e-mail with people all around the world. You can join an online service or bulletin board system and tap into electronic discussions and conferences on virtually any topic that interests you, from collecting depression glass to raising Toucans in captivity. Right now, you can tap into online databases and electronic newspapers, or go shopping and make travel arrangements using an online service.

If you operate your own business or service, you can set up an electronic bulletin board system to communicate with your customers. Students can use online services to research homework projects. Or, you can relax, get online, and just play games. The now-famous Doom virtual reality game has recently been enhanced for play over the Internet, and many other pastimes are available.

To put it mildly, a lot is already happening on the information highway, or at the very least on the dirt trails that we've already beaten through the electronic medium called *cyberspace*. In this chapter and the next we're going to look at the information services that are there today and what they offer.

Just What Is Electronic Information?

Electronic information itself is nothing new. We've received it for years over television and radio. But the electronic information delivered by radio and television is quite different from the electronic information we cover in this book. Traditional radio and TV are strictly *one-way* information sources. The analog radio or television signal beamed into your home via an antenna, cable, or satellite receiver is a one-way signal. All you can do with that signal is watch it or listen to it, and the only actions you can take are to turn your radio or TV on or off, adjust the volume, or change the channel.

Cable and satellite television have added another action: the ability to pay for special or additional programs on a "pay-per-view" basis. But "pay-per-view" is still a one-way service. You don't use your television to respond to the pay-per-view offer. You use your telephone or a modem to call the cable or satellite service to authorize the additional charges and turn on the program you want. Home shopping networks are another recent phenomenon on TV that give you an opportunity to interact with the program by purchasing products. But again, you use your telephone to close the loop and make your purchase, so the TV home shopping shows are still a one-way source of information.

The electronic information that will travel over the information highway will be exclusively *digital* information—information in the form that computers can handle. Unlike information traveling over traditional radio or TV, this electronic information will move *both ways.* It will be information that you can respond to from your computer or from a device attached to your TV that essentially turns your TV into a computer. This device is called a *set-top converter* or *set-top box.* We'll discuss the difference between digital and analog information, set-top converters, and other technical details later. For the moment, the key point is that the information highway involves computers and information that computers can work with. This information can include movies, newsclips and documentaries, games, electronic books and newspapers, electronic mail, and all sorts of other documents and transactions.

Moving from one-way to two-way information is potentially a huge step forward for our society. Since the advent of TV, educators and social critics have bemoaned its ill effects, particularly on children. According to those critics, television has engendered a cultural wasteland and has turned us into passive receptacles of mostly meaningless advertisements and entertainment. It's not surprising that TV is called the "idiot box."

Digital information has the potential to dramatically change the traditional role of television. Sure, you'll still be able to sit down and watch a movie or a TV show as we have since the 1940s. But you'll be able to be a lot more selective about what you watch, and you'll be able to use your TV set for much more than simply passive entertainment. Not only will you watch or listen to the information—you'll actively search for and select information from a larger universe of digital data, as well as create information yourself and make it available to others. The information highway will turn your TV into a powerful communications and learning tool.

What Electronic Information Is Available Now?

A dirt path can still get you there—and there's a lot of electronic information available right now, albeit slow and limited compared to what will come in time. If you have a computer with a modem and communications software, you can tap into all kinds of information services. Although we'll discuss modems and communications software later, if the topic is totally new to you, pick up a copy of the book, *Modems for Dummies* [1], or a similar introductory book on communications.

Electronic information is available today by "getting online." To get online means to connect your computer at your home or office to another computer system somewhere else by way of common telephone lines. Usually you connect to an "online service," but you can also connect directly to the computers of colleagues or associates to exchange information. When you're online with another computer dedicated to being an online service, you can send and receive messages and read information posted on the online system. Many services provide electronic mail (e-mail), so you can send and receive private messages to other service subscribers using a personal electronic mail address. We'll discuss electronic mail later in this chapter.

You can usually download programs or files from online services. To "download" means to get information from another computer and store that information on your own computer. Uploading is the opposite route: taking information from your own computer and sending it to another computer system for other people to use. The information you download can range from a simple text message to a complete program that you can run—such as a game or a utility for organizing your hard disk.

The World of BBSs

Any computer can provide an online service with the proper communications software and hardware. In fact, many individual computer users set up bulletin-board systems, or BBSs, to serve a particular interest group or community. For example, in the small town where I live, there's a local PC user group that operates a BBS. You can dial into this BBS from your computer and read announcements and messages from other user group members. If you're just getting started with online communications and want to experiment with getting online, a good place to start is with a local BBS. There is now a BBS in almost every town with more than a few thousand residents. Many local BBSs are completely free of charge or at most charge a small monthly fee.

A local BBS usually operates on a simple personal computer similar to the one you might have in your own home or office. The computer runs special BBS software that allows it to answer incoming phone calls and post messages as specified by the BBS operator, who is often called the sysop (short for system operator). (See the *Resource Guide* at the back of this book for more information about BBSs.) Accessing a BBS is usually a simple matter of dialing the BBS phone number through your computer's modem and following the instructions that are sent down your phone line and display on your screen. These instructions usually include entering your name and assigning yourself a password, and may also require billing information if there are charges.

The capabilities of the BBS are limited by the power and capacity of the computer that hosts it. Most local BBSs have a limited number of phone lines (in many cases, just one) and limited information storage capacity. They're called bulletin-board systems because that's pretty much what they're used for: posting announcements and messages among subscribers.

In most cases, BBSs serves special interests, such as user groups, social clubs, political and religious groups, hobbyist groups, and so forth. But very valuable services are also available on BBSs. For example, the People's Electronic Exchange provides a huge collection of job listings. Another example is a BBS in the state of Washington called Legal Ease, which provides the complete text of state laws and regulations as well as "fill in the blanks" legal documents that users can download from the BBS.

BBSs are also becoming increasingly popular as customer service tools, even for commercial concerns that have nothing to do with computing. Many companies set up a toll-free customer hotline on BBSs, allowing customers to call in with questions or requests for service or product support. Companies also use BBSs to provide updated product information and service bulletins on products as diverse as microwave ovens and camping gear.

One interesting example of a commercial BBS is Wieck's Photo Database of Carrollton, Texas, which provides photographs to news media. With a constantly updated library of photos from the New York Times, Associated Press, and other major press organizations, smaller newspapers can dial up Wieck's Photo Database to get a photo to go with an interview, for example, or an ad agency can get a photo of a Chevrolet for a brochure.

Some BBSs are large, serving users from all over the country. For example, the Aviation Total Information Systems BBS serves flying enthusiasts nationwide. There are retail BBSs such as Movies-By-Modem and Book Stacks Unlimited, through which you can purchase movies and books, choosing from lengthy lists of titles. Federal agencies such as the Internal Revenue Service, the Small Business Administration, and the National Aeronautics and Space Administration also operate BBSs. A list of some of the more popular BBSs and their phone numbers is provided in the *Resource Guide.*

FidoNet

While BBSs are primarily stand-alone systems, many BBSs are set up to communicate with other BBSs via the FidoNet network. FidoNet is not an actual hard-wired network of computers, but rather an enormous group of individual BBSs that cooperate and exchange information with each other over ordinary phone lines. The FidoNet system coordinates the transfer of messages and data. FidoNet is called a store and forward system, in which messages originating on one BBS are automatically forwarded via the phone line to other BBSs on the network.

FidoNet allows BBS users to have a FidoNet e-mail address at their local BBS, which can be accessed by other FidoNet BBSs all over the world, as well as through the Internet. FidoNet BBSs also share conferences and messages from member BBSs on the network. (These shared messages are called echoes.) FidoNet BBSs are basically a throwback to the early days of telecommunication between personal computers back in the late 1970s and early 1980s. The biggest attraction is that many FidoNet BBSs are free, and you can actually have a totally free e-mail address, although not as fast or reliable an address as you'd have on a commercial service.

There are other BBS networks, but FidoNet is by far the largest. Other noteworthy BBS networks are RelayNet, SmartNet, and ILink.

Commercial Online Services

Local BBSs are at one end of the online spectrum. At the other end are national and international commercial online services such as CompuServe, Prodigy, Genie, and America Online (AOL). These big commercial services use much more powerful mainframe and minicomputers than standard desktop PCs, and can accommodate thousands of users simultaneously. These services have from hundreds of thousands of members to over a million, and offer a much wider range of services than typical BBSs. (Prodigy and CompuServe have memberships in the range of 1 to 2 million while AOL just recently hit the one million mark.)

While most BBSs are free of charge or cost a nominal fee, commercial online services are definitely in it for the money. Online services have a variety of payment plans, either charging by the hour that you're connected or charging a lump sum per month, quarter, or year, for unlimited access time or for access time up to a certain number of hours.

A key feature of services like CompuServe or AOL is that they operate a central computer system or group of tightly linked systems that serve all subscribers. This setup is in contrast to the Internet, which is a global network of peer computers accessible through government and academic organizations, as well as commercial services and commercial access providers. The shape of the Internet is similar to the shape of FidoNet; machines linked through the Internet pass messages and data from one to another without passing through a central routing point.

Figure 2.1 shows the difference between the configuration of a commercial service such as CompuServe and that of the Internet. While no one knows for sure, it is estimated that Internet has over 15 million users, making it by far the most widely used online system in the world. But the Internet is really a completely different animal than the BBS or commercial online services we're discussing here. We'll discuss the Internet separately in the next chapter.

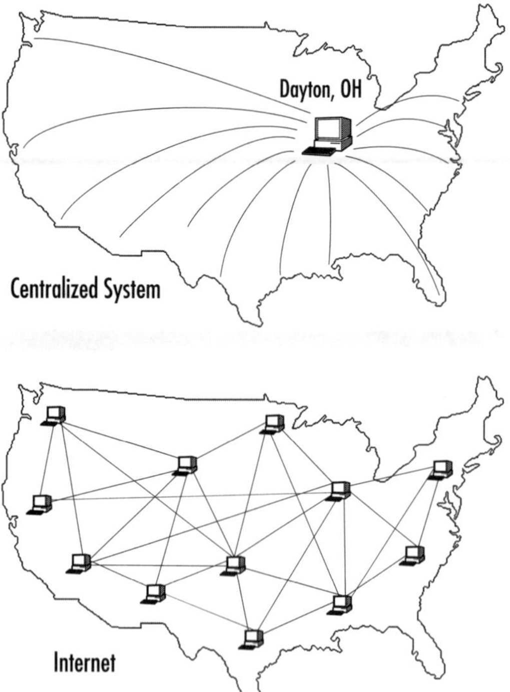

Figure 2.1 *Comparing the configuration of a commercial online service with the configuration of the Internet.*

So What Do You Do with These Services?

Big commercial online services are like hundreds of BBSs rolled into one. In other words, they offer hundreds of separate discussion topics and often include special interest groups that operate as part of the online service. These topics and interests are usually offered as separate conferences, forums, or sessions on the system, which, as a subscriber, you are free to join and participate in. Topics cover everything from current events to scuba diving to cooking to model railroad building to computer support groups to professions such as law and medicine. In addition to general topic conferences, many special interest organizations and companies offer forums or conferences on these big services. For example, both the Democratic and Republican parties have forums on CompuServe, as do many paper publishing houses and large software companies.

As a subscriber to an online service, you can join topics and participate in online discussions with other subscribers. Messages are stored on the system and you can read them, comment on them (by adding a message of your own), or search them for a particular word or phrase. A typical session on CompuServe is shown in Figure 2.2. You can capture the information scrolling across your screen and print it on paper or store it on your computer for future reference. Most of these services also offer a chat mode, in which you can exchange comments in real time with other people online at the same time you are—in other words, you can have a live electronic conversation with other people typing at their keyboards. CompuServe's famous CB Simulator is the best-known example of a chat service, and a huge revenue source for CompuServe, since chatters typically pay by the hour.

Most online systems also offer a variety of additional services such as online newspapers and magazines, up-to-the-minute news, weather, sports, and financial reports, games, software, and retail shopping services. Some of these additional services cost something extra on top of the base monthly fee, while other sources are included. With the fierce competition among online services, more features are included in the basic package all the time, while hourly rates are gradually decreasing.

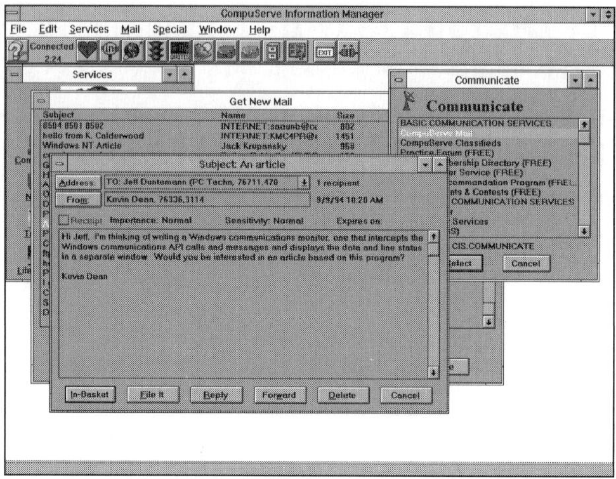

Figure 2.2 *A typical session on CompuServe.*

For example, CBS used the Prodigy online service during the 1994 Winter Olympics to get feedback from viewers. Halfway through the Olympics, CBS claimed to have received some 7,000 messages. Both NBC and ABC also offer services through Prodigy and AOL, including a viewing guide, previews of upcoming shows, and the opportunity for viewers to express their opinions of programming. CompuServe offers news commentaries such as the Beck/Smith Exclusive, which covers the entertainment and media industries.

Many of the software packages and games offered online are in the *public domain*, meaning that their authors have willingly foregone copyright protection and literally release their material for public use without any desire for compensation. The majority of the freely distributable items available for downloading from online services are called *shareware*. Although you can download shareware and try out the games or software without charge, you are expected to send the product's owners a registration fee if you plan to use the program on a regular basis. Some downloadable programs are actually limited demonstration versions of commercial products, distributed with the intent of familiarizing online people with the full versions of the products, which you can purchase after trying out the limited versions. Sometimes there are features left out of the demo versions, or sometimes they can store only small files or perhaps not store a file at all; some people call such demo software "crippleware."

Premium Services

A rapidly growing segment of commercial online activity consists of independent for-pay service providers, who use the big online services to provide some particular information to subscribers. These services usually cost an additional premium on top of the basic fees. Just to give you an idea of the breadth of the services available (and this is only skimming the field) here are some of the services that have recently been introduced.

Master's Program in Journalism

CompuServe offers a Master's of Journalism degree program in association with the University of Memphis. The courses include subjects such as "Journalism Administration and Management" and "Public Relations Principles and Issues." Tuition for the online courses is $1,000 each, which includes texts, videotapes, and other course materials.

Online Discount Brokerage

CompuServe offers the Quick & Reilly and E*TRADE discount brokerage services. CompuServe members can place, buy and sell orders for stocks and other securities 24 hours a day. Portfolio management and a variety of other investor services are available, including performance information and current and historical pricing for stocks, bonds, and options.

Homework Helper

This service, available through Prodigy, is an electronic library aimed, as its name suggests, at students for use as a research tool. Students can type simple questions in English and get back detailed answers from the extensive database. The system includes over 35 newspapers and magazines in electronic form, digitized photographs and CNN television transcripts, graphic images and maps, over 700 literary works, and several reference resources such as *Compton's Multimedia Encyclopedia.*

Bed and Breakfast Guide

CompuServe now offers Pamela Lanier's *Bed and Breakfast Guide.* Based on *The Complete Guide to Bed and Breakfasts, Inns, and Guesthouses in the United States and Canada,* which has sold close to two million copies, the service provides information on more than 9000 inns in North America. You can search the online bed-and-breakfast service by geographical area, name, vacation activities (skiing or fishing, for example), and so forth. The service includes a Bed and Breakfast forum where you can share experiences or direct questions to the guide's publisher.

Online Yellow Pages

Nynex and Prodigy have teamed up to offer the Yellow Pages online for the New England and New York region, listing 1.7 million businesses, as well as display advertising. The service lets you search by business category and by geographical location. The restaurant section also supports searches by type of cuisine. Prodigy hopes to strike deals with other telephone companies to make the service nationwide.

Interactive Grocery and Drugstore

AOL has joined forces with Shoppers Express, one of the country's largest home shopping services, to offer online grocery and pharmacy shopping, with home delivery Monday through Friday. Shoppers Express contracts with supermarket and drug store chains throughout the country to provide the service.

The Growth of Services

The variety of services available online keeps increasing at a staggering rate. In terms of services and conferences, CompuServe is currently the most comprehensive online service, particularly for business and professional users. It's been around the longest and has an enormous number of topics and independent service providers. For example, CompuServe claims that over 400 computer software and hardware companies offer customer support forums on the service.

In spite of CompuServe's dominant position, the competition is fierce and the various services have begun to specialize in serving particular audiences. For example, Prodigy is very popular with home users and families with children, with a lot of games and educational offerings. AOL competes on price and, although smaller than CompuServe, is growing at a very rapid rate.

Specialized Online Services

So far we've discussed the two ends of the online spectrum: small BBSs and large, commercial services. But there are all kinds of services in between. First of all, there are some smaller commercial services that have loyal followings but are far more specialized than CompuServe or Prodigy.

The BYTE Information Exchange (BIX) and ZiffNET are aimed at people primarily interested in computing for its own sake. BIX was originally a spin-off of *BYTE* Magazine and is now operated by Delphi Internet Services. BIX has a wide variety of conferences on all kinds of topics, but its primary user-base consists of *BYTE* subscribers and veteran computer users. ZiffNet is operated by Ziff-Davis, the publisher of *PC Magazine*, *MacUser*, and other magazines, and is targeted at Ziff's readership. While ZiffNET's main function is to provide online versions of Ziff-Davis publications, the company is adding a new service called the Interchange Online Network, which will compete with the more broad-based online services like CompuServe and AOL.

Apple Computer has joined the fray and now offers an online service to Macintosh users called eWorld. eWorld offers the familiar Macintosh interface and attractive graphics, as well as typical applications, such as electronic mail and conferencing. The service is clearly targeted at the Macintosh community. Microsoft is expected to introduce a similar online service.

While you can get many of the specialized services through the big commercial services, some services are available only on separate networks or smaller centralized online systems. For example, CompuServe operates a credit rating service, but it's not available on the regular CompuServe service. It's actually a separate packet network connected to the National Information Bureau in Princeton, New Jersey. We'll talk more about packet networks later.

Home banking is another specialized service that is provided by some local banks, particularly in larger metropolitan areas. The bank that you use provides you with software for your computer that allows you to dial up the bank and perform transactions, such as paying bills or transferring funds from your savings to your checking account. Home banking services publish comprehensive lists of companies that will accept payment through the service. For example, Bank of America's home banking service supports payment to major credit card companies, telephone and utility companies, garbage collection services, many mortgage and insurance companies, and so forth.

Online Databases

The backbone of present information services and of the information highway of the future are the online databases. After all, the main goal of any online service is fast and easy access to information—and most of that information is stored somewhere in a computer database. In fact, the online movies and games of our future living room entertainment centers will themselves be stored in online databases. Online databases are simply collections of various types of data (including text, but by no means limited to text). These databases reside on computers with online connectivity, either through a direct-dial connection, a commercial online service, or the Internet.

There are literally thousands of online databases already in existence, with many more still to come. It's estimated that the text of close to 4,000 newspapers, magazines, journals, and other periodicals is available online. [2] There are legal databases, medical databases, databases containing indexes and abstracts, airline schedule databases, patent and copyright databases, financial information databases—the variety is endless. The problem is figuring out which database to use.

Part of that decision may be dictated by price. Big commercial online databases can be very expensive to use, with hourly rates exceeding $100 per hour. On the other hand, many of the BBSs we discussed earlier are essentially online databases, such as the Legal Ease BBS in the state of Washington. Some of the commercial online services, particularly CompuServe, have developed their own online databases, which may be less expensive (although less comprehensive) than some of the commercial online databases.

Probably the best known commercial online databases are Dialog, LEXIS/NEXIS, and Dow Jones News/Retrieval. Dialog operates over 400 databases covering a wide range of professional topics. Included are the Los Angeles Times, the New England Journal of Medicine, Peterson's College Database, and TRW Business Credit Profiles. [2]

LEXIS/NEXIS are databases operated by Mead Data Central. LEXIS is a legal reference database, while NEXIS is primarily news oriented. LEXIS/NEXIS is highly regarded among researchers and lawyers but charges a hefty hourly fee.

The Dow Jones database specializes in news and financial information. The *Resource Guide* at the end of this book gives you a list of some of the popular online databases.

Large libraries support commercial online databases designed specifically for libraries. The Online Computer Library Center (OCLC) and the Research Library Information Network (RLIN) are two of the major database providers for libraries. While the primary function of these databases is to replace library card catalogs, library databases are rapidly expanding to include full text abstracts and indexes of all sorts of publications. Some libraries also have accounts with Dialog or LEXIS/NEXIS and may offer these services at a discounted rate.

As we shall see in the next chapter, many online databases are available through the Internet.

E-mail

As mentioned earlier, probably the most popular use of online services is for electronic mail (e-mail). As a member of an online service, you can have an e-mail address and send and receive electronic messages to other holders of e-mail addresses. Many people use online services exclusively for e-mail and make little or no use of services beyond e-mail. One of the most popular online services is MCI Mail, whose primary function is to serve as an electronic mail service, although MCI Mail does provide some additional news services. Electronic mail is becoming an increasingly common form of communication in all walks of life, but particularly in large companies and institutions such as universities and government bodies.

E-mail offers a lot of advantages over both the telephone and regular postal service paper mail. You don't play telephone tag with e-mail. You can communicate the substance of your message without having to physically connect with the recipient of the message. The recipient can view the message at some later convenient time. E-mail is faster than postal mail. An e-mail message usually gets to its destination within a few minutes (at most an hour or so), if not immediately. You can send information on e-mail that the recipient can work with on the computer. For example, you can send a report by e-mail to a co-worker, who can then edit the report on a word processor and send the edited version back by e-mail—a far more efficient process than working with a paper version of the report, or trying to dictate its contents over the phone by voice. E-mail is also extremely useful if you need to send a message to multiple recipients. With e-mail, you can write the message once and tell your e-mail program to send the message to multiple addresses.

E-mail has one significant drawback: its lack of security. Since e-mail messages are passed from one computer system to another, sometimes requiring human intervention for routing or bad address processing, it is very easy for unauthorized people to read other people's e-mail messages. Of course, there are millions of e-mail messages transmitted throughout the world each day, so unless someone has some explicit reason to snoop through your e-mail (such as the journalists at the 1994 Winter Olympics who read Tonya Harding's electronic messages), it's unlikely that it will be tampered with. Nevertheless, it is wise to only send e-mail of a non-confidential nature.

Although virtually all commercial online services provide you with an e-mail address, some of these services have more versatile e-mail functions than others. In particular, some services only allow you to exchange mail with other e-mail addresses within that service. More versatile services allow you to exchange e-mail with online services other than the one that you belong to, often at an additional cost, and usually through the Internet. The way this works is that the service has its own e-mail address on the Internet and its users can communicate with other services through that Internet address, as shown in Figure 2.3.

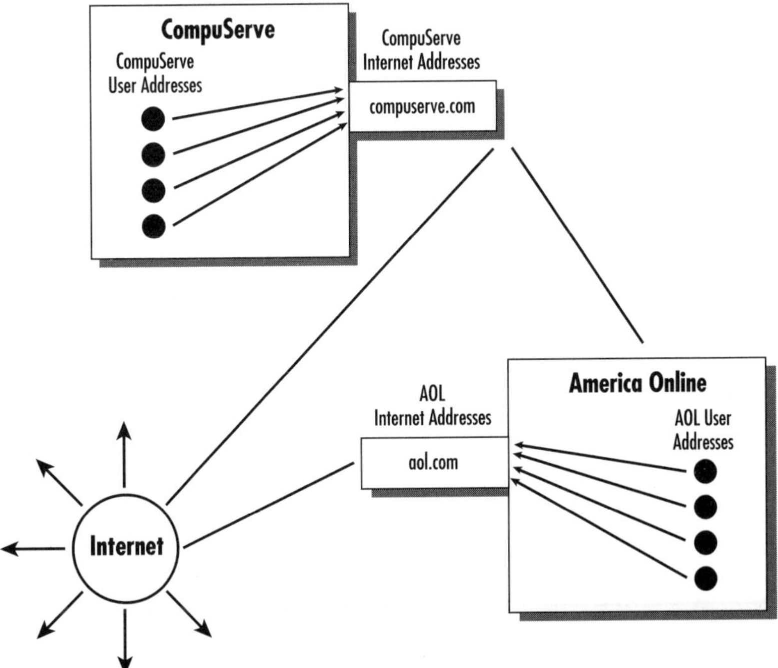

Figure 2.3 *How online services communicate via the Internet using e-mail.*

Video Conferencing and Private Networks

Our survey of what currently exists on the information highway wouldn't be complete without mentioning video conferencing and private information networks. Private networks are set up for a particular company or profession and provide a communication system for conducting "electronic meetings" or for broadcasting information to multiple sites. Satellite transmission is currently the most widely used medium for private networks but telephone connections are also used.

Many companies use private satellite networks to broadcast to employees around the country or the world. In the computer journalism profession, there's a satellite network called Interactive Information Network (IIN), which broadcasts press conferences to the sites connected to the network with a KU-band satellite dish provided by IIN. I live in a remote area and, thanks to the IIN system, I can watch press conferences and product announcements from my home office. Often, a toll-free telephone connection is provided so that the satellite audience can phone in questions.

You may have noticed that most auto dealers that sell and service "Big Three" cars and trucks have a satellite dish on the premises. This is because most dealerships are connected to the factory by a private satellite network that provides parts and service updates as well as video training sessions.

Video conferencing allows participants at remote sites to see one another and converse as though they were in the same room. It also allows the display of graphic images or other visual aids for all the participants to see. Video conferencing systems range from relatively low-cost (and low resolution) personal-computer-based systems that use regular phone lines for transmission, to high-performance commercial systems that use satellite transmission or dedicated phone line hookups. These high-performance systems are usually leased or charged for by the hour.

A typical PC-based system for use in video conferencing consists of a video capture board that plugs into the computer, a camera and microphone, speakers, and a device called a coder/

decoder (codec). Such a system can run across a local area network (a network within one building or a set of adjacent buildings) or on a high-speed phone line, and costs in the neighborhood of $5,000 per system.

One of the most interesting applications of video conferencing networks has been developed in the medical profession. United Medical Network, MCI, and PictureTel have teamed up to provide a "telemedicine" network, allowing physicians and patients from around the world to link up for consultations, diagnostics, and other exchanges of information. United Medical provides the medical know-how, with MCI providing the network service and PictureTel supplying the video-conferencing technology. The system can be used to view medical images such as X-rays, CAT scans, and pathology slides. This means that, for example, a rural hospital without a specialist in a particular field like orthopedics or endocrinology could link up via this network with an expert at a major urban hospital for a consultation.

Other medical organizations are working on similar projects. For example, several Pittsburgh medical centers are working with Westinghouse and the Carnegie Group to develop an online database and network for breast cancer diagnostics and research. The system will allow both physicians and researchers to exchange information such as the most recent laboratory findings, diagnostic and treatment procedures, and so forth.

Telemedicine promises to be one of the most immediately useful and productive applications of information highway technology. Telemedicine has strong supporters in Congress who want to enact legislation providing funding for rapid development of telemedicine networks.

Summary

In this chapter, we've covered the basic information services available today, with the significant exception of the Internet, which is involved enough to require a chapter of its own. We'll get to that next. Electronic bulletin board systems (BBSs) represent the most basic online services, but also provide some extremely valuable information. Large commercial online services are like hundreds of BBSs rolled into one. They cost more, but they offer a lot more diversity and variety of topics and information services. Online databases are really the backbone of the information highway and will reappear in several chapters in this book. Video conferencing and private satellite networks provide an early glimpse of where the information highway is heading, as we shall see.

The Sprawling Internet

The King Who Will Not Rule

> *"The No. 1 bumper sticker on the digital highway for the foreseeable future will read: WELCOME TO THE INTERNET. NOW GO HOME."*
>
> **David Plotnikoff, *San Jose Mercury News*, April 4, 1994**

Not every king accepts his crown willingly. Time and again, commentators in the press and other media have declared that the Internet is in fact today's information highway, and that it will become the information highway of the future, only to meet with howls of denial from those who have worked to build the Internet and those who use it the most. The fury of those denying any connection between the Internet and the information highway is itself telling, and indicates that there are far more than simple technical issues at stake here.

Whether or not the Internet becomes the information highway, it has certainly taught us many valuable lessons about what works, what doesn't, and why; and it has been the cradle of innumerable technologies that will in fact be incorporated into the information highway once it is built. For these reasons, it is well worth becoming familiar with the world's largest and most far-flung data network, how it is used, who uses it, and what its very significant limitations are.

The Weak King

Both its critics and its partisans are more than willing to admit that the Internet has some serious weaknesses. It is difficult to use, especially for non-technical people, and it lacks adequate data security. There's no consistent format for graphics and video, making transmittal of graphic images and multimedia documents a complex process. And while a nearly unimaginable amount of information exists on the Internet, it's hard to locate the information you want when you want it, and when you do find it, it may be hard to avoid drowning in its riches; what some have termed "information overload."

No one really controls the Internet. It operates in a fashion that some have appropriately dubbed cooperative anarchy, without any significant means of resolving disputes or of efficiently allocating costs to users. Most of the information available on the Internet is available without cost, and the notion of information as a protectable, marketable commodity is utterly alien to the Internet's core user community. It has no chief executive officer or president. It also has no centralized financial source of expenditures and income. It has no governing standards body with any power to enforce compliance with a standard.

In fact, many who understand networking look at the Internet and shake their heads in wonder that it functions at all.

Nevertheless, the Internet will play a major role in the development of the information highway, if only as an object lesson and a conceptual model. It is a remarkable example of how a government-funded research project can evolve into something that benefits society as a whole without creating a bureaucracy or a catalog of tax-funded entitlements. And in spite of its limitations, the Internet remains tremendously useful. It provides access to thousands of databases located around the world. It links many university and public libraries around the world so that you can browse their card catalogs or locate articles on obscure topics.

An estimated 20 million people use the Internet to exchange electronic mail, and the volume of network traffic is increasing at a rate of about 15 percent per month, according to estimates. [1] More and more schools around the world are gaining access to the Internet, allowing students to exchange messages with fellow students, scholars, and researchers, or even astronauts in space. In the recent Los Angeles earthquake, seismologists used the Internet to send seismic data to colleagues in Japan. During the 1994 Winter Olympics, Internet users could get comprehensive updates of competition results from an Internet node in Oslo, Norway.

The king may be reluctant, but he is nonetheless actively serving his subjects.

The Magic of Cooperative Anarchy

You might wonder why the Internet seems to be so much more popular than other online systems. A big part of it is simply the cost of access, which for many people is zero. For the Internet's most fanatical users, the account is a bundled benefit of their job or school system that carries no extra out-of-pocket costs to them. The Internet's greatest single distinguishing characteristic, in fact, is that it is not a private enterprise; CompuServe and America Online are private enterprises that exercise complete control over the services offered and what those services cost.

An advantage related to the Internet's public nature is its vast, globe-spanning extent. Virtually every college and university in the United States has an Internet connection, as do thousands of universities around the world. Government agencies such as NASA and the Library of Congress are on the Internet. Millions and perhaps tens of millions of electronic mail addresses reside on the Internet. (There is, remarkably, no way of generating a truly exhaustive list of e-mail addresses recognized by the Internet, so no one is quite sure how many there actually are.) And, as we shall see, there is a grassroots movement to make the Internet something akin to the public library system and available to everyone without charge.

So what, then, is the Internet? The Internet is a large and very free-form association of independent networks and computer systems that adhere to a set of protocols defined by committees and published in a series of electronic documents freely available to anyone who wants them.

These protocols and the basic architecture of the Internet makes a computer system nominally a part of the Internet, while remaining completely independent in all other ways. Some of these independent parts of the Internet are commercial enterprises, selling Internet access to businesses and private individuals. (These commercial enterprises are called access providers.) Although the commercial segment is growing rapidly, most of the Internet is comprised of networks sponsored by government institutions, colleges, and universities. There are volunteer organizations that act as regulating or governing bodies of the Internet, but none of them has ultimate authority. Technical changes and changes to standards are decided by committee, in particular, the Internet Society, the Internet Engineering Task Force (ITEF) and the Internet Architecture Board (IAB).

The Internet grew out of a laboratory experiment in the late 1960s, sponsored by the Advanced Research Projects Agency (ARPA) of the U.S. Department of Defense. Called ARPAnet, the experimental network's primary objective was to allow scientists and researchers doing defense-related work to share information that resided on computers scattered all over the country. The idea was to link up all these computers via telephone lines, so that any user on the network in any location could access information on any other computer on the network, and send messages to any of its users. This was to be an interactive network, meaning that a network user could connect "live" and in real time to another computer on the network and execute programs or open files on that computer.

Packet Switching

To realize the concept of an interactive network, ARPAnet needed a new way of transmitting data via telephone lines that would increase the bandwidth (that is, the speed and capacity) of data transmission across the network. The solution to this challenge was the development of a data transmission technique called *packet switching*, in contrast to the conventional circuit switching technique used in familiar voice telephony. Packet switching passes data gathered into independently routable bundles called *packets*. This concept was a major technical breakthrough in networking technology. It is the primary data transmission technique used in wireline-based computer networks, as well as in packet radio and satellite networks. For an excellent discussion of the ARPAnet project by one of its founders, see the article "Networks for Advanced Computing," published in *Scientific American.* [2]

TCP/IP

The other key challenge in the ARPAnet project was to enable different types of computer systems and networks to communicate with each other without compatibility problems. The solution to this challenge was the development of a common network protocol called TCP/IP, which stands for Transmission Control Protocol/Internetworking Protocol. A network protocol is a set of procedures and data formats governing the exchange of information among computers or networks of computers. The IP portion of the acronym (Internetworking Protocol) is essentially a translator that allows dissimilar networks to communicate with one another. It is from the TCP/IP protocol that the name Internet arose and was adopted.

These developments took place in the late 1960s and early 1970s. The first public demonstration of ARPAnet took place in 1972. Although ARPAnet remained the obscure province of defense researchers and scientists in those early years, it laid the groundwork for the proliferation of packet-switched networks. And proliferate they did. Research organizations, government entities, and universities around the world began establishing packet-switched networks. Today there are are thousands of independent packet-switched networks that together comprise the Internet

The National Science Foundation and NSFNet

While packet switching and TCP/IP were the enabling technologies behind the Internet, the primary network that shaped the

Internet as we know it today was NSFNet, created by the National Science Foundation (NSF) in 1987. The NSF created NSFNet to link supercomputers across the country and to encourage their use for scholarly research. The high-speed network connecting these systems was the so-called backbone of NSFNet, with regional or "mid-level" networks providing access to the NSFNet backbone.

At the same time, the National Aeronautics and Space Administration (NASA) created a network called the National Science Internet. These and other government sponsored networks became the primary "backbones" of the Internet system, providing high-speed dedicated lines across the United States and serving the computers of many research organizations around the world.

BITNET

Technically not part of the Internet, but certainly instrumental in its popularity, BITNET was established in the early 1980s and became one of the most popular networks among universities. Originally based on a network of IBM mainframe computers, BITNET does not use the TCP/IP protocol but is connected to the Internet via IP gateways. While the name BITNET is still used, it is now officially called the Computer Research and Education Network (CREN). BITNET connects over 2300 academic and research institutions around the world.

Private Incursions

As we mentioned earlier, the Internet was not conceived as a commercial enterprise. In its early years, the only way you could get on the Internet was through a government agency or an academic institution. Nevertheless, private commercial networks eventually gained access to the Internet and sold access time to private individuals and businesses. Today, commercial networks around the country sell access to the Internet in a way similar to the commercial online services discussed in the previous chapter. In fact, most of the big commercial online services provide their users with at least an e-mail connection to the Internet. Many are in the process of providing more comprehensive Internet access so that their subscribers may search for data and read the documents that the Internet contains.

Although commercial organizations have gained access to the Internet, there still is strong resistance in the Internet community to commercial use of the Internet. Based on an Acceptable Use Policy (AUP) instituted by the NSF when it started NSFNet, there remains a code of "appropriate usage" on the Internet, and this code precludes blatant advertising or promotion of products and services on the Internet. When users violate this code, they are likely to receive public condemnation by other users or unpleasant e-mail telling them to cease and desist. Remarkably, this sort of mailbombing of transgressors is the only generally available means of disciplining Internet participants. While it is possible for institutions that support the backbone portions of the Internet to refuse access to systems that violate the acceptable use policy, in fact this happens rarely. Such sanctions are rapidly becoming a thing of the past.

The code of appropriate use itself may not have much longer to live. With government funding for the Internet beginning to dry up, it seems inevitable that intense commercial activity will drive control of the Internet into the private sector.

Internet's Far-Flung Kingdom

In the previous chapter, we described commercial online services as analogous to hundreds of bulletin board systems combined into one. The Internet is like hundreds of these large online services combined into one enormous network. It is very difficult to define the Internet because it is such a huge and loosely defined amalgam of resources and information, and its configuration changes all the time. Because the Internet is a network of networks, the underlying network structure is completely flexible in the sense that new networks and systems become part of or (much more rarely) drop away from the Internet all the time.

This protean flexibility is both a weakness and a strength. It is a strength because it makes the Internet virtually indestructible, simply because it is so widely distributed and loosely linked. If one part of the network fails, the rest of the network can still operate. The Internet's flexibility and vastness is also a strength because it virtually ensures a democratic sort of a system (which the cynical would prefer to call anarchic); it would be extremely difficult for any single entity to gain control of a significant portion of the Internet.

This lack of control is also one of the Internet's weaknesses. It makes it very difficult to ensure any sort of data security among systems linked through the Internet. In its current state, the Internet is not secure enough to support financial transactions or even confidential electronic mail. It is also extremely prone to sabotage by way of computer viruses, which, while they cannot disable any major portion of the Internet, can still cause tremendous havoc. One of the most notorious of such incidents occurred in 1988 when Robert Morris, a student at Cornell University, managed to disable several major university Internet networks using a computer virus called a "worm."

Related to the lack of control on the Internet is the real possibility that well-financed and powerful commercial enterprises, such as phone and cable companies, could carry enough Internet traffic to have significant influence on (if not outright control over) the Internet way of operation.

The Internet presents a virtually endless array of information resources. We're going to touch on the some of the most important ones here, but we encourage you to consult some of the references at the end of this book, for more about Internet resources.

E-Mail

By far the most widespread use of the Internet is for electronic mail (e-mail). There are close to 20 million electronic mail addresses on Internet. However, it's not always easy to find a person's e-mail address. Some directories of Internet e-mail addresses are available in bookstores and libraries, but in truth there is no all-inclusive Internet "address book" listing every valid e-mail address across the Internet. Most of the time, you establish electronic mail addresses by word of mouth, by exchanging business cards, or some other mode of contact apart from Internet e-mail.

As mentioned in the previous chapter, you don't necessarily need an Internet account to exchange e-mail with other Internet users. Many online services such as CompuServe and MCI Mail provide e-mail "gateways" to the Internet. For example, users of MCI Mail all have an Internet address consisting of their MCI user name followed by an @ symbol and the suffix (also called a domain name) mcimail.com. My Internet address at MCI Mail is nbaran@mcimail.com. America Online also provides an Internet e-mail gateway, and other online services of any significant size doing the same.

In spite of the anarchic nature of the Internet, the e-mail system is amazingly well organized. Electronic mail addresses are governed by an organization called the Internet Assigned Numbers Authority (IANA), based at the University of Southern California Information Sciences Institute in Marina Del Rey, California. An excellent discussion of how addresses are assigned and what they represent can be found in the book, *The Internet Guide for New Users.* [3]

Usenet and Its Newsgroups

In the last chapter, we mentioned conferences and forums on online services, where you can read and post messages centering on a topic of your choice. This type of message conferencing is also available on the Internet through Usenet. Usenet is an enormous and constantly growing conferencing system accessible through the Internet. What other online systems call conferences or forums are referred to in Usenet jargon as *newsgroups.* Newsgroups are broad-subject categories that have hundreds of subcategories.

There are eight major newsgroups on Usenet: comp (computers), misc (miscellaneous), news (current events), rec (games and hobbies), sci (science and research), soc (social issues and politics), talk (debate and controversial topics), and alt (alternative). You can join discussions on virtually every topic imaginable, from sexual behavior (that's in the alt category) to cooking to astronomy.

To use Usenet, you need special software called a *news reader,* which runs on your personal computer. There are several versions of these news readers available without charge on the Internet, and there are also more elegant and easy-to-use news readers available as commercial products. Usenet has historically been difficult to use, but some of the more recent news reader products make it about as easy to use as any other online conferencing system.

One significant problem is that the volume of information on Usenet can be overwhelming. For example, several years ago, I published a newsletter covering the NeXT computer. There was a newsgroup called comp.sys.next devoted to the NeXT computer. I would check in on the conference a few days each week, and there would be perhaps 200 new messages since my previous session. Now consider some of the newsgroups with broader appeal than the NeXT computer. These newsgroups might have several hundred new messages per day to keep up with.

List Servers

Another major source of news and information on the Internet is public mailing lists, which are available through a function called Listserv. As an Internet user, you can join mailing lists to receive electronic mail on a topic you choose. Articles and messages regarding this topic are posted by other Usenet users and automatically sent to all members of the mailing list. You join mailing lists by "subscribing" to them.

There are thousands of topics accessible through Listserv. For example, during the recent revolt in the Chiapas region of Mexico, journalists and other observers posted hundreds of messages to the indigenous peoples' list server. Many of these list servers exist on BITNET, which is where the list server concept originated, but are accessible throughout the Internet.

As with Usenet, the problem with many of these list servers is the sheer volume of messages they receive. When you retrieve your electronic mail from an active list server, you may be faced with several hundred thousand lines of text to download!

Databases

The Internet is connected to thousands of databases around the world. Most of these are free. Others are commercial databases that charge by the minute of connect-time. The Internet supports a function called Telnet, which allows you to reach out across the Internet and connect to faraway computers (in other words, do a remote log-in). Access to other computers ranges from unrestricted to requiring a government security clearance. In any case, because you can "telnet" (the names of Internet utilities are used as verbs in informal parlance) to other systems, you can gain access to a large number of databases.

For example, if you're willing to pay or if your institution has an account, you can tap into the LEXIS/NEXIS or Dialog databases from the Internet. Many universities maintain databases that are accessible free of charge. For example, the University of Minnesota maintains the CIA World Book of Facts database, which is available to most Internet users.

File Transfer Protocol (FTP)

File Transfer Protocol (FTP) is the protocol used to download and upload files on the Internet. FTP is a set of Unix-like commands for accessing computers all over the Internet, listing files, changing directories, and copying files to your computer.

Files ranging from legal documents to computer games reside on FTP "sites" (Internet jargon for computers) all over the Internet. Some of them are off-limits or only accessible to certain qualified individuals. Others are available to all users free of charge. Depending on the nature of your Internet account, you may also be able to place files at certain FTP sites for others to use.

Searching for Information on the Internet

With such an enormous volume of information available, there's an obvious need for tools that allow you to search for information, and several such tools exist. Probably the most widely used search tool is called gopher, which is essentially a library card catalog searching tool. Gopher consists of hierarchies of menus, each menu leading to a submenu until your search is narrowed to specific articles and so forth. There are thousands of gophers on the Internet. These gophers can lead to other gophers, which can lead to still other gophers. Using gopher itself can become a tedious undertaking! A complementary tool is veronica, which helps you narrow down searches of gophers.

Archie is still another popular tool for searching for files on FTP sites. Other search tools include the Wide Area Information System (WAIS) and World Wide Web (see the next section). There are also tools for finding addresses and people on the Internet. These include finger, whois (who is), netfind, and knowbots. These tools are all described in the books on Internet listed at the end of this book.

The World Wide Web

One of the most recent enhancements to the way that the Internet itself works is the World Wide Web, often abbreviated WWW or simply called the Web. The Web was initially created at CERN, a European lab for research in particle physics. The whole idea of the Web is to create a system for viewing the Internet as a world-spanning hypertext document. Hypertext is the concept of linking documents according to common or associated words or phrases. Web documents include special fields that contain the addresses of other documents elsewhere on the Web. These fields display names of people, places, or concepts pertinent to the document being read—by selecting the special field, a link is made to another document that contains more information on the entity named in the field.

For example, a document about American poetry might have only a paragraph on the work of Robert Frost, with the name

Robert Frost highlighted. As an experienced Web user, you know you can click on the highlighted field containing Frost's name and read a longer and more detailed biography of Frost. You only have to click. You don't need to know that the biography will be loaded and displayed from elsewhere on the Web, perhaps from a place on the opposite side of the planet.

The World Wide Web is still very new, and its full impact on the Internet is not yet known. Many people consider it an important prototype for accessing information on the information highway, and interested readers should research it further.

The Ease-of-Use Issue

Ease of use is a relative concept. If you're willing to plow through one of the many introductory books on the Internet and if you have a free account where you can play around and learn Internet commands and procedures at your leisure without fretting about the ticking of the meter, the Internet might become easy to use after a while. To appreciate this, just ask a veteren Internet user how to do something:

"Hey, no sweat! You just Telnet to eelib@vsi.hsi.lib.edu and do an anonymous FTP! Oh, and make sure to set your terminal emulation to VT-52! Nothing to it!"

Right.

On the other hand, if you're just an average person and just want to get the information you need (and especially if you're paying by the hour), the Internet can be a nightmare. A *Wall Street Journal* reporter tells about searching for information on the leaning tower of Pisa, using gopher. She entered *Pisa*, and then *Tower*. What came on the screen was information about an oriental witch in a tower. It turned out that the reporter had accessed the card catalog at the University of Pisa. [4]

The Internet wasn't designed with ease of use in mind. (There are those who explain this by saying that the Internet wasn't really designed at all—but rather evolved in a context where ease of use was an insult and not an advantage.) The Internet network runs on host computers that almost all use an operating system called Unix. Unix has been in existence since the late 1960s, and although it is a proven and very robust operating system, it is difficult to use. When Steve Jobs and NeXT Computer introduced NeXTStep, which was a graphical user interface and programming environment that worked with Unix, the sales pitch was that NeXTStep offered "Unix for mere mortals." In other words, until the arrival of NeXTStep, only Unix experts could use Unix. And this pitch had an element of truth to it.

Although you don't have to actually use Unix to use the Internet, many Internet commands and procedures are based on Unix counterparts. And some Internet features, like Telnet, actually place you at the Unix command line, which makes the DOS command line look like child's play. You have to deal with slashes and directory trees and terse commands that resemble nothing in any human language. You have to install special software on your system before you can use certain Internet tools such as Usenet or gopher (you need a news reader to use Usenet and you need a "gopher client" on your system before you can run gopher).

This doesn't mean that you actually need Unix itself on your personal computer or workstation to use the Internet. When connected to the Internet, your system behaves like a remote terminal connected to a host computer. Your communications software provides the required "terminal emulation" so that your computer can communicate on the Internet. The remote system is the one that must actually run Unix—you and your terminal must simply understand it.

Terminal emulation brings up another major source of difficulty on the Internet—namely, graphics and video. The Internet was born long before there were any consistent graphics standards. While certain formats have become standard on PCs and Macintosh computers, Unix workstations often produce graphics in other, less common formats.

In addition, graphics files can get very large, even with digital compression, and many users are still accessing the Internet at 2,400 bits per second. This is far too slow for serious graphics in any format. The bottom line is that you can obtain graphic images on Internet, but not always easily.

The information highway of the future is supposed to include pictures and video on demand, presumably without having to worry about graphic formats or conversion programs—and without waiting minutes upon minutes for a single image to appear on the screen. The Internet is a long way from instant access to graphics and video.

New Easy-to-Use Tools

The Internet's archaic interface and esoteric command structure have not gone unnoticed by software developers and access providers. New products that make the Internet easier to use have begun to appear and to the amazement of the rest of old Unix priests. These new tools are achieving fast and wide acceptance. These tools do not actually change the ways that the Internet itself works, but instead, are interfaces or "front ends" that shield you from the Internet's inherent complexity. This approach makes it possible to perform fairly complex tasks by simply selecting a menu item or clicking on an icon.

One of the most popular of these tools is Mosaic. Mosaic provides a multimedia-capable graphical interface for accessing World Wide Web hypertext document files on the Internet. Mosaic's decidedly un-Unix like user interface is shown in Figure 3.1. Developed at the National Center for Supercomputing Applications at the University of Illinois, Champaign-Urbana, Mosaic is distributed without charge from several places on the Internet, and has been included in commercial collections of Internet software by publishers such as O'Reilly & Associates of Sebastopol, California. While Mosaic is extremely easy to use once it is set up, someone familiar with the Internet has to perform the initial configuration. It is also very hungry for connection bandwidth,

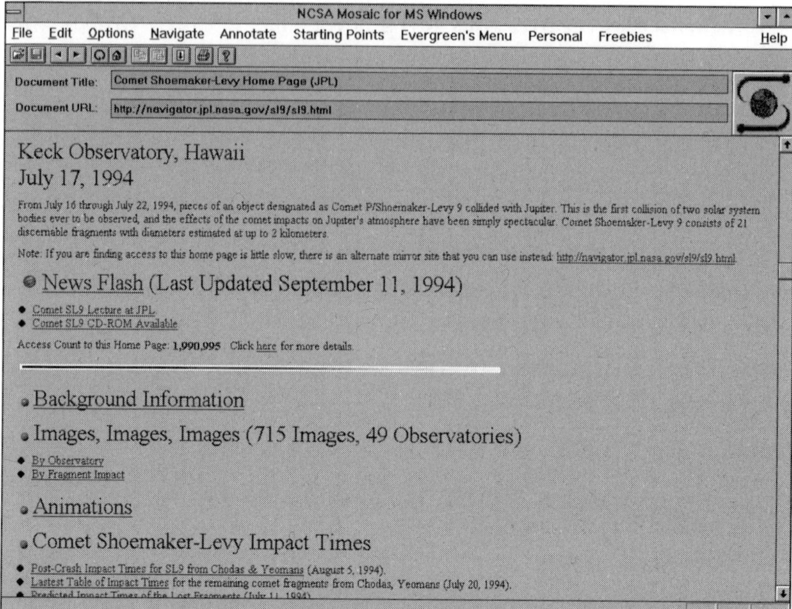

Figure 3.1 *Using Mosaic to navigate the Internet.*

and works best over T1-style, high-speed connections between machines. Like many of the newer Internet tools, Mosaic is simply hopeless at 2400 bps.

Variations on the Mosaic interface concept are beginning to appear. Perhaps the best known of these is Cello, a graphical hypertext browser available free from the author's Internet host machine.

Another tool that recently hit the commercial market is Internet Anywhere for Windows, from Mortice Kern Systems of Waterloo, Ontario, Canada. This interface suite runs on Microsoft Windows and includes a news reader, an electronic-mail interface, and tools for automated operations such as logging into the Internet at night and downloading newsgroup messages. Again, this tool requires some setup that requires knowledge of the Internet. A similar product is Internet-in-a-Box from O'Reilly & Associates.

CompuServe has announced plans to release a user-friendly Internet interface that will be available to CompuServe subscribers who want to use the Internet. Like the Windows interfaces just described, the CompuServe tool will provide easy access to

Usenet and also navigation tools for using search utilities and protocols such as gopher and the World Wide Web.

Certainly these interface tools are a positive step and will help novice users gain access to the Internet. But it won't solve the ease of use problem entirely. As we stated earlier, ease of use is a relative concept. To a savvy Windows user, Internet Anywhere for Windows may be the answer. But there are millions of potential Internet users who don't even know how to use Windows. And if Internet is going to be the information highway of the future, it will have to be much easier to use than even Windows.

Information Overload

Directly related to the general difficulty of using the Internet is the problem of accessing too much information. What do you do with 100,000 lines of text per day? As John Webb of the Washington State University library put it, "what good is a search on a certain topic when you get 20,000 hits?" (A "hit" is a successful "find" based on your search criteria.) These are tough problems to solve, and they will be equally big problems for other forms of the information highway. "Channel surfing" through 500 channels may be a bit much for most people who also have lives away from the tube.

Security

An article on Internet security in the March, 1994 issue of *Scientific American* starts:

> Someday the Internet may become an information superhighway, but right now it is more like a 19th century railroad that passes through the badlands of the Old West. As waves of new settlers flock to cyberspace in search of free information or commercial opportunity, they make easy marks for sharpers who play a keyboard as deftly as Billy the Kid ever drew a six-gun. [5]

And that little analogy sums up the situation beautifully. The Internet is not a secure system. Even though some parts of the system use encryption and other security techniques, mischief makers and criminals can easily get access to user names and passwords and then impersonate those users to gain access to confidential business or personal information. There are also people whose main goal in life is to crack encryption systems—and the more complex the algorithm, the more attractive a challenge it is to crack that algorithm.

As we mentioned earlier, electronic-mail messages are not secure because they are simply blocks of ordinary ASCII text, and can be read by system operators all along their route as they are handed off from one electronic mailbox to another. In addition to these basic security problems, the Internet has grown so rapidly that no one really knows how many users it has or even the exact number of networks connected to the system!

The Clipper Furor

As with the ease of use problem, there is no shortage of proposed solutions to the Internet's security problem. The most prominent and controversial is the Clipper chip designed and promoted by the federal government. This chip was designed by the National Security Agency (NSA, the federal agency specializing in secure communications) for use in telephones and computers on networks.

In the Clipper system, data packets are scrambled during transmission so no unauthorized persons can reassemble the original data. The data packets are then re-organized at the receiving end using an encryption/decryption algorithm called SKIPJACK, which is implemented in the Clipper chip and the hardware device containing the Clipper chip. The encryption and decryption key pairs generated by and used with the SKIPJACKalgorithm are to be created by the U.S. government and held in escrow, so law enforcement agencies can gain access to these encryption keys under court order for wiretapping. The government has stated its intent to require that all communications with government agencies, and work on all government projects must be encrypted with Clipper. A great deal of Internet traffic is government or government-research related, so if adopted, the Clipper system will become a significant presence on the Internet.

Naturally, there has been a major uproar over the Clipper chip, with virtually all non-government companies, professional groups, publications, and commentators (including the American Civil Liberties Union and Computer Professionals for Social Responsibility) lining up solidly against the Clipper system. Because the key escrow system depends entirely on the trustworthiness of several government agencies, the private sector has doubts that the integrity of the key escrow system can be maintained. And because the algorithm was developed in secrecy and never revealed in detail, many have darkly hinted that the NSA has built a trapdoor into the SKIPJACK algorithm, allowing them to decrypt any Clipper-encrypted material in real-time, without even needing the private keys. The NSA cannot prove that this is not the case without revealing the algorithm, which they have thus far refused to do. It is worth noting that SKIPJACK is the only encryption algorithm ever seriously proposed without detailed public scrutiny, implying that the government does indeed have something to hide.

Regardless of one's political orientations and views of the Clipper chip, many experts in the network business think that it's doomed to failure anyway. First of all, its use will be voluntary outside of government business—and without strong adoption in the private sector, it will not be attractive to manufacturers. Secondly, someone is bound to crack the algorithm on the Clipper chip, or at least identify flaws rendering it weaker than the governments claims. Bob Metcalfe, one of the inventors of Ethernet networking technology and founder of 3COM Corporation, wrote in the March 22, 1994 issue of *The Wall Street Journal:*

> I am against Clipper simply because it will not work and it will cost an unnecessary amount of tax money to outfit government computers with the chips. The success of Clipper will depend on its wide adoption, which is unlikely, and the secrecy of its SKIPJACK algorithm. This secrecy will make the chip expensive and inflexible, and I'm willing to bet someone will figure out SKIPJACK eventually.

Later reports in *The New York Times* and elsewhere documented the identification by Bell Labs researchers of weaknesses in the Clipper/SKIPJACK system. We'll have a lot more to say about security later in this book. For now, we're just suggesting that security is one of the major challenges facing Internet, and could be a serious obstacle to its adoption as one of the primary lanes on the information highway.

The Question of Access: Commercial versus Public

As we stated at the outset, the Internet is the closest thing there is to an information highway in existence today. Sure, commercial online services and BBSs are useful, but they are not even in the Internet's league in terms of numbers of users, volume of information, and diversity of access, particularly on the international scene.

Because of the Internet's unique position, there is a mad scramble to get a piece of the action on the Internet. And people are scrambling from all directions. At one extreme, we have a cable service offering an Internet connection starting at $125 per month for home cable subscribers, and more than $2,000 per month for businesses, depending on the access speed. [6] At the other extreme, we have communities setting up FreeNet networks with Internet access that is free to community residents.

There is a clamor from commercial enterprises to commercialize the Internet and de-regulate it. There is a clamor from the government to develop a National Information Infrastructure and a National Research and Education Network (NREN). There is a clamor from the Electronic Frontier Foundation and Computer Professionals for Social Responsibility, warning against the takeover of the information highway by big corporate interests, who would then control the content of the information highway.

Indeed, these are all important issues, and we'll come back to them again and again. But the first thing to recognize is that the Internet is already becoming commercialized. Parts of the Internet are operated and maintained by private companies. For example, MCI, IBM, and Merit, Inc. maintain NSFNet under the auspices of a company they formed called Advanced Network & Services, Inc. (ANS). Although these services are contracted by the federal government, ANS also sells access to the Internet, and is well positioned to establish privately funded Internet networks. Some of the regional telephone companies are in the process of establishing links to the Internet that will allow them to sell access time. Cable companies and satellite network providers are also getting in on the action.

The Internet itself is already being used for commercial purposes. In spite of the Acceptable Use Policy mentioned earlier, private companies and business entrepreneurs post messages announcing the availability of products and services. Mailing lists (list servers) have already been established for all kinds of commercial ventures, from mail order catalogs to online legal services. In the case of list servers, there is no obvious violation of the AUP since membership on list servers is completely voluntary (as discussed earlier, users must subscribe to the mailing list of a particular list server to receive its messages). In addition, many list servers are technically on BITNET, which is not subject to the AUP.

In the case of messages promoting products posted on Usenet, discretion has been the key. Basically, if your message isn't too blatant an advertisement, you can probably get away with it. For example, a booming mail-order software business got most of its customers by word of mouth on the Internet. [7] Several publications are devoted to doing business on the Internet, [8] so there is no shortage of information on using the Internet for commercial ventures.

The Academic Backlash

An inevitable side effect of the commercialization of the Internet is the strong resentment towards commercial interests from the established core Internet community of researchers and students. There are people in laboratories and academia who have literally made the Internet a way of life. In fact, some people spend so much time on the Internet, you're left to wonder if they ever do anything else in their jobs! The Internet has traditionally been a haven for computer enthusiasts (true hackers in the original sense of the term) who feel severely threatened by the commercial encroachment into the Internet. They feel, rightly or wrongly, that commercialization will force the freewheeling nature of Internet into a more controlled, less spontaneous mold—and perhaps lead to the suppression of viewpoints and activities looked upon as too far from the mainstream. These "culture clashes" are inevitable and the culture clash on the Internet will probably force the real hackers and enthusiasts to move on to some other technology where they can continue to be apart from the mainstream. I suspect that they in turn are hoping that commercial interests will depart to form an entirely separate information highway, and leave the Internet to those who created it. No one is yet sure which way it will fall, but it is worth noting that as the Internet balloons into an enterprise of vast proportions, the National Science Foundation is developing a new high-speed network called the National Research Education Network (NREN), which is likely to become the successor to the Internet for researchers and scientists.

Community FreeNets and Grassroots Networks

On the one hand, we have entrepreneurs and commercial interests jumping on the Internet bandwagon, and on the other we have community organizers and grassroots volunteers, educators, and public officials such as librarians. These people have a completely different agenda from that of the commercial advocates. Community organizers comprise a growing movement in the U.S. and Canada (and also in other countries) dedicated to establishing community networks connected to the Internet. These networks, often called FreeNets, enable citizens of a community to set up conferences and bulletin-board systems for local issues and events, as well as to connect to the Internet and exchange information all over the world. Local school districts are often connected to the FreeNet and thereby gain Internet access.

The FreeNet movement is spearheaded by an organization called the National Public Telecomputing Network (NPTN) based in

Cleveland, Ohio. The movement has its origins in a series of research bulletin-board systems established at Case Western Reserve University in the mid 1980s. The mission of NPTN is to help communities start FreeNet systems. [9]

There are about 35 FreeNet networks in the U.S. and Canada, as well as one in Germany. There are also about a dozen educational computer networks affiliated with the NPTN. One of the most successful FreeNet networks is the Heartland FreeNet in Peoria, Illinois. The Heartland FreeNet provides an array of local information conferences, as well as a connection to the Internet and several public schools in the Peoria area. Among other services, Heartland FreeNet operates a medical database sponsored by the local hospital, an automotive diagnostics conference, sponsored by local auto shops, community bulletin boards, and community outreach programs. It's mainly operated by volunteers and funded through donations and grants from local businesses and institutions.

Other FreeNets that have been successful include the Cleveland FreeNet in Cleveland, with more than 35,000 users, and Big Sky Telegraph, based at Western Montana College in Dillon, Montana, a community network with funding from several private sources and the strong support of rural educators.

Running a FreeNet system isn't cheap. The NPTN estimates an annual budget of $125,000 to $150,000 to operate and maintain one of these networks, assuming a worst case scenario where nothing is donated and everything has to be purchased retail. Communities near colleges and universities that already have an Internet connection have a major advantage because it is often possible to connect the community to the institution's Internet connection at relatively low cost. In any event, FreeNets require community involvement and funds.

Is There Enough Bandwidth?

We're going to discuss bandwidth, that is, data transmission capacity, in greater detail in the next chapter. But since we're on the subject of the Internet, we should point out that lack of data transmission capacity is an increasing problem all over the Internet as the number of users continues to grow astronomically. A major university near where I live reports frequent overloading of the system, with data movement on the screen slowing to a crawl. Many universities are undertaking major rewiring projects to increase campus network capacity as more and more students and faculty want access to the Internet. Parts of the Internet run across networks with tremendous capacity, but other parts operate over lines that have been stretched to capacity for years now. Bandwidth will continue to be a major problem on the Internet as it keeps growing, and the Internet has certainly been an object lesson in the effects that limited bandwidth has on the speed and effectiveness of any far-flung network. As we shall see in the next chapter, there are alternatives that may solve this problem.

How Vulnerable Is the Internet?

We stated earlier on that the Internet is indestructible because it is so widely distributed, so that the system as a whole will keep running in spite of local outages or breakdowns. However, local failures and system crashes are quite commonplace on the Internet, and can be disastrous for users who dial in through the unreliable systems. Except for some of the major Internet backbones, most local-level Internet systems do not have high levels of redundancy or fault tolerance, in which a backup or mirror image system takes over when the primary system fails. Such computer systems are used in banks, the telephone system, and in other mission-critical applications where breakdowns cannot be tolerated.

Here is a typical scenario of an Internet breakdown as reported by a college computer system administrator:

> The specific problems we had a couple of weeks ago were twofold. We had some misconfigured machines that were retransmitting all IP packets so they looked like they were constantly changing their addresses. But the main problem was hardware. We added another department to our network and the entire house of cards came crashing down. As a result of all this, my manager decided to rewire our network, to try to clean up the

> rat's nest that had developed over the last few years. He hooked things up *exactly* as they were before, but with the rat's nest cleaned up. Parts of our network stopped working. It took a lot of tinkering around to get things back to a stable configuration.
>
> One lesson to learn from this is that the less you try to tax the capabilities of your network, the better off you'll be. We routinely run at the 'maximum useable' capacity of Ethernet coax, which is supposedly around 30% of the *real* maximum capacity. We could really use a more high-performance network medium like FDDI, but that, of course, takes money.

If anything, the Internet networks will continue to be taxed more and more, and unless additional capacity is added, will become more and more unreliable.

Where Does the Internet Fit In?

The Internet is an admirable example of the technical ingenuity and pioneering spirit of the computer science community. It is also an example of the federal government's and American universities' generosity that has allowed the Internet to become the global network of networks that it is today. And there's no question that the Internet will play a major role in the development of a future information highway, regardless of what form it takes.

My publisher commented early on when we were discussing Internet that it reminds him of the CP/M operating system, which was basically the first operating system for mass-marketed personal computers, long before MS-DOS came along. It was primitive and hard to use, but it got the job done. Decades from now, we'll look back at the Internet the way we look back at those early days of CP/M, or to the early days of the automobile. We may remember that we got things done, or that we got where we were going, but we will often find ourselves wondering how.

The twin questions of how the Internet will change as technology advances, and whether or not the Internet will in fact become the envisioned information highway, are in fact a single question. As the world's communication infrastructure improves, the Internet will improve automatically, because Internet traffic rides the same lines as all other communication services. Greater bandwidth and faster data transmission rates will make things possible on the Internet that are simply not possible today. Mosaic, for example, is capable of playing real-time video clips—but our communications infrastructure is just not capable of delivering them to the Mosaic user's computer quickly enough for them to be useful. If most or all of the Internet were suddenly to operate over fiber optic cable, Mosaic or something similar could deliver feature-length videos in real-time. Given the sort of infrastructure envisioned for the information highway of the future, the Internet could become that highway.

But should it? One of the best arguments brought against the canonization of the Internet as the world's future information highway is that the Internet was never intended to be a vehicle for mass communication. The Internet was conceived as a tool for scholars and scientists, not for consumers searching for interactive video games. Adding such traffic to the Internet could crowd out what the Internet does best: bring the world's best minds together in an anarchic but miraculously fruitful maelstrom of electronic interaction. (As mentioned earlier, the NSF's NREN network will probably serve that purpose, since the Internet becoming a vehicle for mass communication seems to already be inevitable.)

Perhaps the Internet will someday ride the same fiber optic pathways as the envisioned information highway. The two can coexist, after all; the fiber, like a freight train, can carry many different kinds of load. It is helpful to remember that the Internet was once called the Research Internet—and if we look to the Internet as a testbed for the sorts of advanced technologies we will need to build the future information highway, it will have served us well beyond its creators' most optimistic imaginings.

Getting Inside

The Technology behind the Highway

> *"Now comes the interesting part. Builders of the information highway have created a media sensation with their plans for wiring America. But to deliver on their promises, they will have to meet challenges on unprecedented complexity and size."*
>
> **Bart Ziegler, *The Wall Street Journal*, May 18, 1994**

In Chapter 1, I discussed several likely mass-market uses of the future information highway. One of these was "video on demand." To refresh your memory, the scene goes something like this: A few years from now, or maybe even sooner, you're sitting in your living room and selecting a movie to watch that evening from a menu of movie titles that appears on your TV screen. You click on the name of the movie that you want to watch, and within minutes of making your selection, you're sitting back with some microwave popcorn watching the opening credits.

Of course, the phone rings. You pause the movie and go answer the phone. Remember, this movie is not on a tape inside your VCR. It's being transmitted from the computer of your service provider, and you can pause and rewind the movie at will. And you're not the only person watching that movie. Many other customers in your service area may be watching the movie and may have started watching it twenty minutes earlier or half an hour later. Those people are also pausing and rewinding at will.

Video on demand, like many of the other functions and services of the information highway, requires some very complex and powerful technology. For example, video on demand requires powerful computers called *video servers*, which can store hundreds of movies in compressed digital form and can send those movies across the telephone or cable TV lines to the decoder device on top of your TV set, called the *set-top box*.

We're going to take a look at the technology behind the information highway in this chapter. We're not going to bombard you with a lot of acronyms and abbreviations and big words. We're going to keep things simple, but we will cover some fairly technical material. Hopefully, by the end of this chapter, you'll have a basic grasp of the main technology.

The Buzzword Is *Broadband*

When executives and analysts in the telecommunications industry talk about the information highway, they often call it a *broadband network*, or they talk about "broadband services" or "broadband communications." "Broadband" is a buzzword whose meaning few people really understand, but the term certainly shows up a lot in the press. In a nutshell, "broadband" means "broad bandwidth," or to put it another way, "large transmission capacity," measured per unit time. (Don't worry, we'll define bandwidth more clearly.) And "broad bandwidth" means you can transmit a lot of information at once—movies, telephone calls, electronic mail, home shopping orders, all sharing the "bandwidth" of the telephone wires and television cable that enters your home. As we shall see, it takes a lot of bandwidth to transmit all these types of information to your computer or television set. The way the telecommunications industry plans to supply this bandwidth is by building broadband networks. This may all seem very confusing at the moment, but by the end of this chapter, it should make sense.

Another bit of jargon that we want to clarify is *video dial tone*. This term has its origins in a ruling by the Federal Communications Commission (FCC) allowing the local exchange carriers (local telephone companies) to provide "video dialtone service." The term keeps creeping into the marketing and technical background materials from telecommunications companies as if everyone should already know what it means.

The idea of a video dial tone is to make access to video as ubiquitous and straightforward as the dial tone on your telephone, which is the signal that must be present before you can make and receive telephone calls. Going back to our video on demand example, the cable coming into your house would be ready to transmit or receive video with the push of a button. A video dial tone means that the basic "common carriage" transmission services would include the capability to send and receive video.

Technology and the Technology behind It

There's a rule of thumb that applies to virtually every development in high technology: the more powerful the application and the easier it is to use, the more complex the technology behind it. For example, the Macintosh was considered a major breakthrough in ease of use for computer users. Compared to the IBM PC and its DOS operating system, the Macintosh provided a far more intuitive system for operating the computer, using a mouse to point and click on graphical icons and menu items that represented programs and commands. But for programmers who wrote the applications that ran on the Macintosh, the Macintosh system was extremely complex and difficult to program.

The information highway takes these opposed forces of ease of use and technical complexity to another and higher level. The information highway will have to be far easier to use than the Macintosh—and it will have to deliver far more powerful applications. If the information highway is to succeed, it must offer push-button simplicity and it must effortlessly deliver a huge array of information. The technical complexity of the information highway will have to be completely concealed from the ultimate consumer.

Even after all these years of supposed "computer literacy," basic technology is still too hard to use for most workers and consumers. Many computer users don't know how to operate a computer independently. They can follow a set of instructions given by their supervisor or in-house computer expert to perform specific tasks on the computer, but they may be paralyzed by basic tasks like copying a file to a floppy disk if they've never had to do it before and have never been told how.

The great majority of Americans who own video cassette recorders (VCRs) don't know how to program them to record a television show at a later time. In fact, many VCR users don't know how to record television shows at all. The majority of VCR users use their VCRs strictly for playing rented movie tapes, and the daunting problem of making the "flashing 12:00" go away has become a standard gag item on the stand-up comedy circuit. Most home entertainment users are now faced with a bewildering set of remote control devices—one for the TV, one for the radio/amplifier, one for the VCR, yet another for the CD player, and so forth. Babysitters need a training session before they can watch TV!

If we take this current state of affairs a step further and add the services of the information highway without some significant advances in simplicity and ease of use, the living room could become an electronic nightmare rather than the new paradigm for home entertainment and education.

Some proponents of the Internet claim the information highway is already here—we just need to keep building upon the Internet. But if consumers have trouble programming a VCR, they are not likely to have the patience to learn how to navigate the Internet using Internet utilities like gopher or FTP, or even something as well-designed as the Mosaic navigator program.

The Big Three

Three broad categories make up the technology of the information highway: hardware, software, and information content. Hardware includes everything from satellites to telephone cable to TV sets—in other words, the hardware comprises the equipment, devices, and cabling that make up the information highway.

The software provides the interface on the TV screen or computer that enables you to access the information highway. Many people are confused by the term "interface." Basically, an interface is how two unlike things communicate. In its initial definition, the two unlike things were human beings and computers. The interface between the computer and a human being is the software that enables the human being to give commands to the computer and to receive the results from those commands. The information highway is likely to include many different kinds of interfaces, depending on the application.

The information content is what you receive on your TV or computer. Information content includes movies and video games, television shows and newscasts, electronic mail and online conference messages, book abstracts and magazine articles, electronic newspapers, and so forth.

Before we get into these categories, we need to define some important digital and analog concepts and terminology. The following topics provide a very cursory treatment of some technically complicated material that would normally be covered in a physics course or in an introductory course on telecommunications. If you find it's over your head, don't worry. The key points are summarized at the end of the section and are all you really need to know.

Analog and Digital Information

Information is transmitted electronically in two forms: analog and digital. Before the advent of computers, virtually all electronic information, such as that broadcast on radio and television, was transmitted in analog form. An *analog signal* is a signal whose magnitude continually varies with time. A typical analog signal, such as a sound wave, is shown in Figure 4.1. If you move along the time axis in the figure, the magnitude (or value) of the

Figure 4.1 *An analog sound wave that shows how the amplitude varies continuously with time.*

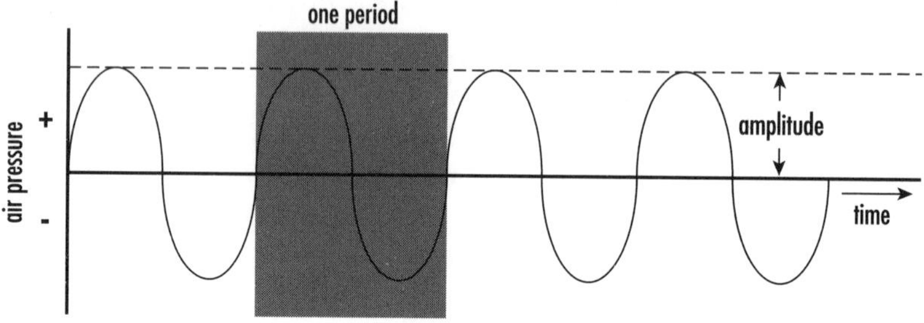

wave changes continuously. Most natural phenomena, such as sound, light, temperature, fluid motion, and pressure are measured and transmitted in analog form. The period is the time it takes for the wave to travel the complete wavelength. The number of times per second that it travels its complete wavelength is called the frequency (this is the reciprocal of the period). If the period is one-half second, the frequency is 2 cycles per second.

Computers, however, are not designed to work with analog signals, but rather with digital signals, which are far less complex than analog signals. [1] A digital signal is composed of a sequence of separate elements that can be in one of two states: on (1) or off (0), as shown in Figure 4.2. A digital signal is also called a *discrete* signal, because it does not vary continuously with time, but rather consists of separate and discrete elements that can have only one of two values. These two values are expressed in the binary number system, in which there are only two digits: zero and one.

Each on or off signal (1 or 0) is called a *bit* (short for "binary digit"). We can use a sequence of digital bits to represent codes or other more complex information. The International Morse code

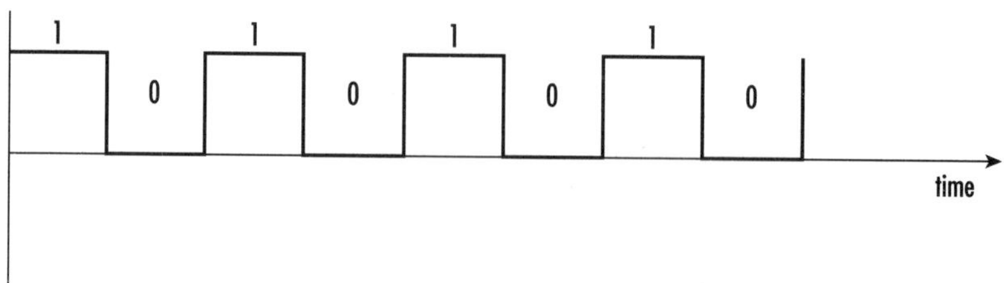

Figure 4.2 *A digital signal has one of two values: zero or one (on or off).*

is perhaps the world's oldest digital code that survives, and goes back to the nineteenth century. Instead of pure on or off states, Morse code consists of sequences of short tones and long tones, which are created by depressing a telegraph key for a short time or a slightly longer time. The sequence of short tones (which could be called 0-bits) and long tones (which could be called 1-bits) determines the meaning of the signal. For example, long-short-long-long (1-0-1-1) means "Y," which is something entirely different from long-long-short-long (1-1-0-1), which means "Q."

By convention, eight bits taken together make up a *byte,* and a byte is large enough to represent a single character or a digit. The American Standard Code for Information Interchange (ASCII) is the standard code for defining the sequences of bits and their corresponding numbers or letters. For example, the number "6" is represented in ASCII as 00110110. The letter "H" is represented by 01001001. Using every possible combination of 8 bits, you can represent 256 (that is, 2^8) numbers and characters. Modern computers today usually can work with 32 or even 64 bits at a time, allowing billions of distinct combinations of bits.

With this enormous number of available bit patterns, digital signals can represent sounds, colors, shapes, as well as characters and numbers, and can therefore represent complex and detailed analog information. This is accomplished by a process called analog-to-digital (A/D) conversion. The basic idea is to approximate the shape of the analog wave by a series of discrete values (numbers) that are expressed in binary form. The concept is illustrated in Figure 4.3. With today's powerful computers, digital informa-

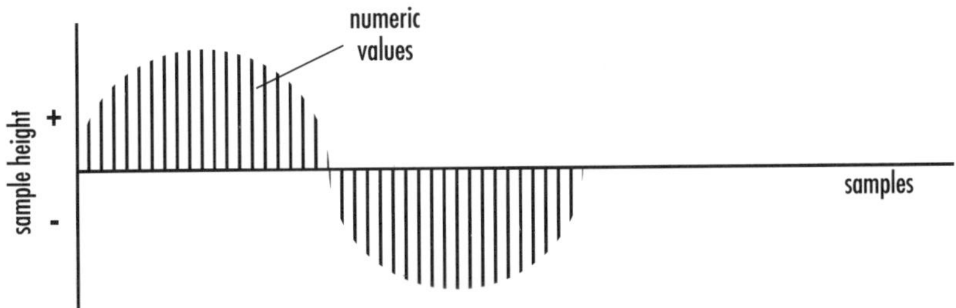

Figure 4.3 *The analog signal of Figure 4.1 is approximated by a series of numbers that can be expressed in binary form (this is also called sampling).*

tion can be used to produce high-quality reproductions of traditionally analog phenomena, such as music, complex color artwork, and full motion video.

Televisions, stereo systems, and telephones are analog devices. Thus, information transmitted digitally to these devices must be converted to analog form, unless the information is going directly to your computer—and even on the computer, digital sound has to be converted to analog before you can actually send it to the speaker to play it. The device that performs this digital to analog conversion is called a *digital-to-analog converter* or DAC. One of the primary components of the set-top box that goes on top of the TV is a DAC.

Because telephone systems are primarily analog, the opposite procedure is necessary to send digital information produced on a computer across the telephone lines. Both the sending and receiving computers each are connected to a *modem* (short for *modulator-demodulator*), which is connected to the telephone line. At the sending end, the modem converts the digital signal from the computer to an analog signal for transmission on the phone line, which is then converted back to a digital signal by the modem attached to the receiving computer (see Figure 4.4). For the foreseeable future, you will need a modem to connect to online services and networks such as CompuServe and the Internet, unless your company or organization has a special digital line called an *ISDN* (Integrated Services Digital Network) line. Modems con-

Figure 4.4 *Modems attach to the computer and the telephone line, and allow digital information to be transmitted on analog telephone lines.*

nected to standard telephone lines pose a severe limitation on the data transmission capacity (the bandwidth) of online services.

As of the mid-1990s, most electronic information is still transmitted in analog form. Radio and television stations broadcast analog signals. Satellite and cable television are primarily analog. Most of the world's telephone systems still use analog transmission techniques, although the availability of digital phone circuitry is expanding rapidly.

In spite of the continued dominance of analog information, the transformation from analog to digital is gradually taking place. There are compelling reasons to switch from analog to digital transmission of information. Digital signals are more reliable and easier to work with. Once information has been digitized (converted to 0s and 1s), all forms of information can be handled the same way—whether the information is a movie, song, or newspaper article, it's represented by a series of bits. Digital information can be stored and manipulated on a computer. It can be compressed so that large quantities of data can be stored and then expanded to their original size when needed.

Digital data can also be organized in little bundles called *packets* that allow more efficient use of transmission lines. Analog signal transmission over long distances requires amplifiers to preserve the signal quality and to avoid signal distortion and noise. Digital transmission does not have this problem. And more importantly, it is possible to transmit digital information at greater speeds and in greater volume than equivalent analog information, simply because digital information can be compressed, and thereby occupy less space and bandwidth than the equivalent analog signals. For example, digital compression allows the broadcast of eight times the number of conventional analog channels on Direct Broadcast Satellite (DBS) systems.

Bandwidth

Transmission capacity per unit time is called *bandwidth*. The term "bandwidth" comes from the term "frequency band," which has its roots in radio. (There are shortwave and longwave bands, for example.) The wider the band, the more stations can transmit at the same time. In computer terminology, the wider the band, the more data can be transferred in a given period of time, and that's the basic definition of bandwidth that applies to the information highway. In a digital world, information and data are virtually synonymous at the transmission level. In fact, the information highway is often called the "data highway," because when they're on the move, information and data are basically the same.

Bandwidth is measured differently depending on whether the data being transmitted is in analog or digital form. In analog systems, the bandwidth is measured in cycles per second, which is a measure of the frequency of the analog signal. A *cycle* is one complete excursion of a signal starting from zero, moving through its maximum value in a positive direction, returning to zero, moving to its maximum value in a negative direction, and then coming back to zero. The frequency of an analog signal is the number of times per second that the signal makes this little dance from zero, through positive max, through zero, through negative max, and back to zero. See Figure 4.5 to see how circuit networks compare with packet switched networks. Notice that circuit

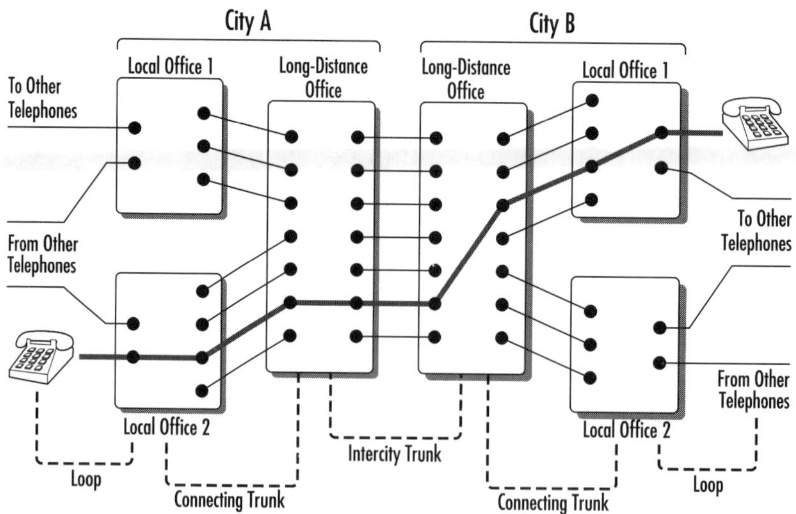

Figure 4.5a *Circuit versus packet switched networks.*

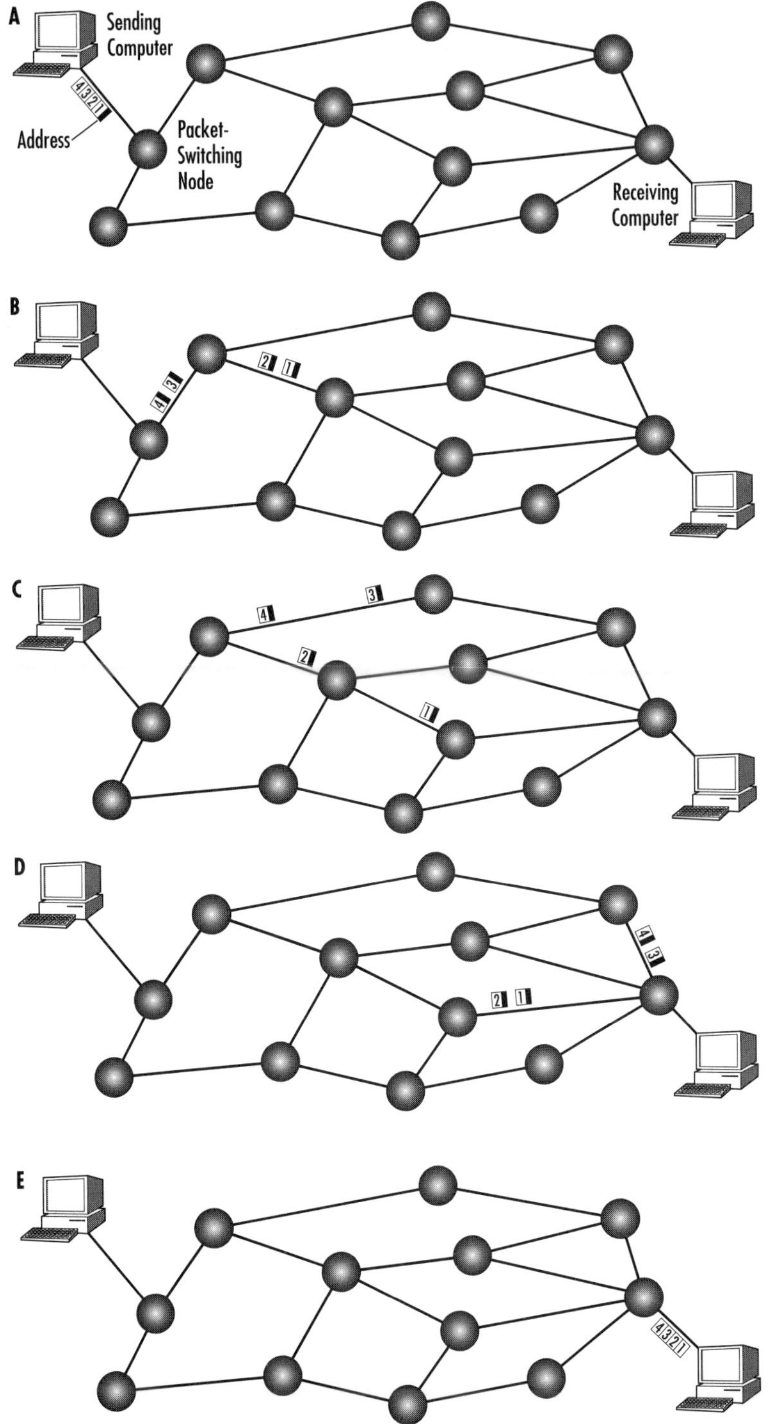

Figure 4.5b *Circuit versus packet switched networks.*

switching requires reserving a portion of an entire circuit, from end to end, for a single connection. Packets travel along any number of circuits and only establish a connection when they reach their destination.

The unit of frequency measurement is Hertz, after the physicist Heinrich Hertz, who laid the foundations for much of what became radio and later television technology. One Hertz is one cycle per second. One kilohertz (KHz) means 1,000 cycles per second. One megahertz (MHz) means 1 million cycles per second, and 1 Gigahertz (GHz) means 1 billion cycles per second.

Electricity and electromagnetic signals (like television and radio waves) travel at the speed of light, which is fairly close to 186,000 miles per second, or 300,000 kilometers per second (exactly the speed in a vacuum such as outer space). The *wavelength* of a signal is the linear distance traveled by the signal during the course of one cycle. If the frequency of a signal is very high, many cycles of that signal occur every second, which implies that each individual cycle takes very little time to complete. If a cycle takes very little time to complete, the signal as a whole will not travel very far in that time, even at the speed of light.

Wavelength is inversely proportional to frequency. This simply means that the shorter the wavelength, the higher the frequency. Radar signals have very short wavelengths and very high frequencies. AM radio signals, by comparison, have far longer wavelengths and much lower frequencies. The wavelength of a radar signal might be only a few inches, whereas the wavelength of a radio station at 1000 on the AM dial is over 1,000 feet. Table 4.1 shows the wavelength and frequency range for a variety of signals.

Here's a useful technical rule of thumb: The necessary bandwidth required to transmit a given analog signal is the maximum frequency of that signal. For example, voice signals used in telephone communications are generally allocated a bandwidth of 4 KHz (4,000 Hertz or 4,000 cycles persecond). The highest frequency of a voice signal that will be able to pass through a phone

Table 4.1 *Wavelength and Frequency Ranges*

Wavelength	3,000 meters	300	30	3	30 centimeters	3
	LF	**MF**	**HF**	**VHF**	**UHF**	**SHF**
Band	**Low Frequency**	**Medium Frequency**	**High Frequency**	**Very High Frequency**	**Ultrahigt Frequency**	**Superhigh Frequency**
	30-300 kHz	300-3,000 kHz (3 mHz)	3 mHz-300 mHz mHz (3 gHz)	30-300 mHz	300 mHz-3,000	3-30 gHz
Uses	Marine and aeronautical navigation equipment	AM radio broadcast; long-distance aeronautical and maritime navigation	Shortwave bradcast; amateur radio; citizens' band radio	Television (channels 2-13); FM broadcasting; private radio land mobile services such as police and fire dispatch	Cellular phones; personal communications services; wireless data networks; specialized mobile radio; pagers; UHF TV channels; microwave long-distance phone transmission	Radar, microwave and satellite transmission; Altair (wireless local-area network system); Cellular Vision (wireless video)
Frequency	100 kHz	1mHz	10mHz	100mHz	1gHz	10gHz

system is 4 KHz. Portions of a voice above that frequency would require additional bandwidth on the phone system (bandwidth that the system simply doesn't have) and are therefore filtered out. 4 KHz is adequate for simple telephone-style voice communications, but considerably greater bandwidth, on the order of 20 KHz, is required for high-fidelity music. By contrast, television channels combining both audio and video require a much broader bandwidth of 6 MHz (6 million cycles per second). There is simply more "stuff" in a television signal; not only is there sound of reasonable fidelity, but enough information to paint 30 color pictures on your TV screen every second. For that, you need a *lot* of bandwidth.

Digital Bandwidth

Digital bandwidth is considered the speed of data transmission. It is analogous to measuring water flow. The faster you pump the water, the greater the volume of water you supply in a given time. While water flow is measured in units like gallons per minute, bandwidth is measured in bits per second (bps), usually expressed in kilobits (1,000 bits), megabits (1 million bits), or gigabits (1 billion bits) per second.

Because analog information is often converted to its digital equivalent, there is a relationship between analog and digital bandwidth. We mentioned that analog-to-digital conversion is accomplished by approximating the analog signal by a series of digital values taken once every given period of time. This process is called *sampling.* This means that at a given instant in time, a sample of the analog signal is measured and converted to a corresponding digital value. The more such samples are taken per unit of time, and the more bits used per sample to represent the value read, the more accurate is the digital equivalent of the analog signal. There is a theorem that states that samples taken at a rate twice the bandwidth of the signal will produce an adequate digital representation of the signal being sampled. This theorem was developed by the American physicist, Harry Nyquist and is called the Nyquist interval theorem.

For example, according to the Nyquist theorem, a voice signal with a bandwidth of 4,000 Hz requires 8,000 samples per second to approximate adequately in digital form. If we use 8 bits per sample to represent the signal, the required digital bandwidth is 8 x 8,000 or 64,000 bits per second (64 kilobits per second). This is the standard bandwidth required for digital voice transmission. High fidelity music is often sampled at 16 bits per sample. If the bandwidth of the music is 22KHz, good-quality digital conversion requires 44,000 samples per second (samples per second or the "sampling rate" is often expressed in Hertz, which in this case would be 44 KHz). This is the audio quality of compact disk recordings, which most people consider to be as good as the human ear can discern.

The digital bandwidth required to transmit CD-quality music is 16 bits per sample multiplied by 44,000 samples per second, which equals 704,000 bits per second (704 kilobits per second). When you consider that a high-speed modem allows you to transmit data at 9,600 or 14,400 bits per second, you can see that the bandwidth required to transmit uncompressed, high-fidelity music is about fifty times greater. As we shall see, even with data compression, high-quality audio transmission still requires considerable bandwidth.

To summarize the key points:

- Information is transmitted by either analog or digital signals.
- Analog signals vary continuously with time, while digital signals can only have two values or states: zero (off) and one (on).
- Digital signals can be used to represent analog signals by the process of analog-to-digital conversion. Digital signals are converted back to analog for viewing or listening using a digital-to-analog converter (DAC).
- Bandwidth is transmission capacity, and must be at least as large as the maximum frequency range of the signal. Bandwidth is expressed in cycles per second (Hertz), when referring to analog systems and in bits per second (bps) when referring to digital systems.

Bits Are Bits—But Just How Many Bits?

We've stated that the trend in information processing and communications is toward digital rather than analog information. As we shall see shortly, the viability of the information highway depends on providing enough bandwidth to handle all those bits of data. Users of the highway will be watching movies that are transmitted live across cable or telephone lines. They'll be receiving online newspapers and other graphic images as well as lots of text. It's useful to get an idea of what quantities of bits we're talking about.

First, let's start with text. As mentioned earlier, there are 8 bits in a byte and a byte is big enough to hold a single alphanumeric character such as a letter of the alphabet, punctuation mark, or digit. On average, there are about six characters to a word in the English language. Therefore, a 1,000 word document would require 6,000 bytes or 48,000 bits. The *Encyclopaedia Britannica* consists of about 53 million words, which is about 317 million bytes, or 2.5 billion bits (2.5 Gbits). Using a fairly typical modem that transmits data at 9,600 bits per second, it would take three full days to transmit the text of the *Encyclopaedia Britannica*, and that's not counting the pictures!

The number of bits required for graphics depends on a lot of factors such as whether the image is in black and white or color and the resolution of the computer screen that will display the image. But to get some idea, many computer monitors today display one million pixels. A *pixel* (from *picture element*) is a single phosphor "dot" on the video screen. As with the dots that make up a newspaper photograph, the more dots or pixels lie within a given space, the greater the resolution of the monitor.

In black-and-white applications, one pixel requires one bit of information. More common than straight black-and-white images are grey-scale images, which display several shades of grey. Grey-scale images require from 4 to 8 bits per pixel. In color applications, depending on the required level of color detail, a pixel requires from 8 to 32 bits. So, using an average of 8 bits per pixel and a monitor displaying 1 million pixels, you get 8 megabits or 1 megabyte per image. A brilliant color image using 32 bits per pixel requires 32 megabits or 8 megabytes per image.

Now, let's say you want to display full-motion video on this same monitor displaying one million pixels on its screen. Smooth full-motion video like that you see from broadcast television requires the display of 30 frames per second. That's a sequence of 30 images per second appearing on the screen. Using the moderate color quality of 8 bits per pixel, you get 8 million bits per frame, and at 30 frames per second, that translates to a data transfer rate of 240 megabits per second. As we shall see shortly, the bandwidth to the home in the near future will be in the range of 3 to 10 megabits per second, 80 to 24 times less than would be required by our one million pixel, 30 frame per second, full-motion video application.

There are ways around this problem. One is to reduce the number of pixels allocated for displaying graphic images. For example, the video might not cover the full screen, but rather would appear in a small window of, say, 350 by 280 pixels (about 100,000 pixels or about one-tenth the resolution of our million pixel display). For some applications, that may be an appropriate solution. But not for movies, where viewers want as large a screen as possible. In fact, for video-conferencing applications, there are two standard video windows called Common Intermediate Format (CIF) and Quarter CIF consisting of 352 by 288 and 176 by 144 pixels, respectively.

The other approach is to reduce the number of frames appearing per second. This is done as a matter of course in the videoconferencing world. Recently introduced video telephones (video phones) for video conferencing displaying 10 frames per second rather than 30 suffer from "herky-jerky" motion and lack of synchronization between the talker's voice and lip movements (lack of "lip sync"). But realistically speaking, even with a reduced frame rate and smaller windows requiring fewer pixels, you still need a little technological magic called data compression.

Data Compression

We mentioned earlier that one of the major advantages of digital data transmission is that digital data can be substantially compressed. *Data compression* is a technique by which the original data is represented by fewer bits than in its original form. This is accomplished by compression technology (which may consist of hardware, software, or a combination of both) specially designed for this purpose. Both the sending and receiving ends must be equipped with coder and decoder hardware devices (*codecs* for short) that coordinate the compression process. Users of the information highway will have set-top boxes that include the necessary equipment for handling data compression.

When transmitted data arrives in compressed form at its destination, it is reconstructed or *uncompressed.* The ratio of the compressed version to its uncompressed version is called the *compression ratio.* For example, if the compression ratio is 10 to 1, then a chunk of data that takes up 10K in its original form will take up only 1K during transmission.

There are two types of data compression: *lossless* and *lossy.* Using lossless compression, the signal is compressed at the sending end and then completely restored uncompressed at the receiving end, with no loss of data whatsoever. Using this technique, relatively small compression ratios on the order of 3 to 1 can be obtained. However, the original quality of the data is preserved, which can be of critical importance in some applications, such as medical X-rays or professional-quality audio. We noted earlier that CD-quality audio requires a bandwidth of 704,000 bps. Using a lossless compression scheme with a compression ratio of 3 to 1, professional audio still needs about 235 kbits per second bandwidth. It should be noted, however, that "lossy" techniques as described below have been used successfully to produce high quality audio at a bandwidth of 64 kbps. Few people have ears good enough to discern the difference.

Lossy compression techniques operate on the principle that some portion of the original image or sound can be discarded without severely affecting your perception of that image or sound. This technique is particularly effective in full motion video applications. In full motion video, you see 30 frames per second. It is therefore possible to "fool" you into seeing much more detailed information than is actually present in those 30 frames. For example, if a sequence of video frames contains a blue sky background, it is possible to save only one frame of the blue sky and use that portion of the frame over and over again in the subsequent frames. This is an example of eliminating redundancies in the data. There are also techniques for exploiting the nature of human vision and how it handles space and time (optical illusions). Using these lossy compression techniques, full motion video sequences can be compressed up to 200 to 1. Still images can be compressed in ratios up to 50 to 1.

Naturally, high lossy compression ratios extract a certain penalty in the quality of the final image. Using 200 to 1 compression of originally analog color movies, the resulting image quality is equivalent to the VHS standard, which is the image quality of movies shown on most VCRs. This video quality is considered adequate for the present but most information providers (such as the entertainment studios) believe that viewers will demand greater video quality in the future and that lower compression ratios will have to be used. As we shall see shortly, this data compression ratio is directly connected to the bandwidth requirements of the information highway.

Lossy compression is being successfully used today to reduce the physical size of compact disc (CD) audio without reducing the number of minutes of audio on a single disk. Sony's new MiniDisc format stores the same amount of audio on a 2 1/2" disc as there is on a traditional CD. It's done through lossy compression; however, the amount of data lost, and the nature of the compression process are so carefully controlled that the sound is essentially as good as on a full-sized "lossless" CD. (The real value of the MiniDisc may turn out to be that it can be recorded on, unlike standard CDs.)

There are currently several competing data compression standards. This could cause some difficulties if various information providers adopt different standards, but the one that seems to be in the lead for most video applications is the Motion Pictures Experts Group (MPEG) standard. A corresponding standard for still images known as the Joint Photographic Experts Group (JPEG) standard has also gained wide acceptance. In any case, assuming that competing standards will always exist, there will have to be tools available in the set-top box for converting from one standard to another.

Modems Won't Cut It

We've seen that the kind of information to be transmitted on the information highway takes a lot of bits. Images and sounds demand transmission speeds far greater than those available from a modem attached to your telephone line. Even with modem speeds climbing recently to over 28,000 bits per second, transmission of the information contained in 3 or 4 minutes of high fidelity music, even compressed 3 to 1, would take *close to an hour.* Transmission of color images still requires several minutes per image. Modems are appropriate for transmitting information consisting primarily of text. Even the current generation of 28.8 kbps modems won't be fast enough for the information highway. In other words, much faster transmission methods will be required.

Circuit Switching and Packet Switching

Before we get into these faster transmission methods, we need to define one more concept: the difference between circuit-switched and packet-switched networks. As we mentioned in the previous chapter, one of the key developments that emerged from the ARPAnet project, which later evolved into the Internet, was the development of packet switching as a means of transmitting digital information more efficiently. Packet switching remains the primary means of sending digital information today, on the Internet or any other digital network.

Traditional telephone communications are made by *circuit switching.* Conceptually, a circuit switch resembles the switch at a junction of railroad tracks. The switch sends the train down one track or the other track. Switches in the telephone system connect a series of phone circuits that end up linking the calling and answering parties. During the telephone call, a portion of the telephone circuit's transmission capacity is reserved for that particular phone call and none other. No other traffic can use that portion of the phone system, even if one of the parties is on hold and no conversation is taking place. The key characteristic of a circuit-switched system is that the connection is end-to-end and reserved for the duration of the connection.

This system has dominated telephone switching for the last 80 years. However, it does *not* foster efficient use of the communications lines being switched. One of the inventors of packet switching, Robert Kahn, wrote, "If circuit switching were applied to roads, and you wanted to drive, say, from New York to Washington, you would call the highway system and ask them to close one lane on the entire stretch of Interstate 95 to all other traffic." [1] Another major drawback of circuit switching for digital communications is that there can be time delays during the circuit switching process. These time delays are inconsequential and barely noticeable in voice communications, but they wreak havoc on digital data transmission, causing lost or garbled data.

The solution to the inefficiencies of circuit switching is a technique called *packet switching,* which resembles (of all things) the postal service more than the phone system. In packet switching, the data (binary zeroes and ones) are organized into *packets.* Each packet has the source and destination addresses encoded into what is called the *packet header*. It also carries information about the packet's sequence in the series of packets being sent. For example, if I send a letter in digital form and it consists of 100 packets, then each packet would contain address information defining the letter's destination, as well as a number from 1 to 100 (or some other identification symbol) to indicate where the packet belongs in the sequence of packets that makes up the letter.

Using this system, it is not necessary to establish an end-to-end connection between communicating parties. Packets comprising a single message can mix and interleave with packets carrying other people's data, and every packet should (assuming none are lost or damaged) arrive at its proper destination. It's exactly like splitting up a large shipment of goods into several boxes and sending each box separately through the postal system. The boxes are treated as separate parcels by the postal service. Each box has an address label, and in time, all the boxes making up the shipment should arrive at the same place, even though they share trucks and aircraft with tens of thousands of other packages along their way.

Millions of data packets can travel along the same circuits simultaneously. They travel from one *packet switch* to another until they reach their destination. A packet switch is actually a computer on the network that sorts out packets and sends them on their way using the most efficient path. There is never a "busy signal" in a packet-switched network. If one circuit is down or overloaded, the packets can take a different route as determined by the packet switches along the network. (Figure 4.5a and 4.5b show the difference between packet and circuit switched networks.) Following our postal service metaphor, if a mail truck finds that a stretch of Interstate 90 is closed due to a semi-trailer roll-over accident, it can leave the Interstate and find a route around the accident.

Data overloading *can* be a problem on packet switched networks and networks can crash (that is, completely fail or break down). The growing enthusiasm for the Internet has caused severe network slowdowns at many Internet sites. One college librarian told me that the Internet network on his campus gets so slow at times, "you can see the packets crawling across the screen." (This isn't quite accurate; actually, what you would see in a network slowdown are letters and numbers crawling across the screen. The packets are reassembled into a message or data file before they ever reach the screen.)

New packet-switching techniques are on the horizon that promise to greatly increase the speed and therefore the bandwidth of packet-switched networks. [2]

Bandwidth Is the Key to the Highway

The information highway will go nowhere unless there's enough bandwidth on the wires, cables, and radio waves to transmit the vast quantity of information that users of the information highway will require. Sorting out the bandwidth requirements and what bandwidth is available is a bewildering proposition, because there are so many different applications and so many different communications systems. As we mentioned early in the chapter, the information highway is based on the concept of a broadband network, which will transmit everything from simple "yes/no" responses to plain text to full-motion video. The information will be transmitted on fiber optic cable, standard copper telephone cable, coaxial cable, wireless radio waves, and satellite. Some of these links will be analog, and some will be digital.

The information highway will primarily be built on different kinds of cable and wire. Of course, satellite, cellular, and other wireless communications (described later in this book) will also play a major role, but not on the same scale as coaxial cable and wire. The reason is simple: Cable and wire already make up much of the "wiring infrastructure" of the United States. Virtually every home in the U.S. has installed telephone wire and about 60 percent of U.S. households have installed coaxial television cable. The 60 percent of households with coaxial television cable at some point *requested* cable to be installed; in fact, television cable passes close to about 95 percent of U.S. households, meaning that it would be fairly trivial to hook up almost the entire country to coaxial cable if homeowners desired it. And it seems likely that early in the next century, most households will be connected to the information highway by fiber optic cable.

In *Scientific American*'s special issue on Communications, Computers, and Networks (September, 1991), Nicholas Negroponte, the director of MIT's Media Lab, predicted the future this way:

> [Wireless] broadcast spectrum is scarce, whereas fiber, like computing power, is something we can just keep making more of. Those facts mean that the channels for distributing different types of information, as we know them today, will trade places. Most of the information we receive through the ether today [i.e. wireless]—television, for example—will come through the ground by cable tomorrow. Conversely, most of what we know receive through the ground—such as telephone service—will come through the airwaves. [3]

There are three primary types of cable and wire in use today. These are twisted pair copper telephone wire, coaxial copper cable (the kind used for cable television), and glass fiber optical cable, which now makes up most of the long distance telephone lines across the country, called long lines or trunk lines, as well as the primary circuits for an increasing number of local telephone systems.

Fiber optic cable can physically deliver much higher bandwidth than copper wire or coaxial cable simply because fiber optic cable uses light waves as the transmission medium rather than audio signals passing through twisted pair or radio waves passing through coaxial cable. Note that light waves and radio waves are basically the same thing—but light waves have a *much* higher frequency than radio waves. Bandwidth is also affected by the methods used to transmit the information along the wire. These methods, called "transmission technologies," have been refined over the years and new methodologies have been introduced that greatly increase the bandwidth on the same physical cable compared to that obtained using earlier techniques. [2] [4]

Local telephone networks still primarily use twisted pair copper wiring to the home and a mix of fiber optic and copper cabling for branch connections to the main long distance trunk lines. The long distance trunk lines consist of fiber optic cable, coaxial cable, and also microwave radio networks. Microwave radio wave transmission uses the same superhigh frequency range used for satellite broadcasts. The telephone companies use powerful antennas located 20 to 30 miles apart to transmit microwave signals. Until a few years ago, microwave communications made up about half of the "trunk mileage" in the U.S. [5] But the trend is definitely towards fiber optic cable as the telephone companies install thousands of miles of fiber optic cable each year. One source estimates that 97 percent of the long distance lines are now fiber optic. [6]

Cable television companies are also switching to fiber optic cable because it offers some major advantages over coaxial cable. Bandwidth is one advantage, but it's not the primary one when comparing coaxial and fiber optic, since relatively high bandwidths are also obtainable on coaxial cable. The primary benefit of fiber optic for the cable TV industry is that it eliminates the need for signal boosting amplifiers, which not only tend to fail periodically (straight coaxial systems require an amplifier every 2000 feet), but also cause noise and picture distortion. [7] Furthermore, as use has increased, the cost of fiber optic cable has decreased, and fiber optic cable uses a glass material refined from common sand, rather than relatively scarce copper. There are other advantages to glass fiber, including lower weight, less environmental impact during manufacture, and near invulnerability to wiretapping.

Cable companies lay fiber optic cable from the cable provider's main transmission station (called the *headend*) to locations within a mile of a group of cable subscribers and then link up to the existing coaxial cable that connects those subscribers. The location where the fiber terminates and connects to coaxial cable is called a *neighborhood node*, which leads to the catchy phrase, "fiber to the node." These combined fiber and coaxial networks are also called *fiber to feeder* networks or *hybrid fiber/coax* networks.

As mentioned earlier, fiber optic cable delivers the highest bandwidth, with some lines operating today at speeds ranging from 51 megabits up to 2.4 gigabits per second. These high-speed lines use a transmission technology called Synchronous Optical Network (SONET). Other trunk lines, using transmission technologies called T1 and T3, operate at 1.5 Mbits and 42 Mbits per second, respectively. Table 4.2 summarizes the various cable transmission speeds.

Transmission technologies such as SONET are also employed on Wide Area Networks (WANs), which are networks that cover distances greater than, say a college campus, or a complex of office buildings. Transmission technologies such as Ethernet and Fiber Data Distributed Interface (FDDI) are employed on Local Area Networks (LANs), which are networks for limited areas such as a building or campus. In this book, we will have little to say about LANs, because the information highway is primarily a WAN technology.

Telephone companies also offer dedicated leased lines for the exclusive use of the lessee. Frequently costing thousands of dollars per month, leased lines are used primarily by large businesses and institutions to provide high-speed communications between regional offices or other remote locations. The most common leased line operates at 56 kilobits per second and is referred to as *Switched-56*. Higher-speed leased lines such as T1 and T3 are also available, and have come down in price significantly in recent years.

Table 4.2 *The Cable Tranmission Speeds for Different Technologies*

Protocol	**Speed**	**Transmit Time**
Plain Old Telephone	2.4 kb	5 days, 19 hours
X.25	64 kb	5.2 hours
T1	1.5 Mb	13.3 minutes
ISDN	2 Mb	10 minutes or less
T3	42 Mb	28 seconds
SONET OC9	466 Mb	2.58 seconds
SONET OC48	2,488 Mb	0.48 seconds
DSO	64 kbps	5.2 hours
DS1	1.5 mbps	13.3 minutes
DS3	45 mbps	30 seconds
OC-3	155 mbps	7.8 seconds
OC-12	622 mbps	31 seconds
OC-48	2.488 gbps	0.48 seconds

-A digital transmission technology that has gained more popularity in Europe than in the United States is Integrated Services Digital Network (ISDN), which provides up to twenty four 64 Kbps digital phone lines as well as a high-speed data line with speeds ranging from 1.5 to 2 m-bits per second using copper telephone wiring. ISDN services are available through local telephone companies in most major metropolitan areas of the U.S., with growing penetration in rural areas.

However, interest in ISDN has so far been less than anticipated, so ISDN may well be superceded by higher speed transmission technologies in the future. The transmission technology that currently shows the most promise for dominating telephone and other digital networks is called ATM or Asynchronous Transfer Mode (not to be confused in any way with the more familiar Automated Teller Machines). ATM combines features of both packet- and circuit-switched networks, transmitting data in packets, but also able to set up high-speed temporarily reserved circuits similar to those used in circuit-switched networks. Speeds of 622 megabits per second have been achieved in ATM applications, but the technology is still relatively new. [2] [4]

Does Coaxial Cable Have the Edge?

While the telephone companies have lots of high-speed fiber in their long distance networks and local transmission stations (central switching offices), the overwhelming majority of households still have plain old twisted pair copper wire. In fact, the "plain old telephone system" now has the acronym POTS in telecommunications jargon. You can do a lot with plain old twisted pair, but you can do a lot more with coaxial cable, and this is where the cable companies have an advantage.

Technologies such as ISDN and a recently developed transmission technique called the Asymmetrical Digital Subscriber Line (ADSL), allow transmission speeds in the range of 1.5 to 2 megabits per second using a standard telephone line—enough bandwidth to transmit a feature-length movie. Again, compression is the key. In uncompressed form, a feature length movie (about two hours in length) requires about 200 billion bytes (200 Gb) of digital data. Using a compression scheme with a compression ratio of 200 to 1, the film can be compressed to about 1 Gb of data. That's 8 billion bits. To transmit 8 billion bits over two hours requires a bandwidth of a little over 1 megabit per second. Several telephone companies have been running trials using the ADSL technology.

But 1.5 megabits per second won't be enough. First of all, most homes have more than one TV and the kids may want to watch *Lethal Weapon XV* while the parents want to watch *Casablanca* for the hundredth time. Second, it's likely that VHS video quality (which is what you get with a compression ratio of 200 to 1) won't be adequate over the long term. Much higher-quality graphics already exist on high-performance computer systems. Furthermore, home viewers have been reading about High-Definition Television (HDTV) which has been hyped to deliver theater-quality movies on a large, wide screen. When these sets become available, viewers will want the service in their homes. Experts in the entertainment industry believe that the minimum bandwidth into the home will be 3 megabits per second—and the reality may be at least 10 megabits per second, considering that many homes have two or three TVs.

That's where coaxial cable comes in. The cable TV industry has so far primarily used coaxial cable for analog television broadcasts, carrying about 60 channels. But coaxial cable can deliver digital information at rates ranging from 10 to 20 megabits per second. Using compressed digital video, cable companies think they can supply enough bandwidth to provide video on demand, telephone service, as well as other interactive television services and communications services such as the Internet or CompuServe.

The advantages of coaxial cable are not lost on hardware manufacturers such as Intel, which is working in cooperation with General Instrument to build a modem specially designed to connect your personal computer to the cable TV line. General Instrument is one of the major manufacturers of set-top boxes, the nature of which we will be discussing shortly. Intel claims that its cable modem will be able to transmit information more than 1,000 times faster than is possible on a conventional phone line. This claim translates to a transmission speed of about 10 megabits per second, compared to a regular telephone modem operating at 9600 bps. General Instrument plans to work with online services such as CompuServe and Prodigy to offer this high-speed transmission technology. If this technology comes to fruition, it will dramatically change the communications capabilities of PCs, giving PCs enough bandwidth to send and receive documents with high resolution graphic images, as well as full-motion video and sound.

Other services are also targeting the existing cable TV infrastructure, or "cable plant" in telecommunications jargon. Digital Equipment Corp. (DEC) has also embarked on an aggressive program to provide high-speed network capabilities over coaxial cable. One of the company's first products in this area is a cable interface to the Internet called the Internet Brouter. In the previous chapter, we mentioned another service offering a cable connection to the Internet. For music fans, a company called International Cablecasting Technologies offers 30 channels of compressed "CD-quality" digital music piped to your stereo system over existing coaxial cable.

Putting It to the Test

Time Warner Cable is testing the broadband network concept in Orlando, Florida. The Time Warner system, called Full Service Network (FSN), is a good example of how the technology we've been discussing would actually work in practice.

FSN uses the "fiber to the node" concept we discussed earlier. Time Warner has installed some 1,000 miles of fiber optic cable in the Orlando area, which connects to 16 neighborhood nodes serving some 4,000 customers (several optical fibers fit into a single cable so the actual mileage of installed cable is considerably less than 1,000). The neighborhood nodes receive the optical signal from the fiber optic cable and convert that signal into radio frequency signals which are sent along the coaxial cable into the home. The node also converts signals from the home (order requests and messages, for example) back into optical signals that are transmitted back to the Network Operations Center for processing.

At first, FSN will offer video on demand, interactive shopping, and interactive games. Other services such as news on demand, educational services, and more extensive shopping and games services are to be offered later.

The FSN customer's TV is equipped with a set-top box and a remote controller and, in some cases, a color printer. The customer selects services from menus that appear on the TV screen or by navigating through a "spatial, interactive environment," which is like a "virtual shopping mall." For example, one of the choices in the virtual shopping mall might be a travel agency, which, when you click on its icon, opens up an airline ticket reservation application. Silicon Graphics and Time Warner are developing the software for the project and have extensive experience in sophisticated graphics applications.

When a customer orders a movie, the request is processed by the Network Operations Center's *media servers*, which are powerful computers that store and distribute the movies. Up to 1,000 customers can watch movies simultaneously in the initial trial, selecting from a library of about 500 movies. The media server sends the movie data along the fiber optic line in Asynchronous Transfer Mode (ATM) packets. The fiber optic line has a bandwidth of 155 megabits per second and each video stream (individual movie transmission) travels at 3 to 6 megabits per second to the neighborhood node, where it is then sent by coaxial cable to the customer's set-top box. The set-top box reassembles the data packets, decompresses the video, and displays the movie. According to Time Warner, it takes less than a second for a customer to receive a movie after he or she places the order.

Upstream versus Downstream Bandwidth

One of the key requirements of the broadband network is that it be interactive. The user must be able to respond and transmit requests and other information back through the network. Therefore, some portion of the coaxial cable or telephone wire has to be allocated to the user. In telecommunications jargon, this is called *upstream bandwidth.* The upstream bandwidth will be considerably less than that required for the transmission of movies and other data-intensive information "downstream" to the customer.

Figure 4.6 shows Time Warner's planned allocation of bandwidth on the Full Service Network. The "return channels" are for two-way communications, which will include telephone conversations, fax, electronic mail, and other online communications. While the upstream bandwidth requirements may be less than those for the downstream, this disparity is likely to narrow eventually as users start to communicate with one another using video and graphics. Video conferencing itself can eat up several megabits per second of bandwidth. Users will also want to broadcast their own movies or send home videos to relatives across the country. The technology for sending movies from a central location to many subscribers is fairly well understood, but what happens when millions of people start sending home videos to each other is a significant and unanswered question.

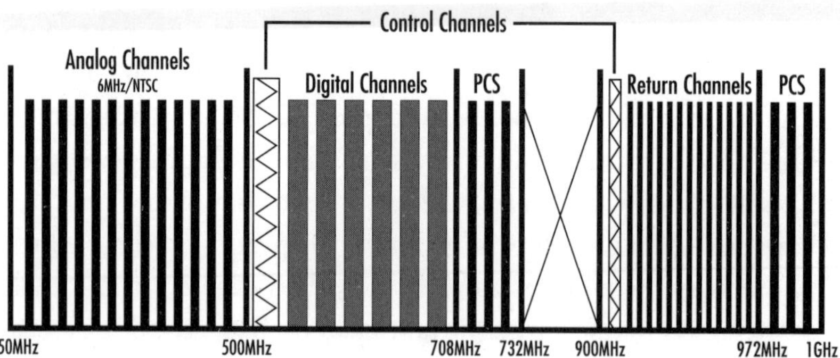

Figure 4.6 *Time Warner's planned allocation of bandwidth for the Full Service Network project in Orlando, Florida.*

Note the category in Figure 4.6 called PCS, or Personal Communications Services. PCS is a communications service still under development, which will allow mobile telephones and other wireless devices to send and receive messages. Time Warner, like other cable companies, anticipates using its fiber optic and cable infrastructure to transmit these wireless communications.

Going with Fiber Almost All the Way

We've briefly discussed attempts to use standard copper wire to provide "broadband" capabilities and we've looked at the Time Warner "hybrid fiber/coax" broadband network. One other technique that garners a lot of attention from the telephone companies is installing fiber optic cable almost right to the house (usually on the poles behind the house or in plenums under the pavement in front of the house) and then going the last hundred feet or so into the home itself with coaxial cable for the broadband information and with standard telephone cable for plain old telephone calls.

This setup is called *fiber in the loop* because it requires installation of fiber optic cable in the local telephone loop (the *local telephone loop* is the set of cables that goes around your neighborhood and feeds into a central switching station). It also requires a "Multi Subscriber Optical Network Unit," which is installed on the sidewalk or on the poles and can service from eight to twelve "living units" (houses or apartments). The system has been developed by a company called BroadBand Technologies (BBT). In its initial implementations, the fiber stops at the sidewalk and is therefore called "fiber to the curb." As time goes on, fiber optic will go directly into the house or "living unit," in which case it will be called "fiber to the home." Figure 4.7 shows a schematic of BBT's Fiber Loop Access System.

Media Servers, Set-Top Converters, and PCs

The transformation to digital information requires computers to process an enormous flow of bits and to transform those bits into text, sound, graphics, and video. This computing is the most complex and challenging aspect of the information highway and also the least proven. Several companies are working on media or video servers that will store and send, on demand, movies and other information. Test runs, such as that in Orlando, Florida, will be the first "proof of concept" of these video server machines.

The different companies working on video servers are taking different approaches, but the goal is to enable users sitting in their living room to control a movie residing on the video server at a remote location the same way they would control a movie residing on their video cassette recorder. They can start the movie any time (while some other subscriber is already watching that same movie) and they can pause or rewind the movie any time. This all happens in billionths of a second (nanoseconds) when

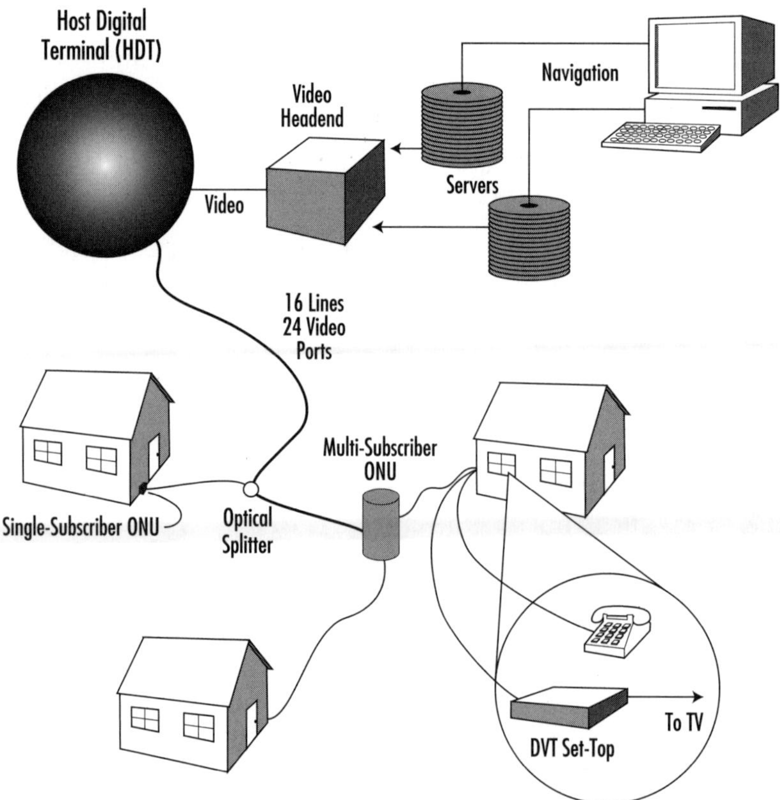

Figure 4.7 *BBT's Fiber Loop Access system, which requires fiber optic cable to be installed "to the curb" near a group of 8 to 12 "living units," which are serviced by the "Multi-Subscriber Optical Network Unit" (ONU).*

the video server receives the request from the user. Basically, the video server is a fast, highly sophisticated video jukebox.

Here's a reasonable question: Why can't the service providers send the whole movie to you before you view it? This would eliminate the pause/rewind problem and the timing issue when different customers order the same movie at different times. There are at least two good reasons. First, it would take a long time to send the whole movie. Assuming 8 billion bits of compressed data for a two-hour movie, even a bandwidth of 10 megabits per second would require about 15 minutes for the whole movie to be sent. That might be acceptable in some situations, but it also assumes that 10 megabit per second bandwidth is always available, which may not be the case on a cold February Friday night with a blizzard underway and everybody at home hiding from the weather in front of the TV. The second and even bigger problem is where to store all those bits when they arrive in your living room. This would require a storage device with a capacity of well over a gigabyte! Such a device is still too expensive to become standard issue for information highway users, even looking ten years or more into the future.

So, back to the video server. The major U.S. companies working on video servers include Digital Equipment, Hewlett-Packard, IBM, Oracle, Microsoft, and Silicon Graphics. Although the technical details are quite different, there is one similarity among all these companies' proposed systems—they use multiple microprocessors, so the video server behaves like a bunch of computers connected together. Microsoft proposes to string together a bunch of personal computers to form a video server. Oracle is using a "massively parallel computer" developed by nCube, which is now partially owned by Oracle. The nCube system can have as many as 8,192 processors delivering up to 25,000 video streams, where each video stream is an individually controllable movie being delivered to the home. [8] Silicon Graphics' system is being tested in the Time Warner FSN project in Orlando. This system, called the Challenge XL, uses 36 high-speed processors and can deliver 1,000 video streams simultaneously.

In addition to mammoth processing and memory requirements for compressing video and keeping track of viewer requests, these servers must have almost unimaginable storage facilities for all those movies. These storage facilities will range from arrays of conventional hard disks to optical storage systems capable of storing terabytes (trillions of bytes) of data. (The Orlando project offers 500 movies, each requiring about 2 gigabytes of storage, for a total of one trillion bytes). It's interesting to note that most video rental stores stock several thousand movies and some of the biggest video rental stores have as many as 10,000 movies on site. If you need one trillion bytes for 500 movies, we're looking at 10 trillion bytes for 5,000 movies—a truly staggering volume of disk storage.

At the consumer end, the information highway user has two vehicles for receiving information: One is a personal computer with a modem, which is likely to be a cable modem capable of 10 megabits per second transmission speeds as we discussed earlier; and the other is a set-top box or set-top converter that sits on top of the TV set and converts digital signals to be viewed on the analog TV set. The set-top box looks very much like the channel selector boxes provided by cable TV companies. The difference is that the set-top box is a powerful computer with a number of special purpose processors for performing compression and decompression, encryption and decryption, digital to analog and analog to digital conversion, and graphics display control. In addition, the set-top box must have several megabytes of memory. Set-top boxes will also have unique identification codes to facilitate billing and filling of orders.

The exact specifications of the set-top box will vary depending on what functions are performed by the media server and what functions are allocated to the set-top box. For example, Oracle's nCube massively parallel computer with thousands of microprocessors offers huge computational capabilities (some critics think it's overkill), and will therefore require a less powerful and presumably less expensive set-top box than perhaps that required by Microsoft's server system. On the other hand, Microsoft's server will be much cheaper than Oracle's.

What's This All Going to Cost?

It's difficult to discuss cost because the costs of computer-based technologies and components change so rapidly. Information highway analysts talk about "cost per video stream." In other words, if a video server costs $300,000 and can deliver 1,000 video streams, the cost per video stream is $300. Cost estimates range from $500 to $1,500 per video stream for the current crop of video servers. Like everything else, this will drop over time, but for early implementations those numbers are considered realistic.

We then have to consider the cost of set-top boxes. Again, it's very hard to estimate, but it's generally agreed that set-top boxes will have to cost under $500 to be make the information highway commercially viable to the majority of Americans, and not simply a premium-cost service for electronic Yuppies. This $500 target seems like a good possibility by 1996, considering that you can buy a basic 486 computer for less than $1,000 today.

Alas, the costs quoted above are just for the computing power on the two ends of the connection. The real kicker is the expense of installing all that fiber optic cable. Of course, the proponents of fiber optic cable claim that costs are now down to a few hundred dollars per home to install fiber optic cable. BroadBand Technologies claims that its fiber in the loop system will cost the telephone companies under $500 per household when installed on a large scale. [9] Nevertheless, there's little doubt that it will cost many billions of dollars to install fiber optic on the scale required by the information highway. There's also no question that consumers will have to carry the burden of those costs.

But Big Hurdles Remain

Even though cable has a big advantage in bandwidth over twisted-pair telephone cable, major technical and political hurdles remain before the existing cable infrastructure could be converted to broadband networks on a large scale. As I mentioned earlier, cable TV is still primarily analog. The coaxial cable lines are equipped with amplifiers to boost the analog signal. The cable company headends are primarily satellite and microwave signal receivers that receive the analog broadcasts of the various channels and then send them to the network's subscribers. In other words, the current cable TV system is not really set up for digital communications.

Furthermore, cable TV systems are not in a position to provide telephone service without major investments in building long distance fiber optic trunk lines or striking deals with the telephone companies to use their lines. These technical problems may be trivial compared to the regulatory hurdles that would have to be overcome for the cable companies to provide telephone service. Another factor that the cable companies have to consider is that they have very few cable installations in businesses and institutions with an existing coaxial cable presence. Their customers are almost entirely residential. So, if cable companies are to provide information services to business, a lot of coaxial cable must be installed. Granted, the cable passes close to most of those businesses and connecting them is therefore not an insurmountable task, but nevertheless a major one.

The Time Warner project in Orlando is one of the first major tests of both the technical and commercial viability of broadband networks. FSN services will be charged on a per transaction basis while basic cable costs are to remain the same. Time Warner says that prices for movies will be comparable to those charged by video rental stores. Considering the investment required to install all that fiber and set up those powerful media servers, it's hard to see how Time Warner (or anyone else for that matter) can make a profit just charging a couple of dollars per movie. Whether Time Warner can make a profit and whether customers actually use the FSN and how they like it remains to be seen.

Similarly, the telephone companies are faced with a large number of their customers having only twisted pair copper cable, which is why the "copper only" solutions such as ADSL seem extremely attractive in spite of their limited bandwidth. A solution such as BroadBand Technologies' fiber in the loop scheme either requires the phone companies to gain access to existing coaxial cable supplied by the cable companies or to install coaxial cable on their own—a massive undertaking.

Regional peculiarities will put an occasional twist to the problem that defies easy characterization. In July of 1994, the city of Seattle announced that it will take quotes on the installation of a broadband network to connect every business and residence in the city of Seattle. The city does not intend to own the cabling—but in contrast to most American cities and towns, Seattle owns all of the poles carrying power, telephone, and coaxial cable throughout the city. It therefore has the power to license the use of its poles to some new conglomerate intended to compete with the existing cable and telephone providers. How much control the liberal-leaning Seattle government will exact for the use of its poles is an interesting and as-yet unanswered question.

None of these problems has an easy solution. Only time will tell how the telecommunication companies meet these challenges.

Wireless Communications

Earlier in this chapter, we cited Nicholas Negroponte's prediction that what we receive "through the ether" today we will receive through the ground via cable tomorrow, and much of what we receive through the ground today (primarily telephone service) will be transmitted via the airwaves tomorrow. Negroponte takes this axiom a step further:

> Two rules of thumb define how information should be distributed. First, use the broadcast spectrum to communicate with things that move: cars, boats, airplanes, wrist telecommunication terminals, dog collars, scuba tanks and the like. Second, deliver information to the desktop or living room by fiber. [3]

Indeed, these rules of thumb make a lot of sense and are largely confirmed by the trends we see occurring today. The fastest growing sector of the wireless communications world is the cellular telephone industry. It's estimated that there are currently over 17 million cellular phone subscribers and this number is expected to double by 1998. [10]

Cellular telephones today rely on circuit-switched analog transmission techniques and are not at all well suited to data transmission. However, this limitation will disappear or be greatly reduced with the advent of a packet-switching technology for cellular telephones called cellular digital packet data (CDPD). Operating at 19.2 kilobytes per second, CDPD will enable cellular telephones to send and receive digital data more efficiently and reliably than is possible using circuit-switched analog techniques. However, 19.2 kilobytes per second is a far cry from the bandwidth required for many of the services of the information highway. (Although in fairness, few experts expect people to demand entertainment video over a cellular link.) In the near term, cellular telephones will primarily be used for voice communications and low-bandwidth data transmissions such as fax and text.

It is estimated that more than one million cellular phone users use their phones for exchanging data. With the introduction of CDPD in 1994, the number of cellular "data users" is expected to double by 1997 or 1998. However, a bigger share of wireless data transfer takes place using paging devices. There are currently some 20 million wireless paging devices in use, and the number is increasing at the rate of about 4 million per year. [10]

Satellite Angst

Satellites make up another major sector of the wireless communications industry. According to Negroponte, "within 20 years, it will be perverse, if not illegal, to use satellites for broadcast television." [3] This could well happen in 20 years, but not in the next 12, because satellites have a life span of about 12 years, and the satellite broadcast industry is in the process of launching new satellites for its Direct Broadcast Satellite (DBS) TV service.

Satellite TV competes directly with cable TV and is also in the process of switching from analog to digital transmission methods, using digital compression schemes. This approach allows transmission of eight times the number of channels possible with analog transmission techniques. But satellite broadcasting has some severe limitations in terms of the information highway. The main limitation is that satellite communications are not interactive. The viewer can't send signals back to the satellite. This problem is somewhat sidestepped by having satellite subscribers call into the satellite service provider to order pay per view, for example, but this is not true interactivity. Also, satellites can't support true video on demand because without interactivity there is no means to provide functions such as pause and rewind. Nevertheless, satellite broadcasting is a major force, particularly in rural areas that don't yet have cable service and will probably be last in line for access to the information highway.

In spite of these limitations, there are ambitious plans in the works involving satellite networks. The most ambitious is being sponsored by two boyhood chums, Microsoft's co-founder and CEO, Bill Gates, and McCaw Cellular's founder, Craig McCaw. They have formed a joint venture called Teledesic Corp. with the intention of launching, by the year 2001, 840 satellites to provide broadband communication services similar to those envisioned on fiber optic cable. Their plan is to support interactivity and high bandwidth with the goal of providing these services to poor and remote areas around the world. Understandably, there are many skeptics. The costs and technical challenges of launching 840 satellites are enormous (Teledesic plans to raise $9 billion). There are currently only about 350 active satellites orbiting the earth. [11] If in fact the network is aimed at poor and remote areas, it will be interesting to see who will pay for these services. As Howard Anderson of the Yankee Group commented in *The Wall Street Journal*, perhaps the whole idea reflects a "midlife crisis" for both Gates and McCaw. [11] Hughes Aircraft has announced a competing plan to expand its $660 million Spaceway satellite project into a $3.2 billion worldwide system (*The Wall Street Journal*, July 29, 1994).

In spite of these ambitious projects, in the context of the information highway, satellite communications will play a more important role in providing wireless telephone, paging, data, and fax services. "Sky phones" are already in use today and operate similarly to cellular telephones. Rather than using ground-based cells for passing the signal along, sky phones use satellites as their primary transmitters. However, satellite telephone service is considerably more expensive than cellular, and is therefore mainly relegated to "niche" markets such as rural markets that don't have cellular phones and international markets, which often don't support the same cellular standards as in the United States.

Spectrum Wars

The biggest problem with wireless communications is that there is limited bandwidth on the radio spectrum. Figure 4.8 shows the divisions of frequency bands for various functions and it is clear that contention for the radio waves will continue to increase. As Mr. Negroponte said, you can always add more fiber optic cable and computing power, but there is only a fixed number of radio frequencies. In the United States, these frequencies are controlled by the (FCC).

The FCC has allocated two bands of frequencies for Personal Communications Services (PCS). These frequency ranges were formerly allocated to emergency services such as ambulance and police. Public safety officials are none too pleased about the decision but the plan is to switch these emergency services to higher frequencies or to move them to fiber optic cable over the next few years. The FCC is in the process of auctioning off these frequencies to telecommunications service providers. The winning bidders will have licenses to provide services such as voice, fax, paging, and data transmission on these PCS frequency bands.

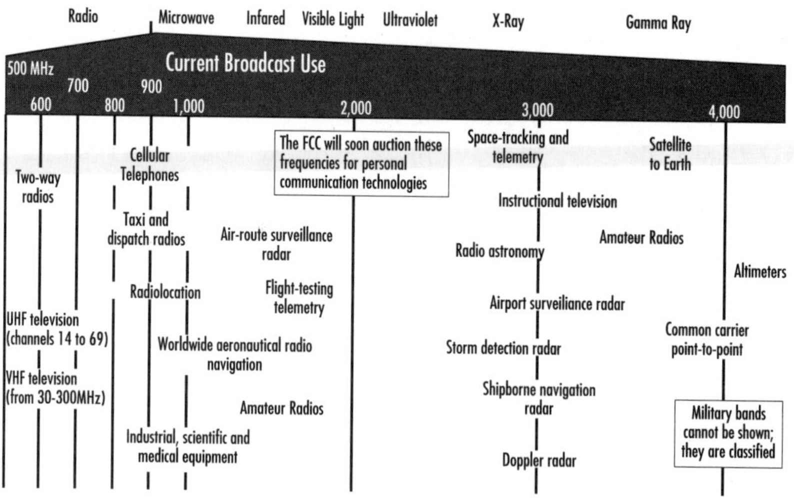

Figure 4.8 *Contention for available radio waves will continue to increase.*

PCS is targeted at mobile and handheld wireless devices such as "personal communicators," pagers, and the like.

The wireless communications market is growing rapidly and is a major source of revenue and business for a growing number of companies. But its role in the information highway is unclear. If Mr. Negroponte is right, the main transmission media on the information highway will be based on fiber optic cable, with wireless media largely reserved for voice communications and mobile data users. Although this model seems reasonable, political and business issues could change the way things turn out. The battle between satellite and cable is far from over. And whether the telephone and cable companies can get together to build the fiber infrastructure for the information highway is also uncertain.

The Software

We've talked about set-top boxes and video servers and video on demand and data compression. None of these things will work without software that lets you tell the hardware what to do. There are two major software components: the software that responds to your requests by controlling events and actions at the "operations center" of the broadband network, and the software that lets you control your TV or personal computer and send commands to the network operations center.

The software required to control the operations center, which we'll call the control software, represents one of the greatest technical challenges that computer programmers have ever confronted. It's somewhat akin to the software required for managing the air traffic control system. In fact, it's worth noting that the Federal Aviation Administration's efforts to modernize the software for the air traffic control system are about six years behind schedule, with a team of 500 programmers at IBM working on the project. [12]

The control software also has something in common with the software used for controlling telephone systems. Millions of transactions must be logged and billed. Data must be routed to millions of destinations. Bandwidth must be allocated on the fly, depending on the load. And, on top of that, the control software must manage thousands of video on demand requests, requests for CNN news, requests for pizza from Marcello's Pizzeria, requests for access to the Internet and other online services, and so forth. Then it must deliver the information, decompress it, and display it on your screen.

On the user side, the software must present an easy-to-use system for making selections. This can either be a system of menus and icons similar to Microsoft Windows or the Macintosh interface, or it can be more a visual environment such as a simulated shopping mall, for example. But it will have to be far more intuitive than Windows or even the Macintosh. Using the system should require virtually no training. Here's what I envision: A simple push-button infrared pointing device (simpler than a VCR control) will control the software. Graphic images that clearly represent specific functions will appear on your screen and you will highlight the function you want with your infrared pointer and push a button.

The software will also have to be intelligent and learn from the pattern of requests you make. For example, if you order an online version of *Newsweek* on a regular basis, the software should put the necessary command at the top level of your menu heirarchy. If you join certain online conferences on a regular basis, the software should have some mechanism for automating this process. If you frequently request certain types of movies (westerns, thrillers, and so on), the software should put those types of movies at the top of your movie menu list.

While perhaps not initially, the software will eventually have to handle queries in English such as "What is the tallest building in the world?" This type of query presumes a transparent connection to a knowledge database; see the next section on information content.

The software must have different intelligence for different family members. It must also be able to lock out children from certain activities on the information highway that, at the discretion of the parents, should be accessible only to adults—things like home banking and adult movies.

Both control and user software must have provisions for security. Billing and transaction security will be critical, and so will privacy. The software must also be highly secure.

Several computer companies are working on software for the information highway. These include Apple, Microsoft, Oracle, Silicon Graphics, Sybase, and a start-up company founded by former Apple employees called General Magic. General Magic has developed software specifically designed for telecommunications between incompatible devices. The software for transmitting documents between these devices is called Telescript and the user interface is called Magic Cap. It will first appear on handheld devices such as Motorola's Envoy personal communicator, but it may well show up in set-top boxes.

With all these different companies developing their own software for different types of media servers, the question of compatibility is critical. The control software depends largely on the type of computer system used for the media server. For example, Microsoft's media server is a huge network of PCs requiring entirely different control software than, the Silicon Graphics media server, which is based on a central system with multiple microprocessors.

The user software, obviously, depends on the nature of the control software. Microsoft's media servers will require different software in your set-top box than that required by Silicon Graphics. As we mentioned earlier, the set-top boxes themselves will vary depending on the functions of the media server.

I've talked about similarities to the telephone system control software, but this diversity of user software and set-top boxes is a major departure from the model of the telephone system. I can only hope that the service providers of the information highway will avoid the compatibility problems that have plagued the computer industry. It will be a real shame if the information highway in Los Angeles can't handle a compressed document from Orlando. Not only would it be a real shame, but it would prevent these expensive and ambitious projects from coalescing into a unified whole. This danger has not gone unnoticed by the American National Standards Institute (ANSI), which has formed a new panel called the Information Infrastructure Standards Panel to developing standards for the information highway. As the President of ANSI told the National Press Club, "unless everyone involved—consumers, manufacturers and content providers—can agree on the standards that ensure interconnectivity and interoperability, we might have an information highway to nowhere."

Information Content

The third piece of the puzzle is the most important from our vantage point as users of the information highway—namely, what kind of information will be available to us on the information highway? We're only going to touch briefly on this topic in this chapter because much of the rest of this book is devoted to it.

If the information highway is to succeed, it must clearly offer more than just video on demand. It must offer a vast assortment of news and information services beyond what is currently available on broadcast TV. It must allow people to share information and communicate in a way that is not possible today, far beyond Internet newsgroups or chat sessions on CompuServe.

How this information content is going to be made available and how it's going to be controlled are perhaps the most critical issues facing the builders of the information highway.

The information content presented on the information highway will likely develop in an evolutionary fashion. It will start with basic news, shopping, and entertainment services familiar from current services, such as CNN, home shopping, video games, and movies on demand. There will be electronic publications available and links to online services such as CompuServe and the Internet. Databases and research facilities will be available through these online services. And long distance learning programs will be available.

Public versus Private

All these services I have just described will be privately funded commercial services that will charge fees. There will also be parallel movements to gain access to the information highway for information services in the public and community sector. We talked about FreeNets, and such grassroot movements are likely to make inroads into the information highway. Once the fiber optic cable is there, it will be difficult if not impossible for the phone and cable companies to prevent free information services from gaining access. The history of community cable channels will probably be repeated in some form.

Into the Great Wide Open

I've covered a lot of territory in this chapter, yet we still only have a glimpse of what is to come. The one thing that seems inevitable is the eventual universal installation of fiber optic cable. This inevitability seems as certain as the construction of interstate highways did forty years ago. It will take some time, but when all that fiber optic cable is in place, the information highway will evolve in ways that are hard to envision. Undoubtedly some of the high-profile, big-investment projects of the telecommunications companies will fail. Some will succeed. Grassroots projects may take us all by surprise. It will be an interesting ride.

The Highway on the Move

New Applications and Merger Mania

> *"There is almost universal agreement both on the importance of the revolution in telecommunications that is now under way and on the actual role of the private sector in bringing it about."*
>
> Gerald Levin, chairman and CEO, Time Warner
> *The Wall Street Journal*, April 19, 1994

Let us hope that there is more to life on the information highway than video on demand. Sometimes it seems that "VOD" is all the press knows of the highway and its implications. Part of the problem is that video on demand is the primary application for a lot of "proof of concept" trials being conducted by various telephone and cable companies around the country, such as the Time Warner Orlando project, discussed in the previous chapter, and other projects that we'll cover in this chapter. Another factor is that video rental is a service that is absolutely everywhere in our country, affecting a majority of Americans and doing a staggering dollar business every day. Online services, if charted on the same graph, would scarcely cause a blip. And although video on demand is a technically complex application, it's not a particularly intriguing one, and it's unlikely to change much in modern culture apart from sending the corner video rental store into bankruptcy. After all, video on demand is basically a high tech version of renting movies. The money will be gathered in novel ways and go to different parties, but the ultimate product delivered is the same thing being enjoyed in living rooms today.

It's better to look at the enabling technology behind video on demand, to see exactly what *else* it enables. If we envision a society connected by fiber optic cable and "broadband services," the possibilities are close to endless. If the "video dial tone" (see the previous chapter) were somehow to enter every home, office, warehouse, retail establishment, hospital, school, and factory, our lives would never be the same.

The video dial tone means having live full-motion video and audio available in every home and workplace, capable of tapping into both public and private information resources. Schools could tap into libraries of electronic books, journals, and films. Engineering firms could tap into libraries of technical data and engineering drawings. Workers at home could tap into company databases and exchange documents or participate in video conferences with colleagues at the office. Designers at different offices could work on the same drawing displayed on an electronic "whiteboard." Sons and daughters could send home videos of the grandkids across the phone lines to their parents, or orchestrate a "live" visit with grandma and grandpa on a video conferencing connection.

Indeed, many of these functions of the information highway are already being tested, and we will look at some of these tests in this chapter.

There are countless compelling applications that could find their way on to the information highway. But there is also the very real danger that mass-market (and some would say, low-brow) applications such as video on demand will dominate the scene. If the information highway is built and controlled by a consortium of powerful telephone, cable, and entertainment companies, it could turn into nothing more than a huge electronic shopping and entertainment mall, totally subject to the profit motives of its controlling interests and lacking in both diversity and quality. In this chapter we'll consider some of the important movements to counteract the commercial control of the information highway.

The Information Highway and the Working World

Because businesses are willing to pay for services that can provide a measurable increase in productivity, many functions of the information highway will appear in the workplace before they do in the home. Many businesses already have fiber optic cable connections and some are already using "broadband services" such as video conferencing and electronic document sharing and exchange.

A survey conducted by IBM found that small companies are generally very interested in the services of the information highway. According to a story in *The Wall Street Journal:*

> . . . the survey reported that the most common uses small companies said they would find for the superhighway would be the ability to take or place business orders, conduct video conferencing, check the market prices or availability of raw materials, and analyze cash flows.
>
> Other favored potential uses included creating and sending manufacturing and design specifications to staff, vendors and customers, gaining access to immediate inventory management, making competitive bids, conducting banking and stock market transactions, paying taxes and gaining access to image technology. [1]

In Chapter 2, we discussed current video-conferencing applications, and in particular some medical applications using video-conferencing technology. Video conferencing is going to become much better and more affordable in the next few years as fiber optic cable becomes more widely available.

Here are a few other examples of workplace applications using broadband technology.

Manufacturing

Developed by Digital Equipment Corp., Times Mirror Cable TV, and Arizona State University, the Electronic Commerce Network

(ECnet) is being tested in Phoenix and Tempe, Arizona. ECnet is aimed at linking manufacturing companies with suppliers and subcontractors using fiber optic and coaxial cable, with full video and audio capabilities. Users of the system can engage in video conferences while simultaneously working with shared resources, such as databases and electronic drawings.

The initial implementation of ECnet links McDonnell Douglas' helicopter division with two of its subcontractors. Using ECnet operating at 10 megabits per second, McDonnell Douglas in Phoenix and a parts supplier in Tempe can simultaneously view and manipulate three-dimensional drawings of helicopter components. According to McDonnell Douglas engineers, this capability allows them to solve design problems in a matter of minutes rather than days and cuts the design and development cycle time for a new part from eight months to six weeks. [2]

Law

American Lawyer Media and Mead Data Central have teamed up to provide an interactive legal counseling service for lawyers, which incorporates Mead's LEXISand NEXIS online research services (see Chapter 3). Called Lexis Counsel Connect, the service allows lawyers to access the LEXIS and NEXIS archives of legal briefs, court decisions, and news, as well as engage in interactive communications with legal experts and access other legal counseling services provided by American Lawyer Media. The service will also offer a personalized electronic newspaper that presents information and news about legal developments based on the subscriber's particular professional interest. [3]

In its initial stages, this service will probably be primarily text-based and operate largely over low-bandwidth modem connections. But it's easy to envision this type of service expanding dramatically with the installation of fiber optic cable, allowing video conferencing with legal experts, exchange of graphic images and film footage, audio transcripts of legal proceedings, and so forth.

The Movie Industry

Pacific Bell is testing the transmission of digitized movies directly to neighborhood theaters. This is a lot like the video on demand scenario we've discussed already, but in this case the digitized movie is going to hundreds of movie theatres from a central video server. The initial test is in cooperation with Sony's movie studios and involves about a dozen Los Angeles theatres.

Pacific Bell claims that its "Cinema of the Future" could save Hollywood about $300 million a year in distribution costs. In addition, it would eliminate the "glitches of a sleepy projectionist who dozes off between reels." [4] However, each theater would need about $100,000 worth of equipment for receiving and decompressing the digital movie and showing it on a high-definition screen. (This service would use a 25 to 1 compression ratio, rather than the 200 to 1 ratio being used for home video viewing. The quality of the video would be much higher than that piped into the home.) And, as we discussed in the previous chapter, there are huge costs associated with digitizing and storing all those movies.

Pacific Bell offers its "Advanced Video Services" to individual customers, as well. For example, using a high-speed data connection set up by Pacific Bell, Steven Spielberg was able to edit film for *Jurassic Park* while he was on location in Poland working on *Schindler's List.*

Telecommuting

Working at home and communicating with the office using computer and modem is called *telecommuting*. Telecommuting is by no means new but has been a relatively slow moving trend in the workplace. Many managers are reluctant to grant employees the independence and lack of supervision that comes with telecommuting—and some employees fear that being detached from the center of the informal office power structures will gradually convert them to outsiders who will be first out the door in any layoff. And until the emergence of broadband networks in the home, there will be limitations on the type of communications that telecommuters can perform from home. Today, what telecommuters typically do is manipulate textual information and make phone calls and faxes.

High-speed, fiber-optic communications will dramatically improve the communications capabilities for telecommuters and will also make telecommuting more attractive to management. From a technical standpoint, it will allow telecommuters to participate in meetings and work on documents simultaneously with colleagues in the office. Offices will be equipped with "electronic whiteboards," which, as the name suggests, are the electronic equivalent of the traditional blackboard. A whiteboard is basically a "big-screen" computer monitor with built-in digitizing capability, allowing users to draw or write directly on the whiteboard or from remote locations using high-speed networks. The input from the remote locations (typed on a keyboard or drawn on a digitizing tablet, for example) will appear on the whiteboard and simultaneously on the screens of the participants.

Many of these advanced capabilities are already available using ISDN or Switched-56 dedicated phone lines. However, as we have seen, true full-motion video requires far higher bandwidth than the 64 kilobits per second available through ISDN. While ISDN bandwidth is adequate for many telecommuting functions, fiber optic connections will take telecommuting to another level, in which participation from a remote site is nearly as good as being there in person.

Many companies and organizations are promoting telecommuting as a means to reduce traffic in congested metropolitan areas. Telecommuting can also alleviate child care problems and give employees the flexibility to make their own schedules. For example, a nonprofit organization called Smart Valley in the San Francisco Bay Area actively promotes telecommuting and helps businesses and employees set up telecommuting systems.

There are some thorny problems with telecommuting. Not all tasks are structured enough to lend themselves well to telecommuting, and work that deals in goods rather than information is obviously tied to the physical location of the goods. Not all workers are good candidates. Some people simply don't work well at home. It can be lonely and also requires a lot of self-discipline and motivation. (Many telecommuters report gaining weight when their "office" is just a short amble down the hall from the refrigerator.) It can be very difficult to separate work from leisure time when the workplace is in the home.

There is also the danger of workers being exploited as telecommuters. Companies are attracted by the idea of hiring part-time telecommuters to do well-defined but tedious tasks such as telemarketing or database entry, thereby avoiding having to pay for office space, as well as full-time employee benefits such as medical care, holidays, and paid vacation. It would be ironic in this age of high technology if we created a new low-paying telecommuting industry similar to the piecemeal cottage industries of the 19th century.

If managed and organized correctly, the benefits of telecommuting far outweigh its negative aspects. Telecommuting saves money for companies and spares employees hours of commuting in bumper-to-bumper traffic, reducing traffic congestion and air pollution in the bargain. The information highway is likely to make telecommuting much more popular than it is today.

Interactive TV

If "broadband" is the buzzword that describes the technology, "interactive" is the buzzword that describes information highway applications. Rather than sitting passively in front of the boob tube, you can interact with the programs that will run on the information highway.

This interaction is not limited to selecting movies or ordering pizza. All sorts of interactive applications are being developed. Much like the early days of the PC software industry, developers are working out of their garages to produce interactive applications that will eventually run on the information highway. There will be interactive games and new forms of entertainment that are part-game and part-movie, allowing the user to participate in the plot of the story. There will be interactive functions for customizing the way you watch a sporting event, allowing you to select a camera angle or viewing vantage point, for example.

Users will also be able to "broadcast" their own information, although to what extent users will be able to broadcast on their own initiative is a major policy issue.

Of course, much of the educational content offered on the information highway will require participation of the user, whether it's a child in the school library or in the living room doing homework or the child's mother taking a "distance learning" class.

We should note that there are already forms of interactive TV available in which television viewers can play along with game shows and sporting events or respond to news polls. For example, a company called Interactive Network based in Sunnyvale, California, offers computerized games that allow you to play along with live television game shows such as Jeopardy or predict the outcome of live sporting events. Interactive Networks provides the subscriber with a specially designed wireless laptop computer that uses FM sideband frequencies to communicate with the centralized network computer. Game questions are transmitted to the laptop's computer screen and responses are sent back to the central computer, which keeps score and compares the subscriber's score with scores of other subscribers.

Basically, Interactive Networks offers a computerized "simulcast" of live TV programs, in which the viewer participates alongside the live program. This interaction is controlled by Interactive Networks' computer system, which is independent of the live TV show. For example, Interactive Networks offers selected live major league baseball games. The subscriber predicts balls and strikes, hits, strategic decisions (such as a bunt or a steal), and the score as the game progresses. The user's responses are recorded by the central computer and the interactive game is scored according to the number of accurate predictions. Interactive Networks awards prizes and holds special competitions to attract new and current subscribers.

While mainly focused on sports and game shows, Interactive Network is broadening its offerings to include interactive TV dramas (for example, guessing "whodunnit" on *Murder, She Wrote*), subscriber opinion polls in response to news programs, and educational programs, such as interactive quizzes and study guides for the Scholastic Aptitude Test (SAT). Interactive Network's strategic investors include A.C. Nielsen, National Broadcasting Co. (NBC), the cable company Tele-Communications Inc. (TCI), and the Gannett Company.

This type of simulcast interactivity might be the first step in the development of truly interactive applications for the information highway. But it's a far cry from the kind of interactivity that will be possible with fiber optic cable and a full-sized TV screen. (The Interactive Network laptop operates at 9600 bits per second and uses a tiny 8-line by 40-character LCD screen.) Nevertheless, Interactive Network is a company to watch. It has backing from the types of companies that are likely to be key players on the information highway and its fortunes may be a bellwether of what's to come.

Aside from Interactive Network, other major cable, telephone, entertainment, and computer software companies are investing heavily in developing the technology and applications for interactive TV. Here are a few examples:

- Microsoft and TCI plan to test interactive applications using Microsoft software and TCI's digital cable network. The first tests will involve Microsoft and TCI employees, to be followed by tests involving TCI customers. Microsoft is working on a number of other information-highway projects, including interface software for interactive TV applications and an interactive energy information service in conjunction with TCI and Pacific Gas and Electric. [5]

- A "Baby Bell" company, Bell Atlantic, is building a studio for interactive TV that will provide services for digitizing and compressing video and audio and for developing new interactive applications. [6]
- TCI recently announced a similar project called the National Digital Television Center, in which TCI is investing $100 million. [7]
- MCI has opened a Developers' Lab near Richardson, Texas, with facilities for application developers to test their applications on MCI's network of both analog and digital lines. Developers must apply to MCI with a detailed proposal before gaining access to its laboratory. [8]

Does Anybody Want This Stuff?

The interesting thing about interactive applications is that no one really knows yet what the public wants. Obviously, some interactive applications will be very popular and successful—others will completely miss the mark. The big telephone and cable companies will get some idea what the public wants from trial projects such as Time Warner's Full Service Network in Orlando. As we shall see shortly, virtually every major telephone company and several cable companies in the U.S. and Canada are planning or have already started similar trials.

For the start-up developers in their garages, it will be more difficult to know the market's needs until the information highway is up and running. But many such developers are introducing CD-ROM versions of their interactive applications, which run on personal computers.

Trials of the Information Highway

While there may be a lot of hype and skepticism surrounding the information highway, there's little doubt that the telephone and cable companies are dead serious about it. Otherwise, they wouldn't be spending millions of dollars investing in trial and experimental networks to gain experience in delivering "broadband services" as well as finding out what customers want. As we mentioned earlier, most of the major telephone and cable companies are involved in some sort of trial of broadband networks.

Consumer-Oriented Trials

Some of the trials, such as the Time Warner Orlando trial, are geared towards video on demand and other interactive services for residential customers or home consumers. Most of the regional Bell telephone companies have launched this type of trial with a few thousand customers in selected communities, for example Nynex in New York City and Rhode Island, Ameritech in Chicago, US West in Omaha, and Pacific Bell in several suburbs in northern and southern California. These trials are testing video server equipment as well as set-top boxes from a variety of manufacturers.

One of the most ambitious of these interactive TV trials is taking place in Canada, sponsored by Groupe Videotron, one of Canada's largest cable TV operators. The network is called UBI, which stands for Universality, Bidirectionality, Interactivity. The first phase of the project involves 34,000 homes in the area of Chicoutimi, Quebec. If everything goes according to plan, UBI will serve some 1.4 million homes in the Montreal and Quebec City areas by the turn of the century.

IBM is providing the set-top converters, which will use the high-performance PowerPC microprocessor (see the book, *Inside the PowerPC Revolution* published by the Coriolis Group) and the Motion Pictures Expert Group (MPEG II) video-compression standard. [9]

The UBI system has the support of a number of partners, including the Hearst Corporation, which is providing online consumer services relating to its publications; *Popular Mechanics*, *House Beautiful*, and *Good Housekeeping*, to name a few. [10] UBI's founding partners include the National Bank of Canada, the Hydro-Quebec provincial power utility, the Canadian postal service, and the government operated Loto-Quebec lottery.

Customers will be able to do home banking and shopping, pay their utility bills, purchase lottery tickets, and send electronic mail, as well as use a host of other multimedia services, such as making travel and restaurant reservations and using electronic yellow pages. Groupe Videotron claims that some 75 service providers have signed on to offer services on UBI. [8]

Unlike the trials in the U.S., UBI will not charge fees to its customers but will instead charge the service providers. They plan to invest over $US 500 million in the next several years. [11]

Another interesting trial in Canada is taking place in Toronto and is sponsored by the Intercom Ontario Consortium. This trial is primarily aimed at a subdivision of new houses in the Toronto area that have been specially equipped from the ground up with advanced communications facilities, such as fiber optic cable, wireless communications, and smart appliances. Eventually, 1,300 new homes will be serviced by the network, as well as some 500 students at York University, which is one of the sponsors of the project.

The project will offer services similar to those in other trials, as well as distance learning from York University and obtaining information from government agencies. Apple, IBM, Bell Canada, the Canadian Broadcasting Company, and others, are participating in the project. Buyers of the new homes, which are moderately priced, will have the option to participate in the project. The consortium plans to keep extensive records of usage to see what kinds of information and services customers prefer. [12]

Business-and Professional-Oriented Trials

The trials we've discussed so far are primarily aimed at the home consumer. Others are aimed at linking up businesses, government agencies, and institutions, such as educational and medical facilities. One of the most ambitious of these network projects is underway in North Carolina under the auspices of the regional Bell operating company, BellSouth.

BellSouth is installing 116,000 miles of fiber optic cable in North Carolina. Using the Synchronous Optical Network (SONET) and Asynchronous Transfer Mode (ATM) transmission technologies that we discussed in the previous chapter, BellSouth is linking more than 50 secondary schools, 35 colleges and universities, 11 medical facilities, and several government and public safety agencies (including the Central Prison), as well as two major scientific research centers in North Carolina (Microelectronics Center of North Carolina and Research Triangle Park).

The project aims at providing many of the educational, medical, and government services we've discussed. For example, rural students in North Carolina will be able to take distance learning classes offered at state colleges and other larger high schools. Telemedicine applications will provide remote examinations and diagnostics and more efficient medical record keeping. A geographic information System will allow state monitoring of environmental and health data. Law enforcement and prison officials will have access to these educational and medical services, as well as information databases.

It should be emphasized that BellSouth is by no means the only Bell operating company working on such an ambitious project. Similar projects are either underway or in the planning stages all over the U.S. and Canada.

The Canadian telephone companies have formed a consortium called Stentor with the goal of wiring the entire country with fiber optic or coaxial cable by the turn of the century at an estimated cost of over $US 5 billion. Stentor has also launched an experimental network linking regional networks similar to NSFnet in the United States, which forms the backbone of the Internet.

Everybody Wants a Piece of the Action

The promise of "broadband services" has generated a gold rush mentality among the telephone companies, cable companies, entertainment providers, and computer companies. They all want a piece of the action. Even the electric power utilities, many of whom have installed fiber optic cable along their power lines for private telecommunications systems, hope to participate in the information highway. [13]

In late 1993 and early 1994, there was a flurry of mergers between telephone and cable companies, both hoping to capitalize on one another's strengths: The phone companies offer transcontinental high-speed "backbones," universal access, expertise in transactional billing, and a lot of cash; while the cable companies offer coaxial cable installations in most neigborhoods of the U.S. and expertise in broadcast programming. It seemed like the perfect marriage. As *The Wall Street Journal* put it, "everyone involved saw nothing ahead but blue sky and big profits." [14]

But as the old saying goes, "the best laid plans of mice and men oft go astray." Indeed, most of these mergers have unravelled; the most famous being the TCI-Bell Atlantic merger, which was initially valued at over $16 billion, followed by the Southwestern Bell/Cox Cable deal, valued at close to $5 billion. [14] Other mergers have been devalued or are being renegotiated. The merger participants have primarily cast blame upon the FCC for lowering cable TV rates and therefore reducing the revenues and stock values of the cable companies, but the reasons are a lot more complicated than that.

Many analysts believe that these mergers were done in haste and were poorly conceived and that the FCC rate ruling was simply an excuse to scuttle the deals. In other words, the players got cold feet and blamed someone else for their desire to get out. Entire books could be and probably will be written on the dynamics of the cable/telephone company mergers, but it seems likely that the information highway will be built whether the cable and telephone companies merge or not. A case in point is that within a few months after the TCI deal collapsed, Bell Atlantic announced an $11 billion project to build a "multimedia network expected to serve more than eight million homes by the year 2000." [15] Bell Atlantic has contracted with AT&T, General Instrument (a set-top box manufacturer), and BroadBand Technologies as major suppliers in the project.

Cable companies are not standing still in spite of their difficulties with the FCC and the failed mergers. Neither are computer companies. We mentioned in the previous chapter the development of cable modems that enable personal computers to communicate over cable TV lines at speeds of up to 10 megabits per second. Intel, which together with General Instrument is developing the cable modem, has announced agreements with several cable companies such as TCI and Viacom to provide these modems on their cable networks. Online services such as Prodigy and America Online also intend to offer their services on cable modems. [15]

It should be noted, however, that these cable modems can only be used in areas where cable companies have upgraded their networks to support two-way communications, which requires fiber optic trunk lines and special amplifiers on the coaxial segments of the network. In other words, cable viewers in small communities and rural areas will have a long wait before their systems can use cable modems.

Computer companies such as Microsoft, IBM, Electronic Data Systems (EDS), Lotus, Oracle, and Silicon Graphics, to name a few, are vying for opportunities. For example, in the summer of 1994, EDS, which is a major computer services and data processing supplier to big business, launched negotiations with Sprint, the long distance telephone company, to merge into one telecommunications giant. The companies ultimately failed to make a deal, but we can expect similar merger attempts in the next few years. AT&T, which is both a long distance carrier and a computer services company, and IBM will also compete in providing services on the information highway.

Software companies such as Lotus and Microsoft are trying to establish their products on the information highway. We mentioned in the previous chapter Microsoft's ambitions in the video server arena, but the software giant is also interested in supplying applications such as electronic mail, word processing, and a host of other office productivity applications. Lotus, the well-known maker of spreadsheets and other software applications, is pushing its Lotus Notes program, which is designed for sharing a wide variety of information (for example, databases, memos, graphics) among users on a network, to be adapted for use on the information highway.

In a volatile industry such as telecommunications, in which mergers, deals, and joint ventures seem to come and go with the wind, we would be foolish to try to place bets on who will be partners, and who will be the winners and losers, and what products will succeed. We will go out on a limb, however, and predict that virtually every home and office in the United States and Canada will eventually have fiber optic cable or at the very least, coaxial cable; probably by the turn of the century or a very few years thereafter. Note, however, that this prediction is disputed by the satellite industry, which claims that an independent study shows that only about half of U.S. households (some 50 million) will have fiber optic cable access by the year 2003—"the cost of wiring America with fiber optic cable is staggering, with estimates of from $200 billion to $400 billion and taking 20 to 30 years to complete." [16]

Who Will Be the Information Providers?

Regardless of their exact relationship, both the telephone and cable companies will play a major role in the information highway, and both will make major investments in the infrastructure needed to make the information highway become a reality. Naturally they will collect usage fees to cover their investments.

But telephone and cable companies are not information providers. They are the means by which information is distributed, but they don't create information themselves. There is, however, the very real danger that they could end up controlling the information that is distributed on the information highway. We'll come back to this point in the next chapter, but, similar to our assumption about fiber optic cable, we will proceed with the assumption that all information providers will be able to distribute their information on the information highway. If democratic forces prevail, the information highway will be open to everyone.

If we assume open access to information providers, these providers will succeed or fail based on the merit of their products, marketing savvy, financial clout, and the other factors that determine the winners and losers in the marketplace.

The Big Boys

Some of the information providers on the information highway are already big name companies in the entertainment, publishing, broadcast, computer, and distribution businesses. Barry Diller's QVC will be a major player in home-shopping services on the information highway. Hearst Corporation and U.S. West's Interactive Video Enterprises also look to be big players in the home shopping market. Walt Disney, Time Warner, Paramount Communications (now a subsidiary of Viacom), and Sony (which owns Columbia Pictures) will clearly play major roles in providing movies and other entertainment. Cable News Network (CNN) and other network television companies will provide much of the news broadcasting on the information highway.

But it's not the big boys that make the information highway an exciting opportunity. As we stated earlier, the information highway will be nothing more than glorified TV if it's left to the big boys. It's the start-up companies, the community networks, the schools and colleges, and businesses working together, that will make the information highway a major social revolution. Sure, the big boys will get their piece of the action. They'll sell their movies and home shopping services and online versions of *Time* and *Newsweek*. But it's the stuff we can't quite predict, the stuff that people are working on in small offices or garages, the small-time movie producers, the community news services, the local business information centers—this is the stuff that will make people want to participate in the information highway.

Smart Valley

An example of businesses working together with communities to build the information highway is the Smart Valley Corporation in the San Francisco Bay Area. Smart Valley is a nonprofit organization with a board of directors composed of representatives from high-technology companies, universities, and government. Smart Valley describes itself as follows:

> Smart Valley is a broad-based initiative to build the first pervasive regional information infrastructure. It will require access to high speed communications lines and equipment, the development of new tools, information services and applications, and the education programs and regulatory environment that will give all members of our community access at a reasonable cost. [17]

By the turn of the century, Smart Valley hopes to have established a broadband network linking businesses, universities, libraries, schools, hospitals, government agencies, and individuals, based on the fiber optic infrastructure being built by companies such as Pacific Bell and TCI. Pacific Bell has announced a project called the California Research and Education Network (CREN) as part of its involvement in Smart Valley. And the city of Cupertino is operating a citywide network called CityNet under the auspices of Smart Valley.

In fact, Smart Valley's goals are strikingly similar to BellSouth's goals in North Carolina, described earlier. But the success of Smart Valley is by no means assured. The chairman of Smart Valley and former chief executive officer of Hewlett-Packard, John Young, was quoted as saying, "Smart Valley is a grassroots effort that will need plenty of nurturing and encouragement from the public in order to be successful." [18] Community support and participation will be crucial in determining the nature of the information highway—whether it ends up being an expensive home entertainment center for the affluent segments of society or whether it becomes a tool that benefits all of us.

Is the Internet Ready for Prime Time?

We devoted an entire chapter to the Internet earlier in this book because it is playing a major role in the development of the information highway. We pointed out its weaknesses, such as poor security, limited bandwidth for most users, uncontrolled and often poor-quality information, and the problem of overloading the system as the Internet's popularity increases at a staggering rate.

But the Internet has its strengths, too. For one thing, quite simply, it *exists*. It is a living, breathing, global network. Millions of people in government, education, and business have electronic mail addresses on the Internet. Thousands of conferences covering thousands of topics add new messages from around the world every day.

And, there is a groundswell of commercial activity aimed at making the Internet much easier to use and more accessible at much higher bandwidths. Software companies are developing tools that make it easier to access Internet. Some of these commercial ventures are offshoots of projects developed at universities, such as Mosaic, the navigational interface developed at the University of Illinois National Center for Supercomputing Applications, or Cello, a multimedia application for the Internet developed at Cornell University. [19]

High-bandwidth connections to the Internet, while still expensive, are becoming available and are significantly dropping in price as they become more popular. For example, cable subscribers in Cambridge, Massachusetts can access the Internet through their cable TV connection, using cable modems provided by Continental Cablevision and Performance Systems International (PSI), an Internet service provider. Pacific Bell in California is offering Internet connections at 64,000 bits per second using its Integrated Services Digital Network (ISDN). Digital Equipment Corp. (DEC) is offering products that enable cable access to the Internet.

While low-bandwidth access to the Internet limits users primarily to text and some graphics images, high-bandwidth access opens the possibility of using the Internet for providing "multimedia" information, including quality digital audio and full-motion video. Carl Malamud, whom *The Wall Street Journal* calls a "computer network architect and self-styled pioneer on the Internet," has been broadcasting multimedia programs on the Internet, including interviews, music, and video footage, which can be downloaded on high-speed network lines. [20]

When high-bandwidth coaxial or fiber optic connections become widely available, the Internet's role could change dramatically. It could indeed become the central repository of the information highway. But as we discussed earlier, many technical, financial, social, and security-related problems would then have to be resolved. Higher bandwidth would strain the resources of the Internet even more. Where would all the multimedia information be stored, when most Internet networks today are running out of disk space for storing text? How would usage be governed and who would pay? Is it possible to provide adequate security on the Internet?

The Internet provides a working model of the information highway, but it will be sorely challenged to meet the demands of a ubiquitous high-speed multimedia network, which will be the reality of the information highway in the next century.

Whither TV and Advertising?

The age of interactive TV poses many interesting questions about the television culture that has dominated our society since the mid-1950s. If users can select from hundreds of channels, if interactive games and educational applications replace passive TV shows as the primary entertainment of children and if users can tap into movies and videos from a variety of sources; what will happen to advertising?

This is *not* a trivial or unimportant question. In modern capitalist society, advertising is the most powerful and most important vehicle for selling products as well as for the financing of creative expression, and television has been the primary advertisng medium for the last forty years. For example, Procter and Gamble (P&G) spends close to $3 billion annually on television advertising. It sells 50 million tubes of Crest toothpaste and 400 million boxes of Tide laundry detergent annually. [21] These products are ingrained into the consciousness of the American people.

P&G spends this enormous sum on advertising because it knows it reaches a huge audience concentrated on a handful of television channels. The certainty of this audience will disappear down the information highway. The chairman of P&G, Edwin Artzt, stated in a speech to advertising agents that "television is the lifeblood of our business" and warned that advertisers and ad agencies need "to get together as an industry to better define the video market of the future." [21]

It is likely that new forms of advertising will emerge to deal with the age of interactive TV. Advertisers will probably supply "infomercials," which offer more content than the glitzy 30-second sound bites of advertising today. Consumers will probably have a choice of whether to view the infomercial or not, by clicking on an icon representing the infomercial. Advertisers will have to compete not only on the quality of their products but on the quality of their advertisments. The positive side of this is that consumers may get more useful information from advertising on interactive TV than they do from TV commercials today.

Grassroots Broadcasts

It's too early to predict the kinds of applications that will appear when the broadband infrastructure of the information highway becomes a reality. Some observers predict the "democratization" of entertainment and publishing, with individuals broadcasting or publishing their work for general consumption on the information highway. There are already examples of this phenomenon on the Internet. But it's hard to predict how people will react to public access. Public access cable TV has generally been a failure. "When cable television was in its infancy, many fantasized about an abundance of choice. It didn't happen. Adults got CNN, teens got MTV, children got Nickolodeon, and the public limited its actual range of choices to perhaps seven or eight channels instead of the old three or four. There still is lots of 'shelf space' on many existing cable systems, and little to fill them. 'Public-access' cable didn't generate a huge burst of creativity from the citizenry: It just put a lot of kooks on the air." [22]

Public-access cable certainly puts plenty of kooks in the public eye, but perhaps understandably, the public eye simply doesn't seem to be watching. Even when it makes its best attempt at interesting programming, public access viewership is as close to nil as can be measured. A recent experimental debate/talk show presentation on public-access cable in Glendale, Arizona (population 500,000) *did not garner a single caller* in an entire hour. Worthy topics such as school vouchers and local "hot button" tax proposals were discussed with measured fairness from both sides of the ledger—but no one seemed to be on the other end of the cable.

No one knows how public access will fare on the information highway, or even to what extent it will be available. We'll return to this and other questions of policy in the next chapter.

A Matter of Policy

Government, Society, and the Information Highway

"The information highway concept is less a blueprint and more an inkblot test into which every interest group projects its own fantasies for funding and policy. Sooner or later one must deliver. The administration, after more than a year of talk, hasn't delivered."

Eli Mo. Noam, professor, Columbia Business School
The Wall Street Journal, April 19, 1994

"In a crisis, even the most dedicated hackers would trade millions of bytes of software for a few bites of bread."

Michael Dertouzos, Director of the Laboratory
for Computer Science, M.I.T.
Scientific American, September, 1991

You've heard this again and again: "If we can go to the moon, why can't we feed the hungry . . . house the homeless. . . end corruption in government . . . create fifty million new jobs . . . " and on and on. Twenty-five years after we went to the moon, we still have all the same problems. In all fairness, few people realize how *easy* it actually was to go to the Moon relative to the complexity of a project like the information highway. The whole enterprise only had about ten or twelve million moving parts, counting the different decision makers and involved organizations. Furthermore, as a purely technical challenge, our moon voyage was very crisply defined. By the time it is mature, the information highway may well have as many as a quarter *billion* users—not counting the numberless different suppliers, governing agencies, and support mechanisms necessary to put it in place and keep it running.

As we've seen in the last few chapters, the information highway presents major technical challenges. But the political and social challenges may be even greater. The technical challenges and their solutions are fairly well defined, while the political and social issues are still difficult to grasp. These issues include universal access and fair pricing, intellectual property rights and copyright issues, control of information content, free market competition, and the role of the government, to name a few.

There are no easy solutions. In a society that is fed up with what it perceives as excessive government spending and taxation, there is little support for a massive federal investment to build or subsidize the information highway. Whatever form the information highway takes, it will be built by private enterprise. Yet low-cost, universal access may be difficult to achieve considering the huge investment of several hundred billion dollars necessary to build a fiber optic infrastructure.

Universal Access Goes Way Back

Universal and affordable access has been a fundamental tenet of telephone service since the passage of the Communications Act of 1934. This act established the Federal Communications Commission (FCC) and pronounced the goal of making "available, so far as possible, to all the people of the United States, a rapid, efficient, nation-wide, and world-wide wire and radio communication service with adequate facilities at reasonable charges." [1]

This principle has been enforced by the FCC primarily through price regulation and controls. Since the break-up of AT&T and the creation of the seven regional Bell operating companies (RBOCs or "Baby Bells") in 1984, the long distance telephone companies have been required to pay access charges to the regional companies. These access charges are assessed for the use of the regional

Bells' local facilities to connect customers to the long distance network. The local telephone companies use the resulting revenues to subsidize low-cost local telephone service. In addition, they use revenues from higher-priced business accounts to further subsidize low-cost residential and rural phone service. There are also two funding pools called the Lifeline and Universal Service funds, to which all telephone carriers are required to contribute. [1]

This system of ensuring universal and affordable access to the telephone system has worked fairly well within the framework of an essentially monopolistic industry. Even with the break-up of AT&T, which was intended to make the telephone industry more competitive, AT&T still dominates the long distance market with about 60 percent of total revenues, while the regional Bells enjoy virtual monopolies in their service areas, controlling about 80 percent of the country's local access lines, with the remaining being operated by independent operators such as GTE, Cincinnati Bell, and Rochester Telephone Corp. [1]

Competition on the Rise

But the rules of the game are about to change. As we've seen, the information highway represents a convergence of cable television and telephone networks. Naturally, the cable companies want to get into the telephone business and the telephone companies want to get into the cable TV business. In addition, wireless communications and computer companies are eager to form alliances with both cable and telephone companies to gain market share on the information highway.

Already, the regional Bells are starting to see more competition in local service areas. For example, Rochester Telephone has begun a project in Rochester, New York to link its telephone network to Time Warner's cable television lines, enabling Time Warner to offer local telephone service. Pending approval from state regulators, who have reacted favorably to the plan, Rochester Telephone and Time Warner will be able to initiate video trials and other "broadband" services in the Rochester area, which is also serviced by NYNEX, the regional Bell serving New York state. [2]

Southwestern Bell is trying a similar project in Maryland, offering telephone service through its cable network in territory serviced by Bell Atlantic. [3] Note that regional Bells may own and operate cable services outside of their telephone service areas. In this case, Southwestern Bell owns an extensive cable network in Maryland, including suburban Washington D.C.

These competitive pressures are sure to force Congress and the FCC to loosen the regulatory restrictions that currently prevent true competition in the telecommunications industry. As of this writing, Congress is in the process of enacting legislation that will allow the telephone companies to provide video services and to own a small percentage of these services, as long as they allow competitors to also use their networks to provide video services. [4] In fact, the FCC has already granted this capability with its "video dial tone" ruling. [5]

However, rules, regulations, and court decisions change so fast that it is impossible to predict what the regulatory landscape will look like a year from now, let alone by the turn of the century or beyond. In spite of occasional digressions and regressions, the courts, Congress, and the FCC all seem to be heading towards greatly relaxed controls on competition in the telecommunications business.

Information Control

One of the most difficult aspects of the convergence of telephone and cable TV services is that they have operated under completely different constraints when it comes to information content. The telephone system is a democratic system. Anybody can use it and, within the constraints of the law, can say anything he or she wants. The telephone providers charge for *access*, but make no money on (and indeed, technically have no knowledge of) the information that passes over their networks. This model is likely to be extended to video services offered by the telephone companies. They will be allowed to offer video services as long as they allow others to do the same on their networks. In other words, the intent is to apply the concept of universal access to the video dial tone.

Cable television companies, on the other hand, are businesses run more like radio or TV broadcasting companies; that is, they have vested interests in the information content that they deliver and are accustomed to controlling what is broadcast on their networks. For example, Time Warner is in the cable television business and also owns *Time* magazine. One of the largest cable vendors, Tele-Communications, Inc. (TCI), owns part of Cable News Network (CNN). Unless forced to do otherwise, these cable companies are obviously going to give preferential treatment to the publishing and broadcasting services that they own in competition with, say, *Newsweek* or NBC News.

The Hazards of Unbridled Competition

No one really knows what will happen when the competitive barriers fall, which they are sure to do over the next couple of years. Proponents of unbridled competition claim that market forces will keep prices down and ensure universal availability. Skeptics say that unbridled competition will simply result in a virtual monopoly controlled by the cash-rich regional Bell operating companies in cahoots with the cable companies, who will provide advanced services in profitable areas and leave out rural and economically deprived communities.

In fact, a study backed by civil rights and consumer groups, including the National Association for the Advancement of Colored People (NAACP) and the Consumer Federation of America, charges that the regional Bells are already in the process of discriminating against poor and minority groups based on their initial broadband network projects, which the study claims are concentrated in affluent and predominantly white neighborhoods. [6]

The regional Bells vehemently deny the claims of the study. In the cited article, a spokesman for US West, the regional Bell serving fourteen western states, put it this way: "To say that we're going to stay out of areas permanently is dishonest and ridiculous. But we had to start building our network someplace. And it is being built in areas where there are customers we believe will use and buy the service. This is a business." [6] Of course, there lies the rub. It is indeed a business, and unless there are some provisions to ensure universal service, the owners of the networks will give preferential treatment to areas where they can realize the greatest return on their investment.

What happens to information content is also anybody's guess. Although there are likely to be provisions for a democratic model on the information highway, the question is how it will be financed and supported when the whole infrastructure is built and paid for. People who have not owned or managed a business may not understand this fundamental truth: *Universal access must come at a price.* If it costs several dollars per minute to broadcast video on the information highway, few people will use this capability. Even if it only costs a few pennies per minute, the operators may have difficulty recouping their investment.

An Interim Solution

One approach that's been proposed by the Electronic Frontier Foundation (EFF), a nonprofit organization dedicated to promoting civil liberties on the information highway, is for the telephone companies to implement a less expensive interim digital network before plunging all of their resources into fiber optic cable. The EFF argues that many of the services of the broadband networks of the future could be realized with existing narrowband technology such as ISDN (Integrated Services Digital Network).

According to the EFF's Open Platform Proposal, "narrowband ISDN, if offered nationwide and tariffed at affordable, mass-market rates, can offer end-to-end digital service without major infrastructure investments. This narrowband technology can also serve as a transitional telecommunications platform until national switched broadband access options become available early in the 21st century." [7]

The idea of the Open Platform Proposal is that ISDN, operating at 64 kilobits per second, would provide adequate bandwidth to support digital communications of text, audio, image, and video data at an affordable price today. ISDN could even support limited video on demand using the higher speed (but more expensive)1.5 megabit per second rate. The main objective would be to make practical digital communications available in the near term. Many of the scenarios we've discussed, particularly in the workplace and in libraries and schools, work reasonably well with the bandwidth of ISDN—distance learning classes, for example.

And the most compelling argument for this approach is that it could establish a public and universally accessible network, before the forces of greed and mindless commercialism conspire to take over the information highway.

The Feds Have a Plan

The federal government is also strongly advocating a democratic system based on universal access. Led by Vice President Al Gore, the Clinton administration has presented its vision of the information highway called the National Information Infrastructure (NII).

Gore's comments have been widely presented in the press, including statements like this in *The Wall Street Journal*:

> Because full and productive participation in American society will increasingly depend on access to information, President Clinton and I are committed to making the benefits of the communications revolution available to all Americans across all sectors of society. [8]

Al Gore's interest in high-speed digital networks dates back to his years in the Senate, where he sponsored the High Performance Computing Act of 1991. [9] This legislation allocated funds for the National Research and Education Network (NREN) and other network research projects. NREN is supposed to succeed the Internet as the government-sponsored network for research and educational purposes.

As Vice President, Gore has promoted an "Agenda for Action"—the government's blueprint for building the information highway. [10] However, this document has been widely criticized for being vague and short on detail. [11] The Agenda for Action advocates lofty ideals such as universal access and linking schools, hospitals, and other public facilities to the network, but it does not propose a means to finance these ideals other than the generous good will of private corporations. As Ken Auletta wrote in *The New Yorker*, "The Clinton Administration wants the superhighway to have public channels, but it doesn't want to expend public dollars to accomplish that; it wants rigorous enforcement of the anti-trust laws, yet also wants friendly relations with corporate America. Sometimes, obviously, such goals collide." [12] Indeed, one of the basic premises of the NII is that it will be built by the private sector. The Clinton Administration plans to spend between $1 to 2 billion annually for "investment in critical NII projects," which is all for the good, but a drop in the bucket compared to the actual investment required for a working national broadband network. [10]

On the positive side, the Agenda for Action calls attention to the important social and political issues that must be considered when building the information highway. Public demand for universal access and democratic principles will have a profound influence on how it is built. On the technical side, the NII initiative has spurred approximately thirty major U.S. telecommunications and computer companies to form a Cross Industry Working Team (XIWT) to work on developing standards for the NII and to share information and resources. [13] Government NII projects such as NREN will provide a testbed for emerging network standards and other technical advances that will be employed on the information highway.

Nevertheless, the government clearly plans to take a hands-off approach. Reed Hundt, the chairman of the FCC, told a National Cable Television Association audience, "the economy and the consumers should have the benefit of full-scale, head-on competition among all voice, video, and data providers, including competition both in content and conduit. And beyond that, the future can take care of itself." [14] ("Content and conduit" is another one of those information highway catch-phrases. We've defined content. "Conduit" means the cables and wires—the physical means of transmission.)

Is Universal Access a Marketing Issue?

Although the NII is to be built by the private sector, it does not need to be a high-priced virtual shopping mall and movie theatre for the rich. There is plenty of money to be made and some of the profits could be put back into the system to subsidize low-cost access. In some respects, it's a matter of marketing, much like the difference between marketing luxury items and low-priced mass-market goods. Luxury items are priced high and, because few units are sold, include a large profit margin. Mass-market items are priced cheap and the idea is to sell a high volume with a low profit margin. It's the mass-market approach that is required to ensure universal access to the information highway. Price the services low and many people will use them. Price the services high and the information highway becomes a luxury item for the wealthy.

The bottom line is that if the government wants universal access on the information highway, the government will have to ensure that universal access is made available. It won't happen by itself. Mitchell Kapor, one of the founders of Lotus Development Corp. and now chairman of the EFF, and Jerry Berman, executive director of the EFF, put it this way in a jointly authored opinion piece in *The New York Times*: "Rather than opposing mergers or blindly trusting competition to shape the data highways, Congress should make the mergers hinge on detailed commitments to provide affordable services to all Americans . . . . The best approach would be to amend these requirements to the Communications Act of 1934." [15] One possible requirement would be for the cable and telephone companies as well as the information providers to put a percentage of their profits into a universal access fund.

Free Speech and the Information Highway

If we assume a democratic information highway, in which all participants are free to disseminate information and have the means to do so, we then face the question of free speech. The right to free speech is, of course, a cherished principle of our democracy. It is protected by the First Amendment to the Constitution, and it is also constantly challenged in court—issues relating to pornography, political extremism, civil rights, personal harrassment, subversive or conspiratorial content, and so forth.

Naturally, issues of free speech will play an important role on the information highway. Free speech is already a major issue on the Internet, our closest model of the future information highway, and on commercial networks such as CompuServe, America Online, and Prodigy. These commercial networks reserve the right to remove any material deemed offensive. But, according to the general counsel of America Online, "it is a delicate balancing act to do so without infringing on First Amendment rights." [16]

What Can We Learn from the Internet?

The Internet is a truly democratic forum. Millions of people use the network every day and can post messages of virtually any sort, covering virtually any subject. There has tradionally been an etiquette on the Internet, which, if violated, can result in public embarrassment by other Internet users. The "netiquette" enjoins users from using the Internet for commercial purposes such as advertising, from using obscene or abusive language, and the like.

But this form of peer-group regulation is rapidly losing its effectiveness as the Internet keeps growing. There's the case of an Arizona lawyer by the name of Laurence Canter, who posted an advertisement on the Internet offering services to help immigrants participate in the U.S. government's "green card lottery" for obtaining residency visas. Using an Internet command for sending messages to multiple newsgroups, Mr. Canter posted his advertisement in literally thousands of newsgroups, resulting in his company receiving some 36,000 e-mail messages in two days, many of them angry rebukes for using Internet for commercial purposes, but also messages responding to his service offering. In addition, thousands of angry messages were posted in the various newsgroups where the advertisement appeared. [17] (Angry messages are called "flames" in Internet jargon.)

In spite of the uproar, Mr. Canter was unrepentent and in fact threatened to sue his Internet service provider after his account was terminated as a result of the ad. Canter argued that there was no legal basis for preventing him from posting his advertisments and that he planned to post advertisements again in the future, apparently pleased with the response to his first commercial foray on the Internet, the outrage notwithstanding. Mr. Canter was quoted in *The New York Times* as saying, "the Internet is changing. People don't like the invasion of what has been their private world. But as long as it's set up the way it is, where anyone has access to it, it's a public forum, and they have to accept anything that comes into it." [18]

The case raises some very disturbing questions. From a legal viewpoint, Mr. Canter is correct that he has done nothing illegal. But the Internet could be ruined if such advertising tactics become commonplace. How is commercial use going to be regulated? When every household in America is connected to a broadband network and presumably an e-mail address, what will prevent a deluge of electronic junk mail?

In Your Face Online

One interesting phenomenon of electronic communications is that people lose their inhibitions. After all, they're essentially anonymous (in fact, many users use a "handle" or fictitious name) and, in any case, are physically separated from their fellow network participants. It's very easy to type at a faceless terminal all sorts of thoughts that one would never dream of saying to someone face-to-face. While this feature of electronic communications can be quite entertaining, it also has a very dark side. People may become abusive online. If they get really angry at a particular person online, they might send abusive e-mail. If they become obsessed with someone online, they might relentlessly pursue them with endless e-mail messages.

An excellent example of the abusive mail problem is provided by John Seabrook, a reporter for *The New Yorker*. Mr. Seabrook wrote an article in the January 10, 1994 issue of *The New Yorker*, entitled "E-Mail From Bill," which was a profile of the powerful chairman of Microsoft, Bill Gates. The article presented his views on the future of electronic communications and the information highway. Some readers (this writer included) thought it was an overly favorable, if not fawning portrayal of Gates. However, Mr. Seabrook probably didn't deserve the following e-mail message, which Seabrook, writing in a later issue of *The New Yorker*, claimed to have received from a "technology writer who does a column about personal computers for a major newspaper:"

> Crave THIS, asshole:
> Listen, you toadying dipshit scumbag. . . . remove your head from your rectum long enough to look around and notice that real reporters don't fawn over their subjects, pretend that their subjects are making some sort of special contact with them, or worse, curry favor by TELLING their subjects how great the ass-licking profile is going to turn out and then brag in print about doing it. Forward this to Mom. Copy Tina and tell her the mag is fast turning to compost. One good worm deserves another." [19]

Mr. Seabrook described the horrible feeling of receiving a message like this in an article entitled "My First Flame." [19] Indeed, it is a terrible experience. And it happens a lot in online communications. The problem is that it's very easy to write something in a total fury and then execute the SEND command. Once the message is sent, it is virtually impossible to retrieve. Of course, it is possible that the writer of this flame wrote it in a deliberate fashion, did a spell check using a word processor (though *dipshit* and *scumbag* aren't in most spelling checker dictionaries), and sent it off, knowing full well what it was about. In most cases, however, people send these kinds of messages before they've had a chance to reconsider and cool off like they could in the world of "snail mail" (paper mail), in which you have to print the letter, put it in an envelope, affix a stamp to it, and take it to the mailbox—all activities that take time and may serve to reduce your blood pressure and fury.

The Specter of Litigation

What with hot tempers and quick-acting SEND or POST commands, one would expect libel and defamation suits to become an increasing phenomenon on electronic networks, and indeed they are. A recent libel suit that's received a lot of attention involves an online newsletter publisher on the Internet and a company called Suarez Corporation Industries. Brock Meeks publishes an electronic newsletter called *Cyberwire Dispatch*, which among other things is a self-proclaimed Internet consumer watchdog, looking out for scams and "suspected snake-oil salesmen" as *The Wall Street Journal* put it. [20]

To make a long story short, Meeks published an article in his newsletter accusing the Suarez Corporation of running a "scam," in which the company offered free Internet access through a "shell company" (Meeks' words) called Electronic Postal Service. However, respondents to the offer didn't receive free Internet access, but instead received a six-page direct mail solicitation from Suarez Corporation, offering a book and software authored by Mr. Suarez for the price of $159. According to Meeks' story, Suarez Corporation was using its free Internet offer to collect e-mail addresses and send unwanted direct mail literature to those addresses. According to the same *WSJ* story, Mr. Suarez has been accused before of using misleading direct mail tactics.

In any case, Mr. Suarez took exception to Meeks' allegations and comments, and has initiated a libel suit against him. The libel suit is "one of the first U.S. libel cases to arise out of the free-for-all on the Internet. If it succeeds, some legal experts say it could spawn other complaints." [20]

The specter of litigation could severely dampen the spirit of free expression on the Internet and has obvious implications for the information highway. With commercial ventures and consumer advocates and everything in between converging in "cyberspace," the picture changes dramatically from the informal grassroots, anarchistic chaos of the Internet of a few years ago. The Internet has entered the more nasty, hardball chaos of the "real world" and the information highway is likely to inherit that reality.

Illegal Activities on the Information Highway

Aside from the problems of "flames," electronic junk mail, and litigation, another thorny issue is how to handle, for lack of a better term, "legally questionable" material on the information highway. While the First Amendment protects our basic rights to free speech, it does not protect us from purveyors of child pornography or terrorists providing instructions on how to build pipe bombs, for example.

Pornography

One of the most controversial issues on the information highway is the dissemination of pornographic material. There are dozens of newsgroups on the Internet that cater to various forms of "electronic sex." Some of these conferences are simply for people to exchange erotic thoughts expressed in text form (for example, rec.arts.erotica on Usenet). Others provide digital pornographic images (for example, alt.binaries.pictures.erotica, also on Usenet).

Such "electronic smut" is readily available. As *The Wall Street Journal* put it, "as advancing technology makes it easier to send high-quality video by computer, electronic smut is traveling to more corners of cyberspace, with prosecutors in hot pursuit." [21]. Obviously, some of this smut is illegal, such as child pornography. In this *WSJ* article, it is reported that the U.S. Customs Service has launched a campaign called called Operation Longarm to crack down on child pornography distributed by computer.

A major problem with electronic pornography is how to prevent minors from gaining access to it. Pornographic retail establishments prohibit minors from entering the store. How do you prohibit a minor from joining the alt.sex.bondage conference?

Political Extremism

The dissemination of politically extreme and cult material is also widespread on electronic networks. For example, the *Newsbytes* online news service reported that neo-Nazi literature is finding its away onto the Internet from bulletin-board systems in Germany. [22] Of course, neo-Nazis do have the legal right to publish their views, but the activities of extremist groups are often the subject of legal scrutiny, and the information highway could present a major avenue of collaboration for all sorts of organizations that may engage in illegal activities.

Copyrights and Electronic Information

As anyone who owns a personal computer knows, copyright protection of software has been a long standing issue in the computer industry. In the case of online networks, the copyright issue extends not only to software but to all sorts of other information published on the network, such as databases, newsletters, and books. In the early days of the personal computer, software companies tried to enforce their copyrights by using copy protection schemes that would prevent users from making additional copies of the software. This tactic resulted in a lot of angry customers who couldn't make duplicate disks for backup purposes—and the spawning of a new industry dedicated to breaking those same copy protection schemes. Eventually, the software industry virtually abandoned copy protection and turned to law enforcement as a means to control illegal copying of software, with primary emphasis on mass marketeers of illegal software (many located overseas, notably in Taiwan and South Korea) and large companies that might make hundreds of copies of a particular software package for use internally.

The issue of copyrights becomes even more controversial in the world of electronic networks. In the old days (a few years ago), the primary method of illegal copying was making duplicate diskettes. On an electronic network, you don't even need a diskette. You can just download the program or the document. Illegal copying becomes a trivial exercise. Another daunting aspect of copyright law on electronic networks is that these are for the most part global networks, in which information crosses national boundaries and in doing so becomes subject to different copyright laws.

As mentioned earlier, the copyright issue is also greatly complicated on electronic networks because of the wide variety of information available. Protection of "intellectual property" has become the battle cry of information purveyors of all kinds. For example, if you download data from a database and then publish it in some other document, have you violated the database vendor's copyright? In an excellent article in *Scientific American* addressing such legal questions, Harvard communications lawyer Anne Branscomb writes:

> . . . unless Congress or the states clarify what in a data base can be protected, information providers will have to continue to rely largely on contracts with their users. It is not entirely clear, however, whether a contract that appears momentarily on the screen prior to use is valid if the user has had no opportunity to negotiate the terms . . . . Giving away the fruits of intellectual labor without fair and equitable compensation is a policy not destined to survive the rigors of a market economy. [23]

The question of "fair and equitable compensation" has become critical to authors whose works appear on information networks. In a case that may signify a trend, Random House has established a new contract for authors in which the publisher would retain all electronic publishing rights and pay authors only five percent royalties (about half of typical paper book royalties) for material appearing in electronic form. A representative of the Author's Guild called Random's House new policy "a brazen attempted land grab on the electronic frontier." [24]

Several writers are suing publishers over the same issue, as quoted from *The Wall Street Journal*:

> The battle over electronic publishing rights escalated as 10 free-lance writers sued five companies, including the New York Times Co. and Time Warner Inc.'s magazine group, claiming that articles they wrote were published in electronic databases without their permission and without compensation. [25]

Copyright protection and compensation will remain major issues on electronic networks. Just trying to differentiate between "free information" and information published for profit is a challenge in itself. For example, many electronic bulletin-board systems provide "freeware" or "shareware," which is intentionally distributed at little or no cost. The same BBS may also pedal illegal copies of commercial software. Unknowledgeable users could easily download illegal copies of software without even knowing it.

There is similar confusion between information that is formally published and that which is posted for casual consumption. Quoting Branscomb:

> . . . without question, computer bulletin boards are an electronic hybrid, parts of which may be looked on either as public or private, depending on the desires of the participants. These are analogous to mail, conversations, journals, chitchat or meetings. Under normal circumstances, this electronic environment might be considered more like a street corner where one is entitled to make informal remarks to one's intimate friends.
>
> But many bulletin boards are accessed by users intent on 'publication' for the record—scientists pursuing common interests in a research project, for example. The cooperative writing may therefore have substantial historical, political, or scientific value as a publishable research paper or journal article or treatise or textbook. [23]

Branscomb concludes that the legal system for electronic information will develop "from community standards and consensual observance as well as from litigation and legislative determination." The oft-used analogy of the Internet being the electronic equivalent of the Wild West frontier, with highwaymen and bandits, where folks made laws as they went along, seems quite appropriate. The laws and rules by which people behave and do business on the information highway will evolve through experience and trial and error (literally and figuratively), involving both legal and social conventions.

Many Questions, Not Many Answers

In this chapter, we've posed a lot of questions—but provided very few answers. The fact is that no one has the answers, and the questions themselves are in a constant state of flux. And that is what is so fascinating about the information highway. In many ways, its evolution seems akin to that of the automobile, evolving from its primitive beginnings of hand crank starters and dusty dirt roads to the sleek cars of today cruising on four lane highways. If we look at the IBM PC of 1981 and its 64K of memory (at best!) and two floppy drives, and compare that to the set-top box of the nineties, it is remarkable how far we've come in such a short time. Technical progress and innovation is inevitable. The social and political changes that will go with it seem less certain. Our society will face some significant choices in constructing the information highway. There's no question that the technology will be there, but whether the information highway serves the common good or becomes a toy for the rich, remains to be seen.

Education and the Information Highway

A Golden Opportunity

> *"I have no doubt that as pervasively networked intimate computers become common, many of us will enlarge our points of view. When enough people change, modern culture will once again be transformed, as it was during the Renaissance. But given the current state of educational values, I fear that, just as in the 1500s, great numbers of people will not avail themselves of the opportunity for growth and will be left behind. Can society afford to let that happen again?"*
>
> **Alan Kay, personal computer pioneer, Apple Computer fellow**
> ***Scientific American*, September, 1991**

Perhaps the most meaningful measure of the information highway's success will be its impact on education. There is no field of endeavor that could benefit more from the information highway than education—not only in this country, but all over the world. As broadband networks proliferate, the opportunity exists to simulate the classroom experience across the network, allowing students and teachers to participate in what is called *distance learning*. This capability has broad implications for all levels of education, from grade school to college to professional training in the workplace.

Networks have already proven their worth as tools for education. They are widely used at the college level to exchange electronic mail and to share resources among faculty, staff, and students. Many college dormitories are now equipped with networks and PCs in every room, allowing dorm residents to share a laser printer or tap into campus databases and libraries, as well as the Internet.

The few projects that have enabled K-12 students to use networks have thus far been great successes. For example, the *National Geographic Kids Network* lets young students collaborate on scientific experiments, sharing their results on the network. One project involved a study of acid rain with students around the country "collecting rain samples from their area and testing the level of acidity, and reporting their findings on the network." [1]

A FreeNet network in Montana lets kids in rural schools "get online" on the Internet and exchange e-mail with kids in Russia. They can exchange stories and experiences with students from all over the world. With an Internet connection, kids in New York can read messages from students in Florida who experienced Hurricane Andrew.

The Imperiled Promise of Broadband

These examples all involve low-bandwidth, text-based networks. The possibilities open into the realm of the truly amazing if we imagine our schools connected by fiber optic cable and able to bring full-motion video applications into the classroom or laboratory. One of the most compelling capabilities of today's high-performance computers is the ability to do simulations—simulations of flight and aerodynamics, molecular behavior, and all sorts of physical phenomena. Imagine these capabilities being accessible in every science classroom. Alan Kay, one of the early pioneers of personal computing and a strong advocate of computers in education, gives the following example of what future science education could include with the use of virtual reality:

> The surface of an enzyme can be felt as it catalyzes a reaction between two amino acids; relativistic distortions can be directly experienced by turning the user into an electron travelling at close to the speed of light. [2]

In the fields of social science, language, and music, computers could have a dramatic impact on education. Computers make excellent "language labs." They can be used to teach history by way of compelling visual and audio presentations tied to the text. And of course, computers are excellent research tools. With the advent of CD-ROM, computers can provide a wealth of text, video, and audio information on virtually any subject studied in school. For an excellent discussion of both the potential benefits and pitfalls of computers in education (covering issues apart from the information highway) see Alan Kay's article. [2]

Broadband and Adult Education

While the information highway could benefit elementary and secondary school students in many ways, it could have an equally or perhaps even more profound impact on adult education. Most adults have daytime jobs, making continuing education a real hardship, in a physical if not financial sense. Anyone who's worked an eight-hour day and then gone off to night school knows how exhausting that can be. Imagine being able to take all your classes at home—or taking an hour off from work during the day and "attending" a class electronically, directly from your workplace.

But in spite of the promise of the information highway as a tool for education, major financial obstacles stand in the way. If anything, the resources for educating our people seem to be shrinking rather than expanding. With few exceptions, public schools and community colleges all over the United States suffer from shortages of books and supplies, let alone computers, as well as crumbling buildings and demoralized teachers. Cities are closing libraries to satisfy budget cuts, and many rural communities don't have the resources to build the infrastructure needed to connect to the information highway.

Before the information highway can really make an impact in our schools, the schools will need more computers. A recent study published in *The Wall Street Journal* shows that Wyoming leads the nation with an average of 8.3 students per computer, while New Hampshire is at the bottom with 22.3 students per computer. Surprisingly, the state of California is in the bottom five with 19.8 students per computer. [1] Even the best ratio of about 8 to 1 is inadequate if computerized learning is to take place on a large scale; it's virtually hopeless when the ratio is up around 20 to 1.

Indeed, it is depressing to consider how little impact computers have made in the education of our students in spite of the PC revolution that began almost 15 years ago. Part of the problem has been lack of equipment and resources; the other part, which is directly related to the first, has been the inadequate training of teachers in how to use computers as part of a program of instruction. A study prepared for the Congressional Office of Technology Assessment and cited in the above referenced *Wall Street Journal* report, finds that "with all the investment of time and money that has gone into putting hardware and software in place in schools, students still spend most of their school day as if these tools and information resources had never been invented." The study says further "that at any one time, fewer than five percent of students are present in classrooms where computer technologies can make a substantial contribution to their current education."

The information highway could open up a wealth of learning resources and at tremendous cost savings, allowing people in all walks of life to continue their educations and enhance their employment opportunities either from their homes or from local "distance education centers." But it will require the vision of communities, educators, and information providers to make the necessary investment up front, or this opportunity could slip away.

In this chapter we'll look at some of the success stories and some of the problems of implementing electronic education. First, let's look at what's shaping up to be a success story in New Brunswick, Canada.

A Model Project in New Brunswick

The province of New Brunswick, Canada, is proving that distance learning over the network is a powerful educational tool. Jointly sponsored by the Canadian national and New Brunswick provincial governments, New Brunswick is spending $10.5 million over four years to launch a project called TeleEducation, which links up the province's educational facilities such as universities, colleges, and secondary schools to local "distance education sites," where students can take classes electronically. The TeleEducation system is nothing fancy, using standard PCs, conventional phone lines, and narrowband fax-modems operating at 14.4 kbits per second.

As of this writing, there are close to 50 distance education sites scattered around the province, which is about the size of Maine and has a population of about 700,000, making it a relatively sparsely populated area. These sites are generally located in publicly accessible buildings such as libraries, community centers, hospitals, schools, and college campuses, and some are provided by private companies.

Each site consists of one or two 486-based personal computers running a video-conferencing system called SMART 2000 [3], which operates under Microsoft Windows. Each computer is equipped with a digitizing graphics tablet so that the student can send notes or annotations during the class. For larger groups of students (more than ten), the video image is transferred from the PC to a 32-inch TV monitor. Some of the sites have additional equipment such as printers, CD-ROM, scanners, and so forth.

Some of the equipment is provided by the TeleEducation project but there is a strong emphasis on community involvement and volunteerism, with the local communities coming up with the distance learning sites and, when possible, at least some of the equipment.

As of this writing, some 2,000 students are taking "distance learning" classes on the New Brunswick TeleEducation network.

A wide variety of courses are offered in both French and English, and are broadcast from the various colleges and universities in the province. To give a few examples, Mount Allison University offers courses in astronomy and computer science. The University of New Brunswick offers degree programs in nursing and education. Moncton Community College offers courses in computer-aided drafting and quality control.

New Brunswick residents can take high-school equivalency classes and tests on the TeleEducation network. Professional training programs are also offered or in the planning stages. For example, the hospitals of New Brunswick are using a distance education program developed by Health Sciences TV Network in Texas. The Department of Fisheries and Agriculture is working on an electronic training program for fish plant workers. [4]

Success on the Network

It doesn't take a lot of convincing to see the benefits of distance education. A classic story is that of Corina Balcom, a resident of Newcastle, New Brunswick. Twenty-five years ago, she earned a nursing diploma, and recently went back to school to get her bachelor's degree in nursing. She did 90 percent of the coursework at a distance education site in Newcastle, although the program originated in Fredericton, about two hours away by car. "I have a family and could never have left them every week to travel to Fredericton for classes. It took getting used to, being in one place while our instructor spoke to us from another over a speaker phone. But it worked great. And, I was able to get my degree without leaving my family." [4]

Future Directions for TeleEducation

The narrowband network in New Brunswick may not be ideal, but it's a major step forward and lays the groundwork for the next step, which, according to Rory McGreal, the director of the TeleEducation project, is to gradually convert the network to fiber optic cable. Northern Telecom in cooperation with the Canadian Stentor consortium has embarked on a $300 million project to have 60 percent of New Brunswick wired with fiber optic cable by 1998. [5] It is worth noting that in conjunction with Northern Telecom's press announcement of its plans, the New Brunswick government announced its goal to make basic computer literacy a required component of the province's school curriculum.

In the meantime, TeleEducation is experimenting with the Internet and dedicated lines to offer higher bandwidth applications on the network. The Internet network in New Brunswick, called NBNet, already has linked many of the province's public schools and libraries, allowing students and teachers to access the resources of the Internet.

Like many areas of North America that depend on pure resource industries such as fishing and timber for jobs, New Brunswick is going through tough economic times. The TeleEducation project opens up the possibility of retraining segments of the work force for different careers and opportunities. As the government position paper on TeleEducation states, "there is a pressing need in all regions of the province for adult upgrading." New Brunswick is also a largely rural province with many of its residents living in isolated areas. "TeleEducation NB is a way of empowering rural communities, reducing the historical inequities caused by distance and isolation." [4]

TeleEducation is just part of an ambitious plan to establish a true information highway in New Brunswick. Eventually, government and health services will be available on the regional network, and kiosks will be set up in shopping malls and other public areas, allowing citizens to obtain government information, as well as to take care of things like vehicle registration or payment of fees.

Nevertheless, New Brunswick faces many of the same policy issues that exist in the United States (discussed in the previous chapter)—for example, universal access and affordable rates. But TeleEducation is an impressive start. It actually works using modest resources and technology. New Brunswick appears committed to broadband services for all of its citizens. TeleEducation will offer better capabilities and access as fiber optic cable becomes the primary telecommunications infrastructure in the province.

In the United States: Lots of Projects, Not Enough Funds

What New Brunswick is doing is by no means unique. Similar projects are going on in the United States that represent virtually every aspect of New Brunswick's plans—we have kiosks in California, an educational network in Texas, and a FreeNet in Montana, called Big Sky Telegraph that connects rural schools. [6] But what stands out about New Brunswick is that the government has a comprehensive strategy and appears willing to spend some money. Students are actually taking classes for credit from remote sites electronically, which is still rare in the U.S. (although some courses by satellite TV are available in this country). [7]

In contrast to New Brunswick, there isn't a comprehensive strategy in the United States for implementing distance learning. Instead, there is a haphazard conglomeration of projects going on all over the country, competing for limited funds. One educator, who requested anonymity, told us that the problem is not so much the lack of funds, but that too many people are trying to do the same thing. There are federal and state agencies, and a host of grassroots organizations all competing for funds to set up educational networks. The result is that available funds are spread very thin and nobody has enough funding.

One of the best sources of information on distance learning in the United States is the United States Distance Learning Association (USDLA), which publishes a monthly journal and sponsors a variety of conferences on the subject. [7] Another source is the Society for Applied Learning Techology (SALT). [8] Literally dozens of educational network projects are going on in the United States and we'll highlight a few of them. Some of these projects show great potential, but have a long way to go before they have a major impact on our educational system.

The Texas Educational Network

One of the more prominent projects is the Texas Educational Network, sponsored by the Texas Educational Agency. The network links up most of the state's school districts on a low-bandwidth, text-based network that is primarily used by teachers. Called TENET, the network provides a gateway to the Internet, e-mail, and access to various educational databases. Teachers who use the network say it's been a great help in sharing ideas and information with other teachers, collaborating on lesson plan and research project ideas, gaining access to reports and articles in their fields, and so on.

But the Texas Education Network, which serves the entire state of Texas, has operated on a budget of $6 million since 1989. [9] According to TENET's director, the budget for the 1994 fiscal year was $2.5 million. New Brunswick is spending roughly the same amount of money ($10.5 million over five years) in a province that is one-tenth the size of Texas in area and has one twenty-fifth the population (700,000 versus over 17 million).

The result is that only five percent of the classrooms in Texas have access to phone lines. "The average Texas school has three to six phones: in the administrative office, the principal's office, the athletic office and the library," says a report in *The Wall Street Journal.* [9] The bottom line is that TENET will primarily serve teachers for many years to come. There's nothing wrong with that as far as it goes, and TENET may well help teachers do their jobs, but it doesn't do much for bringing the benefits of the information highway directly to students.

PBS Learning Link

Another project that's garnered considerable attention is the PBS Learning Link, which is primarily distributed by public television stations in the United States. Learning Link is also a text-based network providing educational services to schools, day-care centers, home schoolers, and the like. It was first developed at the WNET public television station in New York as a two-way communications system to accompany educational programs on public television. Learning Link then received a grant from the Corporation for Public Broadcasting and was redesigned for widespread use in local communities. [10]

Learning Link is not a television service. It's similar to an electronic bulletin-board system, with a central computer providing the educational services, and users dialing up from a modem on a personal computer. Because of its history, Learning Link is primarily operated by public television stations, with over twenty of them offering the service in their communities.

The content and way that Learning Link is funded varies from station to station. Some stations charge usage fees or provide local funding from other sources or a combination of the two. For example, the Idaho Public Television version of Learning Link offers everything from an online version of *Mr. Rogers' Neighborhood* to information for math and science teachers from the Northwest Regional Educational Labs in Portland, Oregon. Most of the Learning Link networks offer "curriculum specific forums covering topics such as the Rain Forest, Space Exploration, Current Events, the Environment, and the Arts." [11]

In an interview with Idaho Public Television's director for Learning Link, Bob Pyle, the conversation quickly shifted to lack of funding. "Unfortunately, most schools can't afford the toll charges to connect to Learning Link," said Pyle, "particularly if they're at the other end of the state."

In its report on telecommunications and education, *The Wall Street Journal* hit the nail on the head: "While many educators applaud the coming of networks to primary and secondary schools, researchers say only a small percentage of schools nationwide are using the technology. Cost is the biggest obstacle, since many schools are still struggling to get basic computer equipment. In addition to the expense of hardware and software, some networks require schools to pay online fees and long-distance telephone charges." [9]

A Free Lane on the Highway for Education?

One of Vice President Gore's primary goals for the information highway is to "have every classroom, hospital, and library in the U.S. linked to the National Information Infrastructure." [12] And the telephone and cable companies have at least paid lip service to Gore's challenge. Before the collapse of the Bell Atlantic-Telecommunications Inc. (TCI) merger, the two companies had announced plans to offer a "Basic Education Connection" to the 26,000 public schools in their service areas, including free educational TV programming and free access to the Internet. [13]

Quite apart from their ill-fated merger, TCI and Bell Atlantic, as well as other telephone and cable companies, have separately promoted special deals for schools. TCI sponsors a "cable in the classroom" program, offering a variety of discounted educational services. Bell Atlantic has strongly supported educational networks with free equipment and services in Maryland. [13]

One of the most impressive commitments comes from Pacific Bell in California, which has announced a $100 million project to supply high bandwidth connections to most of the 7,400 public K-12 schools, public libraries, and community colleges in Pac Bell's service area by 1996. The plan is to connect all of these institutions with up to four ISDN lines with free installation and free usage for the first year, after which a discounted educational access rate would apply. [14]

Empty Offerings

Nevertheless, critics claim that these acts of good will by the telephone and cable companies are more public relations maneuvers than substantive efforts to bring networks to the classroom. It's one thing to offer "basic connections" to the schools, and another to actually provide the schools with toll-free network nodes and telephone jacks in every classroom. It may look good to provide facilities and services for a handful of schools, but won't make much difference if 95 percent of the schools are left out. Even Pac Bell's project would only hook up two sites in each school and library (in other words, two classrooms or laboratories per school or library) and funding for wiring the rest of the classrooms and paying the access fees would be supplied by private donations.

Public interest groups are trying to force the telecommunications companies to provide free network connections to schools and other public institutions. As of this writing, a proposal before the Senate Commerce Committee's communications panel, authored by the panel's chairman, Senator Daniel Inouye (D-Hawaii), would allow "... federal regulators to set aside up to 20 percent of the capacity [of advanced telecommunications networks] for schools, libraries, public broadcasters and other non-profit groups." [15] The allocated space could then be used for educational services such as distance learning classes at no cost to the providing institution.

Of course, the telephone companies are likely to oppose the proposal. A vice-president of the United States Telephone Association is quoted in the above referenced story as saying "... it's not appropriate to require us to give this away. It's an unconstitutional taking of property." The telephone representative went on to argue that telephone companies already offer discounted rates for fiber optic equipment and other broadband services. While this may be true, it hasn't helped rural parts of the country such as the state of Idaho, where schools can't afford the access charges for connecting to PBS Learning Link.

Professional Education

Use of the information highway for professional training will initially occur on a larger scale in the private rather than in the public sector simply because private enterprise does not have the same degree of financial obstacles that face public education. Of course, private enterprise must also deal with tight budgets and other financial constraints, but there are strong financial incentives for using the information highway for training employees. Private enterprise will be able to save money in many cases by holding training sessions over a broadband network rather than having employees travel to a central training center.

Professional training over broadband networks is already starting to take place. For example, a startup company in Toronto, Canada, called Mentor Networks, is offering a multimedia training course for doctors in the Toronto area on a trial basis. The course is entitled "Chest Pain in the Emergency Department" and was created by two prominent specialists in emergency medicine. "Using personal computers, doctors will be able to work with simulated cases using a mixture of full-motion video, audio, animation, text, and clinical images. They will be able to order electrocardiograms, ultrasound, and X-rays of the simulated patients, as well as use tutorials and reference materials." [16] One of the sponsors of the project is the Canadian Stentor consortium of telephone companies, which plans to use the Asymmetric Digital Subscriber Line (ADSL) technology, which we discussed in Chapter 4, to enable doctors in remote areas to take the training course.

This kind of training is clearly the wave of the future. Of course, there is considerable overlap here with video-conferencing technology that we discussed earlier in this book and which will be discussed again in Chapter 10. As a further example of this trend, the state of California is aggressively promoting the use of video-conferencing by state agencies for meetings, training, and other group activities that formerly required travel. Among the state institutions actively involved in implementing the policy are the California Department of Transportation (CALTRANS) and California State University at Sacramento. "CALTRANS estimates it will save $1 million annually in travel expenses, travel time, and increased productivity." [17]

Libraries

Libraries have historically been one of our primary sources of information and will remain so even in today's electronic information age. Indeed, there are striking parallels between the evolution of the public library and the movement today to establish "public" electronic networks accessible to all. It was the rapid proliferation of books and other printed materials in the late 19th century that spurred the growth of public libraries supported by government taxation. [18] It is the similar phenomenon of the explosion of electronic information that is spurring the "public information highway."

To Enhance, Not Replace

There seems to be a popular misconception that somehow the information highway will replace libraries and make them obsolete. The information highway should make libraries more accessible, particularly on the international level, but it hardly seems likely that the millions of pages of literature, art, history, philosophy, medicine, and social and physical sciences that have been printed on paper throughout human history will be converted to electronic form to any large extent. As the assistant director for library automation at Washington State University (WSU) library, John Webb, pointed out, "the total volume of information on the Internet is about one third the volume of printed information at the WSU library." If we consider that WSU is a typically sized large college library, and then consider the number of large universities in the United States, let alone the major public libraries such as the New York and Boston Public Libraries, each having millions of book titles, and then consider the major libraries around the world, the amount of available electronic information becomes miniscule in comparison to the volume of printed material.

At the moment, libraries are caught between the past and the future, making the difficult transition from being print-based institutions to computerized, digitized repositories of both electronic and printed information. The transition hasn't been easy and is far from complete. Libraries face stagnating or shrinking budgets while at the same time dealing with ever greater quantities of information, both printed and electronic. Says WSU library's John Webb, "Libraries are faced with a dilemma—the volume of both electronic and printed information is increasing and the costs are outpacing our budgets."

The real power of the information highway with respect to libraries lies in the ability to perform searches for material in libraries around the world. If you're a researcher, the prospect of being able to locate an article on an obscure topic in a library in Australia while sitting at a computer somewhere in the United States is compelling indeed. Of course, finding the article is one thing, but getting your hands on it can be quite another. Many major libraries are establishing international loan programs, allowing researchers to obtain articles or other published material from around the world. In addition, it is often possible to obtain printed material by FAX.

Machine-Readable Card Catalogs

Most major libraries around the world have scrapped or are in the process of scrapping the tried and true card-catalog system in favor of computerized search and retrieval systems based on the Machine Readable Cataloguing (MARC) standard format. These search-and-retrieval systems are huge electronic databases that supposedly have the same information as the library's card catalog. I use the qualifier "supposedly" because there is a great deal of controversy concerning the accuracy and reliability of electronic databases that have been converted from card catalogs.

Naturally, there are typographical errors in the converted card entries (just imagine entering the millions of cards of the Harvard Library to an online system) and there are all sorts of problems related to the computer's lack of human intelligence. Computers can't recognize, for example, that Pyotr Iljitch Tschaikovsky is one and the same man as Pjotr Iljics Csajkovsky. "The computer has to be informed of that fact outright; otherwise, symphonies and string serenades will be sprinkled haphazardly over the alphabet and a searcher won't have any idea what he is missing," writes Nicholson Baker in his excellent article in *The New Yorker* on the pitfalls of the conversion from card catalogs to electronic databases. [19]

It is true that the computerized databases replacing these card catalogs are relatively new and are undergoing the process of refinement and "debugging" that can only be gained through experience. In the meantime, library users often encounter exasperating deficiencies and errors in these computerized systems. As we mentioned in the chapter on the Internet, many online search and navigational tools are too slow or their search focus can't be refined enough so that they often produce thousands of "hits" (that is, successful searches), making the search result virtually useless. Says WSU's John Webb, "people can't use current tools effectively. Computer people say that increased power will take care of inefficiencies. Even the more sophisticated search tools haven't been producing significantly better results."

But although some traditionalists such as Nicholson Baker argue for the preservation of the printed card catalog, the conversion to electronic databases is not only inevitable but already occurring on a large scale. As Baker mournfully reports in his article, libraries actually hold farewell parties for their obsolete card catalogs, some of which have included balloon "send-offs" of cards. And Baker has some strong arguments. Mis-typed card entries can result in titles actually being lost in the closed stacks of large libraries. Baker notes wryly that one card conversion project "globally altered 'Madonna' to 'Mary, Blessed Virgin, Saint' as part of an authority-control routine—a change that, before it was corrected, caused problems for libraries interested in cataloguing the recent work of Ms. Ciccone." The Ms. Ciccone in question here is, of course, the fabulously successful pop/rock singer Madonna.

Nevertheless, electronic search-and-retrieval systems are here to stay and their proponents say it's just a matter of time before they become more reliable, efficient, and easier to use. John Webb, although critical of the current tools, agrees that "the more we can make available electronically, the better off we are." He points out that the annual turnstyle count of people entering the WSU library is over one million and that the staff re-shelves some 700,000 items per year. Obviously, the manual labor requirements could drop significantly if people could access more information electronically—although it should be noted that electronic searches are not free of charge, and that most libraries bear those costs.

But some critics see a gloomy future for online catalogs. Writes Baker:

> What we have already begun seeing, in fact, especially at state universities with dwindling budgets, is a kind of self-inflicted online hell, in which the libraries are forced to continue to pay paraprofessionals to convert their huge card catalogues, since they've already pillaged the paper database to the point where its integrity is unrestorable, and yet they aren't able to afford the continuous hardware and software upgrades necessary to make the growing mass of online records function together adequately. They can't go back, and they don't have the money to go forward. [19]

Indeed, an ever increasing volume of information is becoming available electronically. Many newsletters, journals, and other periodicals are now published in electronic form. Abstracts, if not the entire text, of many published articles covering a wide variety of fields and disciplines are also available. For example, the Online Computer Library Center (OCLC) based in Dublin, Ohio, which is the main supplier of MARC format electronic library catalogs, offers a variety of "online journals" for specific professions, such as the *Online Journal of Current Clinical Trials.* A medical library would be likely to subscribe to such a journal. OCLC also offers services such as an online "Table of Contents Service," which provides the subscriber with an online table of contents of a selected professional journal or periodical. The subscriber can select articles from the online table of contents, which appears automatically as electronic mail with each issue of the publication. The selected article is then sent electronically or in printed form.

Again, Bandwidth Is the Key

It seems that the phrase, "bandwidth is the key," could be the slogan of this book. High bandwidth, and of course the funding to go with it, is the key to making the information highway a major component of education—at all levels. Even universities, which are the most advanced of our educational institutions in the application of networks and computer technology, suffer from lack of bandwidth. Many universities rely on a single T-1 1.5 megabit per second line (see Chapter 4 if you're not familiar with that terminology) to connect to the Internet, making high-bandwidth transfers of audio and video (or even high-resolution graphics) virtually impossible without bringing the whole system to a crawl. (Remember that the information highway will require a minimum speed of 3 megabits per second into each home for full video and audio transmission.) In addition, many college libraries don't have enough computers or terminals with the graphics capabilities necessary to allow widespread access to graphics and video. A medical article in electronic form but without the illustrations, for example, is a poor substitute for the printed version.

There is no question that the information highway could greatly benefit students of all ages and in virtually all educational settings. The question is whether the resources will be allocated to make it possible for education to take advantage of the information highway. It's a very complicated and controversial issue. There are clearly outrageous bureaucratic inefficiencies and squandered resources in many school districts (what with custodians in one of our country's largest public school systems earning up to $80,000 per year and with virtually no supervision or accountability [20]), while others simply don't have enough funds to keep up with the technology. Probably everyone agrees that our educational system is in sore need of an overhaul. Part of that overhaul must include meaningful efforts to incorporate computers and information networks into the everyday curriculum of our schools.

Security Issues

Big Brother, Wire Bandits, and the Information Highway

"Our society has made a commitment to openness and to free communication. But if our legal and social institutions fail to adapt to new technology, basic access to the global electronic media could be seen as a privilege, granted to those who play by the strictest rules, rather than as a right held by anyone who needs to communicate."

Mitchell Kapor, co-founder Electronic Frontier Foundation
(*Scientific American*, September, 1991)

"Does the average person really need this kind of security? I say yes. He may be planning a political campaign, discussing his taxes, or having an illicit affair. He may be designing a new product, discussing a marketing strategy, or planning a hostile business takeover. He may be living in a country that does not respect the rights of privacy of its citizens. He may be doing something that he feels shouldn't be illegal, but is. Whatever his reasons, his data and communications are personal, private, and nobody's business but his own."

Bruce Schneier, from the preface to his book, *Applied Cryptography* [1]

Electronic espionage, wiretapping, invasion of privacy, and other security issues involving telecommunications have been a major social and political concern since the invention of the telephone. George Orwell's ominous vision of "big brother is watching you" appeared in his novel, *1984*, published in 1949. Fears of illegal wiretapping and espionage reached unprecedented heights during the McCarthy era in the 1950s. So, it is no surprise that these same issues are of great importance in the development of the information highway. In fact, ensuring security on the information highway is probably the most difficult and challenging task facing its developers. We've already briefly discussed the security problems of the Internet, and those problems are getting worse with the Internet's rapid expansion and growth.

Security Breaches: Illegal, Legal, Unethical

But before we get into the details, let's consider the meaning of "security on the information highway." Breaches of security can take many forms. Some are illegal and some are, strictly speaking, legal—but considered highly unethical. Illegal breaches of security include various forms of wire or telephone fraud such as unauthorized use of someone else's credit card number, or illegal use of the telephone system to make unpaid long distance calls. (This was the realm of the so-called "phone phreaks" like the legendary Captain Crunch, who made this practice famous in the 1960s by fooling the phone trunk switching machinery by whistling into the receiver with a toy whistle he got out of a cereal box.) Until cellular telephone systems switch to digital technology, they are particularly vulnerable to fraud and eavesdropping, since "anyone with the right radio receiver can listen in on calls." [2]

With digital telecommunications such as e-mail and file transfers, a different class of security breaches is also prevalent. Mischief makers on the Internet can masquerade using someone else's user name and password. They can send forged e-mail as a form of sabotage, or they can use the e-mail system to distribute the equivalent of obscene phone calls. As Paul Wallich writes in his article entitled "Wire Pirates" in the March, 1994 issue of *Scientific American*, ". . . electronic impersonators can commit slander or solicit criminal acts in someone else's name; they can even masquerade as a trusted colleague to convince someone to reveal sensitive personal or business information." [2]

Forged Imagery

A particularly dangerous aspect of digital forgery is its use in modifying photographs or other digitized images. Digital manipulation of photographs and video images has made the veracity of photographic evidence open to question in ways it never was before. A photograph or video tape of being "caught in the act" is no longer bullet-proof evidence in a divorce case, for example.

Of course, illegal activities such as blackmail and extortion are encouraged by the ability to create bogus digital imagery. And worse still, forged digital imagery can be used for political purposes to discredit a political opponent or to create a fictitious event. William Mitchell, professor of architecture and media arts at MIT, concludes his article on digital forgery in *Scientific American* with the following caution: "The information superhighway will bring us a growing flood of visual information in digital format, but we will have to take great care to sift the facts from the fictions and falsehoods." [3]

Online Con Artists

Online con artists are a growing phenomenon, both on commercial online services and on public networks such as the Internet. Although commercial services can theoretically control activities on their networks, it's difficult if not impossible to monitor the millions of users on these services. In any case, "a variety of illegal and abusive investment schemes, including stock manipulation, pyramid schemes, and Ponzi scams are already flourishing on commercial online services," says the *Newsbytes* news service. [4] Ohio Securities Commissioner Mark Holderman is quoted in the *Newsbytes* story as saying, "unwary Ohio residents who take the wrong turn on the information superhighway will end up getting cleaned out by high-tech schemers . . . . The danger here is that cyberspace, which could be a beneficial way for consumers to do a better job of informing themselves, will be instead discredited as a haven for fast-buck artists." [4] Regulators warn online users to beware of get-rich-quick schemes and to be careful about giving out names, addresses, and phone numbers.

Invasion of Privacy

Another major security problem, which fits into the legal but unethical category, is invasion of privacy. Invasion of privacy is already a major concern in our society. Residents of the United States find themselves bombarded with "junk mail" because of the practice of shared mailing lists. In fact, U.S. residents receive an average of almost 250 pieces of advertising mail per person per year, about three times as much as the next biggest junk mail country, Belgium, in which residents get an average of 80 junk-mail items per year. [5]

Some of the methods used to compile these lists may not be illegal but certainly raise serious ethical questions. For example, according to a special report on the invasion of privacy published by the *Boston Globe*, the Johnson & Johnson company compiled a list of five million elderly women based on responses to an ad for Serenity bladder control pads, and then offered the list to other companies. The report states further that "buying a product—or simply inquiring about it—is enough to get on such a list. So is filling out an application to operate a car or a boat, or declaring bankruptcy. And you leave a trail for the makers of lists each time you answer those extraneous questions on warranty cards, give your phone number to a cashier, order anything through the mail, or call a sex line or any other 800 or 900 number." [5]

Junk mail is only the tip of the iceberg when it comes to invasion of privacy. Marketing firms, lawyers, private detectives, and anyone else who's interested can obtain all sorts of personal information, from unlisted telephone numbers to medical records, for a price. There are companies that specialize in obtaining this information, and apparently do so by legal means. The *Boston Globe* cites a company in St. Petersburg, Florida, called Telephonic-Info, Inc., which will get you someone's unlisted telephone number for $69. Need to verify a divorce? That's $49. A look at someone's medical records or their personal bank account gets to be more expensive; $249 for the bank account and $299 for the medical records. "And it's all supposedly so aboveboard that even law enforcement agencies use its services," says the report. [5]

Eavesdropping in Cyberspace

Eavesdropping and wiretapping are age-old problems that take on new dimensions in "cyberspace." One of the more renowned cases of electronic eavesdropping took place at the 1994 Winter Olympic Games in Norway, where several journalists were caught reading figure skater Tonya Harding's e-mail. [6] E-mail can be read by others very easily on the Internet, as messages are passed from one node to another. Obviously, imposters who have obtained your password can receive your e-mail directly. And obtaining other users' valid passwords on the Internet is almost a trivial exercise for experienced hackers. One scheme called "packet sniffing" records user names and passwords as they travel across the network, enabling the "sniffers" to gain access to hundreds of computer systems. [7]

An "Electronic Pearl Harbor Waiting to Happen?"

Of course, security is not only a problem on the personal level. A recent book, which would probably appeal to Tom Clancy fans, is entitled *Information Warfare: Chaos on the Electronic Superhighway.* It warns of grave risks to our economy and democracy at the hands of "information warriors." The author, Winn Schwartau, quotes himself as telling a Congressional committee that "government and commercial computer systems are so poorly protected today that they can essentially be considered defenseless—an electronic Pearl Harbor waiting to happen. As a result of inadequate security planning on the part of both the government and the private sector, the privacy of most Americans has virtually disappeared." Mr. Schwartau goes on to warn his readers ominously: ". . . as terrorism now invades our shores, we can expect attacks upon not only airliners and water supplies, but upon the money supply, a sure way to strike terror into millions of people with a single keystroke." [8]

Malicious Software: Viruses, Trojan Horses, and other Rogues

Of all topics relating to computer and network security, software viruses have gained the most media attention and visibility. So far we've looked mainly at security breaches and violations designed for personal gain or to obtain intelligence. Viruses, time bombs, worms, and trojan horses, are in a different category, because their main intent is simply to cause destruction or at least chaos on computer systems and networks. Viruses are more akin to acts of vandalism rather than to robbery or fraud. Programmers who design these programs generally do it because it's a challenge and because it's fun, and they are usually launched anonymously, so that the perpetrator really has nothing to gain other than the satisfaction of spreading chaos and destruction among computer systems.

There are fine distinctions between destructive programs classified as viruses, time bombs, worms, and trojan horses. Viruses and worms copy themselves from one system to another. Trojan horses are concealed within functional software and are generally designed to simply destroy the system on which they reside. For an in-depth look at these various types of programs, see [9].

Probably the most famous virus was the Michelangelo virus that had its moment of fame in March, 1992. Lucikly, this virus caused a great deal more hysteria and hype than actual destruction. It was called the Michelangelo virus because it was a time bomb that was supposed to become active on March 6, 1992, Michelangelo's 517th birthday. The virus was designed to erase data on the host system's hard disk by automatically reformatting the hard disk. Some five million PCs were allegedly infected with the Michelangelo virus, and users were scrambling to purchase "anti-virus" software that can detect virus software and erase it before it causes any problems. In the end, very few PCs actually were infected—only about three percent of the world's PCs. [9]

Another of the most famous incidents was the Internet worm of November, 1988, designed by a student named Robert Morris at Cornell University. Exploiting a deficiency in certain versions of the Unix operating system, which is used by most Internet host systems, the worm copied itself onto thousands of computers on the Internet network. It didn't actually damage data or files. "Rather, the damage caused by the worm was tied directly to the amount of processing caused by its comprehensive and aggressive propagation, which ultimately overwhelmed the processing capacity of each system it successfully entered." [9] The Internet was brought to a virtual standstill for several days while system administrators worked day and night to clean up their systems.

I could regale you with many more horror stories of security breaches and ominous warnings from the experts, but it would be more useful to consider what can be done about these problems. We would do well to remember that the information highway we envision has not yet been built, and it should therefore be possible to create a high level of security during its construction. Certainly this will be a lot easier and more effective than attempting to add security to the information highway after it is in place.

Methods of Security

There are many aspects to building secure computer systems and networks, which is why entire books have been written on the subject. Preventing unauthorized access, protecting sensitive data, and warding off viruses are the three main objectives of security. Virus protection is accomplished by software that detects and erases viruses. There is a constant "arms race" between designers of viruses and designers of virus protection. The other tactic against viruses is to take fast action before the virus spreads. Since the Internet worm incident, a Computer Emergency Response Team (CERT) was established on the Internet, which acts sort of like the Coast Guard to head off assaults before they gain momentum.

In spite of their media attention, viruses and other malicious software are probably less of a threat to the information highway than the other forms of security breaches I've discussed. Viruses primarily destroy data. Your data should always be backed up if it's important, less because of viruses than simple failure of disk hardware—and some measure of virus protection is now built into most computer operating systems. The end result of most viruses is that they cause a lot of inconvenience, whereas fraud and invasion of privacy can do more permanent damage. Let's now turn our attention to methods of security related to access and data protection.

Much in the same way that the military treats matters of security, security on computers can be classified in levels ranging from low to high. High-level security systems involve some form of data encryption. *Encryption*, a security technique that has been used for thousands of years, means to encode or encipher; "to convert (as a body of information) from one system of communication into another; esp: to convert (a message) into code" [*Webster's Collegiate Dictionary*]. "Cipher" is defined as "a method of transforming a text in order to conceal its meaning."

Most Networks Use Low-Level Security

An example of low level security is a simple unencrypted password system. In a low level security system, the password and other data generated on the system exist on the network in their "plaintext" form. If the password is "jonny13," it is stored as the binary equivalent of the string "jonny13" and travels as such on the network. In other words, "plaintext" is unencrypted data, and if an intruder obtains the password (say by electronic eavesdropping), he can not only read it, but use it as though he were the authorized user of that computer system or user account. This type of low-level security is by far the most common in use today, which is why most networks are relatively insecure systems.

Firewalls on the Internet

In between basic low-level password and high-level encrypted systems, there are all sorts of other security approaches. On the Internet, many companies and institutions use a "firewall" system to protect internal computers from the Internet at large, but at the same time allow communications between them. One such system examines all packet addresses coming to and from the system and only allows passage of those headed for specific destinations. "AT&T built a firewall consisting of two dedicated computers: one connected to the Internet and the other connected to the corporation's own network. The external machine examines all incoming traffic and forwards only the 'safe' packets to its internal counterpart." [10] But firewalls have major limitations. They greatly restrict the activities of users of the system, because only certain destinations are permissible. And if users are allowed complete freedom, the firewall can easily be compromised.

Other schemes on the Internet involve various forms of cryptography or "one-time passwords," in which users receive a new password after every use (a second use of the password indicates an unauthorized user). [10] These intermediate-level schemes are stop-gap measures designed to allow companies and institutions to continue using the Internet until something more robust can be put in place, such as a true data-encryption system.

Data Encryption

Data encryption is considered the most reliable form of security, but within the larger topic of encryption are mechanisms offering different levels of security. Bruce Schneier starts the preface of his book *Applied Cryptography* with the following summary of data encryption: "There are two kinds of cryptography in this world: cryptography that will stop your kid sister from reading your files, and cryptography that will stop major governments from reading your files. This book is about the latter." [1] Schneier's remarkably readable book is an excellent text for those interested in the technical details of cryptographic systems.

The basic principle of data encryption is that the data are converted to an encrypted code by means of a so-called cryptographic algorithm or cipher, which is a set of instructions that performs the conversion. In all modern encryption systems, both the sender and receiver need to have a *key* that allows the encryption/decryption process to take place. There are two basic types of encryption algorithms, which are differentiated by their key systems: *symmetric algorithms*, which use a secret key, and *public-key systems*, which use a pair of keys, one secret, and one published in the manner of listed telephone numbers.

Symmetric (Secret-Key) Algorithms

To quote from Bruce Schneier: "Symmetric algorithms are algorithms where the encryption key can be calculated from the decryption key and vice-versa. In many such systems, the encryption key and the decryption key are the same. These algorithms, also called secret-key algorithms, single-key algorithms, or one-key algorithms, require the sender and receiver to agree on a key before the messages pass back and forth. This key must be kept secret. The security of symmetric algorithms rests in the key; divulging the key means that anybody could encrypt or decrypt messages in this cryptosystem." [1] The most widely used encryption system in the United States is a symmetric algorithm system creatively entitled the Data Encryption Standard or DES.

Public-Key Systems

Public-key systems, on the other hand, have a publicly known encryption key, so that virtually anyone can send an encrypted message. A person or organization publishes its public key in some sort of directory that is accessible to anyone wishing to send them encrypted data. Messages and other data may be encrypted by this public key into an indecipherable body of ciphertext. Note that the public key works like a "one-way door"—once encrypted with a public key, ciphertext may not be decrypted by that same key, as is often the case in a symmetric encryption system using a single secret key.

Having encrypted some data with the public key, the ciphertext is transmitted to the owner of the public key. The owner of the public key also has a private key (presumably unknown to others), which is the only way data encrypted with the public key may be decrypted back to "plaintext" or usable form. The public key and private key are generated together, but they cannot be derived from one another. This allows the public key to be freely distributed without threatening the secrecy of the private key.

The best-known public-key system today is called RSA, which stands for the algorithm's inventers (Rivest, Shamir, and Adleman). [1] The RSA algorithm is at the heart of the Pretty Good Privacy product, which is coming into increasingly more common use on the Internet.

Encryption Software versus Hardware

Basically, encryption systems are computer programs. Like other computer programs, encryption systems can operate either as part of the computer's software or in hardware using special processors. The encryption/decryption process can negatively affect the overall performance of the computer system, particularly if implemented in software. Most advanced encryption systems are built into hardware and operate at high speed, having virtually no adverse effects on the performance of the system. However, hardware encryption systems raise the cost and complexity of the computer system or communications device markedly. As I discussed earlier, consumer devices such as set-top boxes will have to be priced very competitively, and it remains to be seen whether the industry will be able to afford built-in encryption hardware on a mass scale.

A Tough Nut to Crack

Encryption systems such as DES and RSA are very difficult to crack. Virtually all encryption algorithms are theoretically breakable, but require so much effort and time (primarily computational effort) to break, that it's not practical to do so for most hackers. Of course, nothing is guaranteed. As Bruce Schneier says, "pronouncing that an algorithm is secure simply because it is unfeasible to break, given current technology, is dicey at best. Good cryptosystems are designed to be unfeasible to break with the computing power that is expected to evolve many years in the future." [1] Breaking encryption systems is the kind of thing that government intelligence agencies with powerful computing systems work on, but good encryption systems eliminate a lot of the small-time "wire pirates" stealing credit card numbers and the like.

Encryption Standards and the Clipper Controversy

Clearly, the sender and receiver of encrypted data must be using the same or at least compatible encryption systems. Standards for data encryption have therefore become a matter of intense controversy. At present, the dominant standard is DES, which is about fifteen years old and has been criticized as outdated and too easy to penetrate. The lack of new standards has greatly hampered the implementation of encryption systems on the Internet.

But much of the controversy revolves around the federal government's policy towards encryption. Before we look closer at this policy, it's important to consider the stakes. What is at stake is the government's ability to conduct intelligence on communications networks. As long as telephone systems were based on analog signals (see Chapter 4), government security agencies could easily (in fact, much too easily) perform surveillance operations. But digital telephony is a different story. Encrypted data on digital phone lines is difficult to decipher without having the encryption/decryption keys. The government wants to control encryption systems by establishing an encryption standard that includes some means for allowing law enforcement agencies to decipher (with proper authorization such as a court order) encrypted code.

The Clipper Chip

The government's encryption system, which is called the *Clipper chip*, has been under development since 1989 under the auspices of the National Security Agency (NSA) at the cost of more than $2.5 million. [11] The Clipper chip is a processor about the size of your thumbnail that uses a symmetric (secret key) algorithm called the SKIPJACK algorithm. It should be noted that although the media refers almost exclusively to the "Clipper chip," there is a second chip developed by the NSA called the Capstone chip that also uses the SKIPJACK algorithm. The Clipper chip is primarily intended for communications devices such as telephones and FAX machines, while the Capstone chip is intended for computers.

Very little is known about how the Clipper system actually works. The details of its functioning are in fact classified as military secrets. What has been revealed is simply how it is to be operated from the outside. The unique and probably most controversial aspect of the whole Clipper/Capstone/SKIPJACK system is the use of a "key-escrow" scheme for allowing legitimate law enforcement access to the keys. Each individual Clipper chip (and hence each Clipper user) will have two unique keys, each of which will be held in escrow by one of two agencies: One key at the National Institute of Standards and Technology (NIST) and the other at the Treasury Department. Both keys are required to decrypt Clipper communications, and storing the keys at two separate government agencies lessens (but hardly eliminates, as critics endlessly point out) casual or corrupt appropriation of the keys. By obtaining a court order, law enforcement officials could gain access to the keys from the two key escrow agencies for the purposes of a sanctioned wiretap. [1]

The Clipper Controversy

There has been tremendous controversy over the Clipper chip for a number of reasons. First, civil liberties advocates oppose the Clipper technology on constitutional grounds, claiming that it violates the Fourth Amendment (unreasonable search and seizure) and the Fifth Amendment (rights against self-incrimination). One of the most vocal opponents of the Clipper chip has been the Electronic Frontier Foundation (EFF), which I discussed in some detail in the earlier chapter on policy.

Another major argument against Clipper is that the federal government plans to prohibit U.S. technology companies from exporting any products that use cryptographic systems other than the Clipper chip. The government's motive is clear. Because it has the keys to the Clipper chip, it can break any system that uses that encryption scheme. On the other hand, it seems highly unlikely that Saddam Hussein or any other U.S. adversary would be stupid enough to buy a system containing an encryption scheme that the U.S. government can break! The upshot is that foreign developers of cryptographic systems will have an enormous advantage over U.S. firms in selling technology that includes cryptographic systems, because they will not have the constraints of having to sell exclusively Clipper-based encryption systems.

There is also the argument that Clipper simply won't work. In Chapter 3, I quoted Bob Metcalfe, the founder of 3Com Corp. and one of the inventers of Ethernet, who claimed that sooner or later the SKIPJACK algorithm would be cracked (or leaked by its creators) and that because Clipper is voluntary, few users would adopt it anyway. The only way to make Clipper truly effective may be to make it mandatory, an action which critics claim would violate the First Amendment, in addition to putting a host of other cryptographic system developers out of business—and eliminating the last shreds of support that the current administration might have in the high-tech community.

Finally, there is the shadowy possibility that the SKIPJACK algorithm, which has not been made public, contains a top-secret "back door" allowing federal intelligence agencies like the CIA and NSA (which created SKIPJACK) to intercept Clipper-encrypted communications without even requiring the secret keys or a court order to obtain them. Critics point out that SKIPJACK is the only encryption algorithm in history that has not been completely published and subjected to the analysis and attack of the worldwide community of cryptographic experts. The RSA algorithm has been published for many years, and as yet has withstood all attempts to defeat it. Critics argue that the only conceivable reason for hiding the SKIPJACK algorithm is that its creators (the NSA, primarily) built a back door into SKIPJACK for its own use. The NSA will not discuss the matter at all, and the critics have not been convinced. Opposition to Clipper can only be characterized as white-hot, with virtually no one outside of government agencies speaking in its favor.

So far, the government is relying on its export regulations and its own promotion of Clipper to make it become a standard. According to a report in *Fortune Magazine*, "the Administration insists that it won't force U.S. companies to build Clipper into their wares. But it also figures a mandate won't be necessary under its two-pronged market solution: First, it buys vast quantities of the chips to create a market; second, it exempts Clipper from otherwise stringent controls on encryption technology." [12]

Meanwhile, the controversy drags on. The government maintains that it needs the capability to perform electronic surveillance of terrorists, spies, organized crime, and other threats to law and order and national security. Critics such as the EFF and the Computer Professionals for Social Responsibility have launched a variety of campaigns to protest the government's policy.

To further complicate matters, a design flaw has very recently been discovered in the Clipper chip, which could force the NSA back to the drawing board and could also delay production of the chip for data-processing applications. Apparently, the flaw won't affect the use of Clipper for telephone conversations. [13] In fact, AT&T has come out with a telephone attachment and a cellular telephone that use the Clipper chip, both priced over $1,000 and mostly being purchased by the Justice Department. [12]

Security Is Up in the Air

Much like the issue of universal access to the information highway, security on the information highway is very much up in the air. The government is adamant about having some control over encryption schemes, which makes it difficult, if not impossible, to establish a robust encryption scheme on the Internet, because it is a global system that crosses international borders. In addition, it would be an absolute nightmare to try to sort out the existing infrastructure of the Internet to the point that a robust security system could be established.

Looking to the future, an agreement on standards for encryption systems will be necessary for large-scale communications to take place on the information highway. The alternative is a maze of "information kingdoms," each with its own "moat" or special encryption systems. This phenomenon is already taking place. Companies are building firewalls, while various virtually unbreakable encryption schemes are available in the U.S. and abroad. One of these, Pretty Good Privacy (PGP) [14] is an RSA implementation that has gained some advocates on the Internet, but it has been mired in licensing disputes and cannot be legally exported from the United States. Security is a messy issue and we won't be able to sort it out here. But it's also of crucial importance for the success of the information highway.

Wireless Communications

Mobility and the Information Highway

> *"Overshadowed by Vice President Al Gore's 'information superhighway' is what has been called the 'information skyway.'"*
>
> —**Lawrence Gasman, President of Communications Industry Researchers, Inc.** ***The Wall Street Journal,*** **June 9, 1994**

The information highway will not be accessible solely from our offices and living rooms. The concept of "information anywhere, any time," means that you should be able to access the information highway when you're on the road—from your car, from an airplane, or from the beach. This capability is made possible by mobile computers and telephones connected by forms of wireless communications: cellular, radio and microwave, and satellite.

Because we're interested in wireless communications as it relates to the information highway, we will focus on *wide area networks* (WANs), which are networks that allow you to communicate over a distance greater than approximately a kilometer; in other words, beyond a complex of office buildings or warehouses. WANs are used to communicate across the country or across town. Wireless local area networks (LANs) are used to provide in-building or very short distance wireless communications. For a discussion of recent developments in wireless LAN technology, see the May 1994 issue of *BYTE.* [1]

The fundamental principle of wireless communications is that it occurs over the airwaves, which are part of the electromagnetic

Table 9.1 ***Range of Frequencies for General Communications***

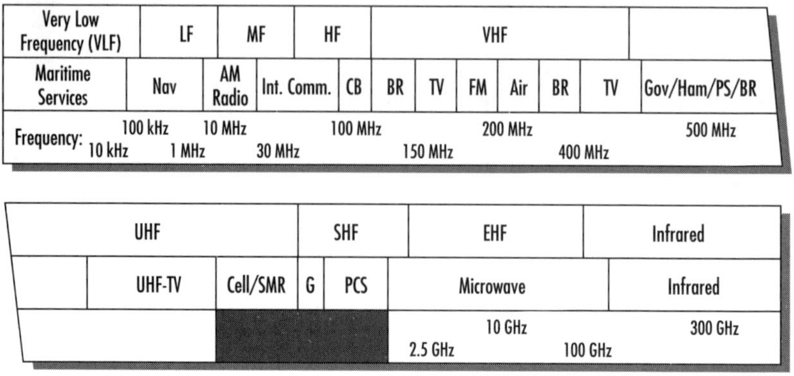

Very Low Frequency (VLF)	LF	MF		HF	VHF						
Maritime Services	Nav	AM Radio	Int. Comm.	CB	BR	TV	FM	Air	BR	TV	Gov/Ham/PS/BR
Frequency: 10 kHz	100 kHz	1 MHz	10 MHz	30 MHz	100 MHz	150 MHz	200 MHz	400 MHz			500 MHz

UHF				SHF	EHF	Infrared
	UHF-TV	Cell/SMR	G	PCS	Microwave	Infrared
				2.5 GHz	10 GHz, 100 GHz	300 GHz

spectrum. As we discussed in Chapter 4, the wavelength of the radio or light wave determines its frequency. Wireless communications are possible over a wide range of frequencies, ranging from the Very Low Frequency (VLF) of 30 Kilohertz (thousands of cycles per second) for maritime services to microwave frequencies of 100 Gigahertz or GHz (billions of cycles per second). Table 9.1 shows the range of frequencies used for communications in general, while Table 9.2 specifies the range of frequencies for data communications.

The important point is that these frequencies are controlled and allocated in the United States by the Federal Communications Commission (FCC). The FCC issues licenses to service providers to operate communications equipment over a specified range of frequencies. Cellular telephone services are authorized to operate in the range of 800 to 900 Megahertz or MHz,

Table 9.2 ***Range of Frequencies for Data Communications***

Cellular	824-849, 869-894 MHz
Private Land Mobile	896-901, 930-931 MHz (Includes RF packet services such as RAM Mobile Data)
Narrowband PCS	901-902, 930-931 MHz
Industrial	902-928 MHz (Unlicensed commercial use such as cordless phones and LANs)
Common Carrier Paging	931-932 MHz (Includes national paging services such as SkyTel)
Point-to-Multipoint, Point-to-Point	932-935, 941-944 MHz
PCS	1850-1970, 2130-2150, 2180-2200 MHz
Industrial	2400-2483.5 MHz (Unlicensed commercial use, such as LANS)

for example. Because these licenses cost substantial sums of money and because service providers are in the business to make a profit, wireless communications are generally more expensive than comparable "wireline" communications.

Note that some frequencies are "unlicensed," meaning that they may be used by anyone complying with the FCC's guidelines for their use. For example, in-building wireless networks use unlicensed frequency bands, as do cordless telephones and automatic garage door openers. But virtually all long-distance wireless communications must take place over licensed frequency bands. One company trying to buck this trend is Metricom, which is using a patented scheme to build a nationwide network on unlicensed frequency bands. [2]

The next important point is that the radio spectrum is a finite and limited resource. While there are virtually no physical limits to the expansion of our wireline communications systems (we can just keep adding cable), we can't add to the radio and microwave spectrum. The communications spectrum is therefore a hotly contested resource. The government, military, public safety and medical services, broadcasting companies, telephone companies, and other commercial interests are all vying for a share of the spectrum.

The Demand for Wireless Is Booming

The limits of the communications spectrum are likely to become an increasingly thorny problem. While some might question the sanity of a society in which people feel compelled to be in contact with information sources at all times, whether they're on vacation at the beach or hurtling down the freeway, there is no question that the demand for mobile communications is enormous and growing at a rapid rate. The growth of the cellular telephone market is a case in point. The number of cellular telephones in this country is expected to approach 40 million by 1998. [3]

Whether we like it or not, mobile and wireless communications are rapidly becoming part of everyday life and often a prerequisite for that "competitive edge" in the business world. In major metropolitan areas, it seems that cellular telephones have become not only useful communications tools, but status symbols as well. Stories are legion of people taking cellular phone calls in movie theatres, restaurants, even classrooms. The *New Yorker* ran a cartoon of a dignified gentleman answering his cellular telephone in the midst of delivering a commencement speech at a college graduation and saying, "Can I call you back? I'm in the middle of a commencement speech!"

While these kinds of excesses make for good jokes and make some cellular users look pretty ridiculous, there is also great utility in wireless communications. Delivery services such as Federal Express and United Parcel Service would be lost without it, both literally and figuratively. These companies use wireless communications (a combination of radio and cellular) to track packages through the entire delivery process. [2] Law enforcement and public safety departments depend on radio communications, as do many other types of services.

Analog Is Bad for Data

Voice communications over wireless media are well-established on radio and cellular telephones. But our main concern here is the communication of data by wireless means. Cellular telephone systems have so far relied primarily on analog transmission techniques. These techniques offer poor performance for transmitting data. If you've ever had a conversation with someone on a cellular phone, especially long-distance, you can hear the pauses and "blank spots" as the signal is "handed off" from one cellular base station to another. (Each base station serves a roughly hexagonal area approximately eight miles in diameter, which is called a cell—hence, the name "cellular.") [4]

These blank spots, while merely annoying during a voice call, can cause serious reliability problems when transmitting data. While it's possible to send and receive data using standard analog cellular telephones connected to a modem, it can be a frustrating experience, with either aborted connections or lost or garbled data. With the cost per minute substantially more than standard wireline access charges, transmitting data by analog cellular can get expensive. Another problem is the lack of security inherent in analog cellular data transmission. Any motivated person with an old-build scanner (prior to 1992) can easily monitor cellular transmissions in their local cell—or even farther, with a gain antenna and an RF amplifier. Tens of millions of such scanners exist, and converters for adapting new-build scanners to the cellular bands (by law, new-build scanners cannot tune the cellular frequencies) are easy to build with a small handful of electronic parts.

Packet-Based Wireless Transmission

Just as digital transmission techniques will dominate the wireline information highway, they are also the trend in wireless communications. Transmitting data packets in digital form is far more reliable than using analog techniques. With packet data transmission, the problem of interrupting the circuit during the signal hand-off is easily circumvented by the error checking schemes built into packet-switching technology. If a packet is lost or garbled, it is simply retransmitted (this whole error checking process happens in milliseconds and is not noticeable to the sender or receiver). It's also easier to implement security measures such as an encryption scheme in a packetized system. It's important to note, however, that the transmission speeds on wireless communications systems are generally far below the three to ten megabit per second rates we can expect on the wireline infrastructure of the information highway.

CDPD: The Answer for Cellular?

In cellular telephone systems, the trend is toward a transmission technique called Cellular Digital Packet Data (CDPD), which makes use of the existing analog cellular infrastructure but transmits data in packets. The CDPD system actually takes advantage of the unused bandwidth during cellular voice transmissions, using a technique called "channel hopping," in which the data transmission "hops" to whatever channel currently has available bandwidth. CDPD supports the TCP/IP networking protocol used by most Internet-based networks, so that data communications with the Internet will be much faster and more straightforward on CDPD cellular circuits.

The maximum transmission speed using CDPD is 19.2 kilobits per second, which makes it competitive with the current crop of high-speed modems on standard phone lines, but hardly fast enough to support video and audio transmissions. On the positive side, CDPD's speed of 19.2 kilobits per second is two to four times faster than most analog cellular transmission modem speeds, which will reduce the access time and the cost of a data transmission session. In addition, CDPD usage will probably be billed separately and at a lower rate than voice usage.

The CDPD standard is supported by a number of cellular providers, including McCaw Cellular and its new partner, AT&T. The problem is that not all cellular phone systems support CDPD and until they all do, it won't become a cellular data communications standard. In fact, CDPD is still a very new technology and has not been tested on a large scale, although it is expected to proliferate during 1995. Says *The Wall Street Journal*: ". . . the cellular strategy to simply overlay digital data atop phone-call traffic is tremendously complicated, and some observers aren't sure it will work as well as proponents promise. The market for wireless data networks has languished, in part, because of a decided lack of user enthusiasm. That could change under CDPD, which offers users the best of both worlds: voice and data."[3]

Eventually, cellular phone circuits will become completely digital using two techniques called Code Division Multiple Access (CDMA) and Time Division Multiple Access (TDMA). These technologies increase the cellular capacity to ten times and three times, respectively, that of analog cellular circuits. [4] But the conversion to cellular digital circuits will take a long time, much like the conversion to fiber optic cable, simply because of the already substantial investment in analog cellular systems.

ARDIS and RAM Mobile Data

Aside from cellular telephone systems, the most prevalent means of connecting to the wireless world is by private data networks such as RAM Mobile Data and ARDIS. These systems operate in the 800-1000 MHz range and provide low-bandwidth data communications using a digital radio network of base transmitters located in most parts of the country. To use these networks, you need appropriate radio modems or other communications devices generally supplied by the network companies. However, some of the mobile communications systems that we will discuss shortly can also connect to these networks, providing services such as electronic mail. Communications speeds range from 4800 bits per second to 19.2 kilobits per second, but are generally closer to the lower end 4800 bits per second.

Compared to the popularity of cellular telephones, these private data networks are small potatoes indeed. While there are some 17 million cellular phones in use, ARDIS had about 40,000 customers in 1993, while RAM Mobile Data had only about 3000. [2] These networks are also expensive, with typical costs in the $100 per month range, although costs have been dropping as the networks compete for electronic mail customers. If CDPD is successful (and that is still a big "if"), these networks could be in for some rough times.

Specialized Mobile Radio (SMR)

Many companies use Specialized Mobile Radio (SMR) services to enable workers in the field to communicate with one another and the home office. Private companies such as NeXTel, Dial Page, and CenCall operate SMR services. [5] Like cellular service providers, these operators have licenses to use radio frequencies in the 800-900 MHz range, and sell access time on these frequencies to customers such as trucking and taxi companies; SMR is particularly well suited for two-way communications between vehicles in motion.

The services available on SMR have been greatly expanded to compete with cellular telephone services. Most notably, MCI has invested heavily in NeXTel, and using a digital technology called the Motorola Integrated Radio System (MIRS), which essentially converts SMR to digital, intends to offer mobile telephones that compete head-on with cellular telephones. As with the private data networks, SMR could face some stiff competition from cellular systems using CDPD.

Destineer

One other competitor in the wireless network business that deserves mention is Mtel's Nationwide Wireless Network, which now has the new name of Destineer. Destineer is scheduled for introduction in 1995. Mtel (Mobile Telecommunications Technologies Corporation) is the parent company of SkyTel, which operates one-way paging services in this country and around the world. [2] The new network will operate on a single 50 KHz channel at a transmission speed of 24 kilobits per second for broadcasts, with a return transmission speed of 9600 bits per second (this is to lower battery demands on portable devices, according to the above cited reference). Mtel has received major investments from Microsoft and separately from Microsoft's founders, Paul Allen and Bill Gates. Because of its pioneering work in two-way wireless paging and voice messaging technology, the FCC has granted so-called "Pioneers' Preference" status to Destineer, which enabled Mtel to obtain a license for PCS services without going through the bidding process. [6]

The Competition Is Heating Up

In summary, the competition for wireless customers is going to get fierce in the latter half of the 1990s. MCI teamed with NeXTel, AT&T teamed with McCaw Cellular, US West in a joint venture with AirTouch Communications (formerly part of Pacific Telesis), and Bell-Atlantic allied with Nynex may well be the "wireless heavyweights," but companies like Mtel could be surprisingly competitive. As *The Wall Street Journal* aptly puts it: ". . . while industry leaders may debate the arcane comparisons of the rival wireless approaches, in the end sheer marketing muscle may determine the winner." [7]

The competition is further complicated by the FCC's allocation of frequencies for Personal Communications Services (PCS).

Personal Communications Services (PCS)

As this book goes to print, the FCC is auctioning licenses for a range of frequencies to be dedicated to Personal Communications Services (PCS). A total of 160 MHz in the 1.85 to 2.2 GHz range (see Table 9.1b) will be allocated for telecommunications companies to provide a new class of wireless data services. There will be fierce competition for these licenses, and the companies that obtain them will be able to offer digital data communications services over the above frequencies. A wide range of new services at much higher bandwidths is expected to be developed for PCS. These services will likely include many of the types of offerings we expect from the wireline information highway: interactive video, home banking, news feeds, electronic mail, and so on. In addition, services for travellers, such as navigational guidance and traffic information, are likely to be part of PCS offerings.

But there are major political and regulatory hurdles to be overcome before these services become a reality. For one thing, the winners of the PCS auction will have to pay for the relocation of "current tenants" within their licensed bandwidth. [4] These current tenants include a variety of industrial and public safety operators who use these frequencies for wireless communications. As relocation may involve the purchase of new or modified equipment, antennas, and employee training, such relocation may be a much greater expense than originally envisioned.

Another twist to the affair is that the FCC will give preference in the auction to small and medium-sized businesses, particularly those with minority or female ownership. "In the next several months," wrote *The Wall Street Journal* in June 1994, "the rules are expected to trigger courtships of small companies by large companies on an unprecedented scale. That's because the cost of building new communications networks will be too high for most independent small companies, and those able to team up with well-financed companies will have an edge in bidding for licenses." [8]

Companies already offering cellular phone or other wireless service may not bid for the PCS spectrum in their current service area, which excludes many of the regional Bell operating companies from bidding. However, San Francisco's Pacific Telesis spun off its cellular services into a separate company called AirTouch Communications, and is therefore able to compete for the PCS licenses. This was announced in a press release as follows: "AirTouch is the new name for PacTel, which recently separated from Pacific Telesis Group to form an independent corporation dedicated to helping people stay in touch through wireless communications." [9]

The result of the PCS bidding war will be a slew of new wireless services by the end of the decade. But some analysts think that PCS will have a tough time competing with cellular services, which will also offer many of the same services envisioned for PCS. Ironically, if Pacific Telesis wins its bid for PCS, it will end up competing against its cellular spin-off, AirTouch, for wireless customers! Cellular telephone systems are also moving away from analog toward digital communications techniques. And as these digital techniques emerge, there is no reason that cellular phone companies can't compete head-on with PCS. The cellular companies also have the big advantage of millions of existing customers.

On the other hand, the FCC's preference for small business could result in some interesting applications. For example, *The Wall Street Journal* reports that ". . . the Small Business PCS Association, a coalition of 60 small firms headed by Kycom, Inc. in Portola Valley, Calif., hopes to build a national 'roaming' network." [10] *Roaming* is a term for operating a cellular phone or modem outside the service area of the organization that bills the phone or modem for service. This approach allows people who pay their cellular bills in Cincinnati to use their cellular phones while travelling on business to Chicago, New York, or anywhere else. Such a roaming network as Kycom envisions would allow nationwide wireless communications regardless of your location.

Pagers Are All the Rage

In addition to PCS frequencies for broadband services, the FCC is also auctioning a range of frequencies for "narrowband services," which mainly involve wireless paging devices. As we mentioned briefly in Chapter 4, paging devices constitute a major segment of the wireless market, and they are selling like hotcakes. The *Wall Street Journal* reports that "pagers are becoming the rage as new models deliver messages along with phone numbers. Devices now can be programmed to beep when a stock price jumps or drops to a certain level and can deliver news stories to users just like computers. Restaurants give pagers to customers waiting for tables, while auto repair shops beep drivers when their cars are ready." [11]

While the functions of paging devices have been fairly basic in the past, new "advanced paging services" will be developed for PCS, "such as zipping data around the country using hand-held computers and delivering voice mail to devices that slip into purses or hook onto belts." [12] Pagers are likely to merge with the wireless equipment that we turn to next: hand-held computers.

Personal Digital Assistants and Communicators

As computers have become more powerful, it has been possible to package their processing power into lightweight, hand-held devices. While portable computers such as laptops have been on the market since about 1984, only recently have lightweight and compact computing devices been available with adequate battery power to be used in truly mobile situations. These new devices are called "personal communicators" or "personal digital assistants" (PDAs) and are the successors to the failed pen-based computer market of the early 1990s. Pen-based computers were a failure in the marketplace because they were too heavy, had poor readability and a short battery life, and featured unreliable and inaccurate handwriting recognition.

Today's personal communicators are a different breed from their pen-based predecessors. The Apple Newton MessagePad and IBM/BellSouth's Simon are examples of new lighter and more energy-efficient systems. Handwriting recognition has been largely de-emphasized because the technology, while improved from its absurd beginnings in the late 1980s, simply isn't good enough yet. For good reason, (especially where the devices are used for estimating and invoicing) users will not tolerate 95 percent accuracy, and until handwriting recognition gets very close to 100 percent accuracy, it will not be a viable technology in any but the small aficionado market. However, these newer hand-held devices are still too expensive to gain widespread market acceptance. With fully configured systems (that is, including communications capabilities) costing $1,000 or more, the market is still confined to "early adopters" and executives who can charge these purchases to their expense accounts (a dwindling breed, to be sure).

A wide variety of hand-held personal communicators are on the market and more are entering the market all the time. Rather than attempt to survey the personal communicator marketplace, I'll focus on one particular product, which I think is representative of the kinds of capabilities that will be provided by personal communicators over the next few years.

The Motorola Envoy

The device that I will describe is the Motorola Envoy Personal Wireless Communicator, shown in Figure 9.1. The Envoy weighs under two pounds and has a 3 by 4.5 inch liquid crystal display (LCD) screen. The touch-sensitive screen has an "on-screen keyboard," which you can access with your finger or with a built-in stylus. Graphical icons on the screen can also be activated with your finger or the stylus.

Data is stored on the Envoy on so-called memory cards, which are about the size of a credit card and about 1/8 inch thick. These

Figure 9.1 *The Motorola Envoy Personal Wireless Communicator*

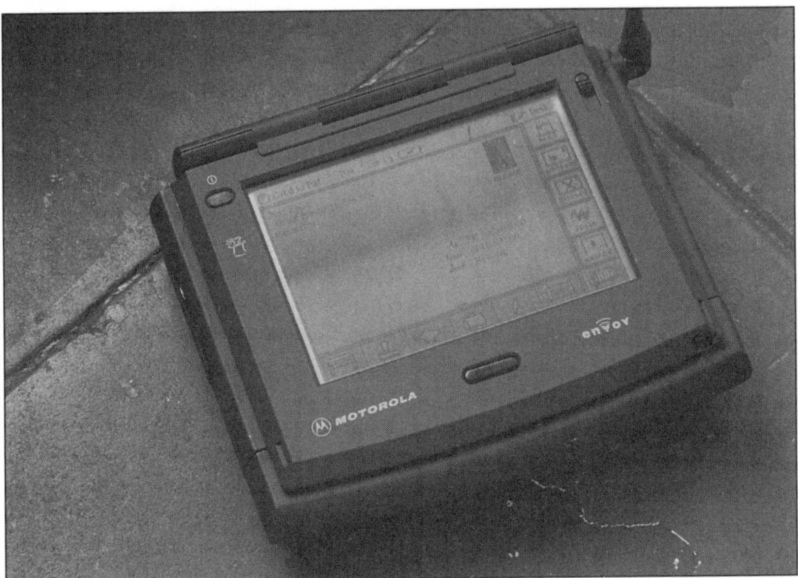

cards, also called PCMCIA cards, adhere to the Personal Computer Memory Card International Association standard, and offer storage capacities of 4 to 16 Mb. As with all storage devices, units with even larger capacity are under development and may be available by the time you read this. PCMCIA cards are not only for storing data but are also the vehicle for loading software applications into the Envoy. The PCMCIA standard is not limited to memory devices alone, and cards are being used as the basis for communications peripherals such as wireless modem and network cards.

The Envoy's battery life is claimed to be about eight hours of continuous use. A standard analog modem and a packet radio modem are available for the Envoy. With either of these modems, you can send and receive FAX, e-mail, and other data.

But more interesting than the hardware by itself is what you can do with the Envoy. It comes with a set of applications for managing personal information and a set of applications for communicating with the outside world. The personal information application suite includes the usual address book and appointment calendar, a notepad with built-in formats for sending form letters and memos, and a calculator. You can also record voice messages of up to 20 seconds in length, which can be included in data messages.

Telescript Is the Lingua Franca

The Envoy's communications capabilities are based on a communications software system called Telescript. Developed by General Magic, Inc., Telescript provides a communications language that can be built into applications so that they can communicate easily with other Telescript-based applications. A Telescript-based application can use "intelligent agents," which can actually perform tasks when they reach their destination. For example, you could send a message to a Telescript-based news service, which includes commands for retrieving a set of news messages that you have specified using a Telescript intelligent agent. These types of messages with embedded commands are called "smart messages" in Telescript jargon. There are also "smart envelopes," in which intelligent agents can handle customized message routing, and "smart stationery," which are messages with embedded commands that can be executed by the recipient of the message. For example, "smart stationery" might come with a video clip, which you open up by activating an agent that appears in the message. [13]

This capability probably sounds more complicated than it actually is. The user does not see all of the complexity that is handled by Telescript. In fact, Envoy users see a graphical interface, also developed by General Magic, called Magic Cap, which is very intuitive, as shown in Figure 9.2. America Online (AOL) is one of the built-in communications options on the Envoy. Simply tapping on the AOL icon with the stylus or with your finger initiates a communications session on America Online. AOL supports Telescript, so that you can customize an "intelligent agent" to automatically perform specific functions when you dial into AOL. CompuServe offers similar capabilities.

One of the major supporters of Telescript is AT&T, which has developed a Telescript-based network called AT&T PersonaLink

Figure 9.2 *The Magic Cap graphical interface.*

Services. Access to PersonaLink is built into the Envoy. Among other services, PersonaLink offers an "advanced messaging service," a news service from Mead Data Central, and an electronic shopping mall called PersonaLink Market Square. AT&T calls its messaging system "advanced" because it can contain special formatting, graphics, and sound, based on the Telescript communications language. For example, you can create a message on the Envoy, draw a sketch as part of the message, and then add a voice stamp. When you send this message on the PersonaLink network, it will appear to the recipient exactly as you sent it, graphics and sound included. This is in contrast to the straight text electronic mail that is generally available on online services and the Internet—which brings us to the Envoy's electronic mail features.

RadioMail

One of the more interesting services in the wireless world today is one called RadioMail. RadioMail connects your wireless communicator using packet radio to virtually all electronic mail services: the Internet, MCI Mail, CompuServe, America Online, and so forth. In the case of the Envoy, RadioMail uses the ARDIS network to transmit messages to and from the Envoy. You can have an Internet e-mail address on the Envoy through a gateway operated by RadioMail. When you turn on your Envoy, RadioMail automatically transmits unread electronic mail messages.

RadioMail also supports RAM Mobile Data and has development tools for supporting RadioMail on CDPD, Metricom, and other networks. Another feature of RadioMail is the NewsFactory, which is a wireless news service providing updated headline and financial news, as well as sports and weather.

Special Applications

Application developers are creating specialized applications for the Envoy. One of these is a wireless health care management system called Med-E-Mail, which includes facilities for issuing prescriptions directly from the Envoy, tracking patient histories, and exchanging mail with other physicians. Another is a navigational system from Navigational Technologies, which supplies "Navigable Map Databases and DriverGuide" technology. Using the system, you enter the addresses of the origin and destination, and the program supplies a map and text-based driving directions.

There's No Free Lunch

Naturally, all of the Envoy's impressive features come at a price. The Envoy itself is priced somewhere around $1,500. To take full advantage of the system, you would need a subscription to AT&T PersonaLink and possibly another to RadioMail so that you could have an Internet address. The costs of these services would vary according to usage, but could add up very quickly.

The Envoy exemplifies the possibilities of mobile computing and communications. Many of the PCSs will be geared towards systems like the Envoy. If Telescript becomes a standard for wireless communications, much of the compatibility headaches of desktop computer communications could be avoided. The Telescript standard would enable easy communication of documents including graphics and sound, which so far has been a messy and complicated procedure in the present online communications environment.

A Work in Progress

Much like other aspects of the information highway, wireless communication is still in an early stage of development, at least with respect to data communications. As we stated earlier, cellular voice telephony is a mature and widely used technology. Andrew Seybold writes, ". . . wireless WANs [wide area networks] are at about the same point as wired modem communications were five years ago." [2] And wired modem communications still need improvement.

The key to both wireless and wireline data communications is the conversion from analog to digital. This conversion is further along in the wired world than in the wireless. For at least the next several years, the maximum wireless data communications speed is likely to remain at 19.2 kbits per second, with most transmissions speeds well below that figure. As we stated earlier, these speeds are generally not adequate for more than plain text transmissions, particularly considering the relatively high per-minute access charges for wireless communications.

The high cost of wireless communications devices is an obstacle to the widespread use of the technology. When machines like the Envoy cost around $500 (which is not impossible but may not happen as soon as we'd like; recall the cost history of CD-ROM drives) we'll probably see a significant expansion of the wireless market.

Personal communications services may be the decisive element in determining whether wireless data communications becomes a mainstream activity or remains a specialized and expensive niche market. PCS provides an opportunity for some innovative new technology to be developed. By the end of the decade, we should see the results.

And What about Satellite?

We discussed satellite communications to some extent in chapter 4—in particular, Bill Gates' and Craig McCaw's plans for having 800-odd communications satellites orbiting the earth in low orbit by the turn of the century. The fact of the matter is that satellites are not well suited for interactive use. According to satellite consultant Richard Peterson of DBS Connection, satellite communications "are good for point to multipoint communications, and in many cases, the telephone line is an adequate return path. Satellite doesn't apply to point to point communications or applications requiring high speed in both directions."

The Rural Connection

On the other hand, satellites serve an important function in areas that don't have high-speed wireline communications facilities. The state of Maine is an example. According to Jack Kilday, who runs the Northern Lights BBS out of Portland, Maine, "it's pretty much an information cowpath up here." Jack was spending hundreds of dollars per month on long distance calls and a special connection to the Internet called UUCP, to provide information from the Internet on his BBS. Then he discovered a company called PageSat based in Palo Alto, California, that transmits Internet newsgroups via satellite. The satellite delivers a "continuous, uncompressed news feed" to Kilday's BBS at speeds ranging from 9600 to 19.2 kbps. Kilday says he strips out the information that he doesn't want, such as the "adult pictures" and other extraneous stuff, and posts the rest on his BBS. "The satellite connection paid for itself in less than a year," Kilday says.

As the information highway develops, satellite communications will play an important role in rural areas and in other parts of the world that don't have the existing communications infrastructure of the advanced industrialized countries. While Gates' and McCaw's vision of a global satellite network has drawn its share of skepticism and even derision, the fundamental idea makes some sense. It could easily be twenty or thirty years before fiber optic cable reaches many parts of the Third World. A global satellite information network could at least allow people all over the world to participate in the information highway. As always, the question is: Who will pay for it?

Multimedia and the Information Highway

The CD-ROM Meets Cyberspace

> *"There's a tremendous amount of baloney being dished up about the future. But I don't think there's any doubt that books will change enormously, or any reason to be nostalgic. The ability to add sound, graphics, animation, and layers of text will alter the experience of what a book is, and I can't wait."*
>
> —Michael Crichton, author of *Jurassic Park* and other best-sellers, *The Wall Street Journal*, March 21, 1994

Earlier in this book, we characterized the information highway as the convergence of telecommunications and computing. Part of that convergence has been made possible by a merging of technologies within computing itself—namely, the convergence of audio, video, graphics, and text processing. Applications that combine these forms of information are called *multimedia applications.*

Unlike traditional computer software consisting of text, graphics, and high-pitched beeps that provide the sole audio effects, multimedia applications come with full-motion video, good-quality voice and music, and high-resolution graphics and text. Multimedia is a mass commodity largely because of the development of the compact disk (CD) as a medium for storing data, which is called CD-ROM (Compact Disk Read Only Memory). The ROM portion of the acronym indicates that the information on these compact disks can only be read—it cannot be erased or added to or in any way modified, much as with compact disk audio recording.

What's unique about CD-ROM is that about 600 Mb of data can be stored on a single compact disk. Video and audio data require a lot of storage capacity, and compact disk offers a convenient and affordable means to distribute multimedia applications. CD-ROM applications range in price from $20 to several hundred dollars and are often heavily discounted when purchased together with the necessary hardware.

A Host of Applications

An impressive variety and rapidly growing number of applications are available on CD-ROM: encyclopaedias, atlases, and other reference books, complete with illustrations; educational applications with video and audio clips, as well as a host of electronic books, video games, electronic shopping catalogs, and much more. In fact, the number of applications on CD-ROM is growing so rapidly that stores don't have enough shelf space to accommodate them all. Estimates vary widely, but, according to *The Wall Street Journal*, at the end of 1993 there were some twelve hundred CD-ROM titles on the market, with close to two thousand expected by 1995. [1] *The San Francisco Examiner* says the number is "anywhere from 6,000 to 10,000 titles in print, depending on who's counting," [2] which confirms Mark Twain's observation that there are "lies, damn lies, and statistics." In any case, there are definitely hundreds and perhaps thousands of CD-ROM applications available.

Just Getting Off the Ground

The term *multimedia* has been bandied about for years, but it is only in the last few years that multimedia is starting to play a significant role in computing. Through much of the late 1980s, CD-ROM was a technology that could never quite get off the ground. Microsoft's Bill Gates was an early proponent of CD-ROM. In defending his optimistic outlook for the information highway, Gates cited his vision of CD-ROM in a speech to the Commonwealth Club:

> I am on the lunatic fringe of believing in this highway. I have had a good track record. Over a decade ago, Microsoft held its

> first conference on software distributed on CDs, that is, CD ROM-based multimedia software. At the time I said that information such as medical information, encyclopedias, catalogs, and phone books would very soon be put onto these very cheap disks, and that a high percentage of personal computers would actually contain drives that would use this kind of software. Although it's taken five years longer than I expected, I can say with confidence that in the next few years this will really catch on. [3]

And apparently, Bill Gates is right. CD-ROM is catching on. The number off "multimedia PCs" that are equipped with CD-ROM drives, audio and full-motion video capability, and high resolution graphics, has gone from about one-half million units in U.S. homes in 1992 to about five million anticipated by early 1995. [4] Sales of CD-ROM drives purchased separately during the same time period have increased from about 1 million to close to five million, which adds up to about ten million CD-ROM equipped systems in use by 1995. And some analysts consider these to be conservative estimates—one venture capital firm's estimate has about 28 million households having CD-ROM drives by 1998. [5] Another source says there are already 8 million CD-ROM drives in use as of mid-1994, "and 14 million are predicted by the year's end." [6]

Industry forecasts always have to be taken with a grain of salt, but there's no question that personal computers equipped with CD-ROM drives are becoming the systems of choice for home users. Somewhere between 30 and 50 percent of all PCs sold today are equipped with CD-ROM drives. Parents are easily sold on the technology because their children can benefit from the educational software available on CD-ROM. Schools and libraries are using CD-ROM-equipped computers to provide reference materials and in some cases, library card catalogs.

Multimedia is also gaining considerable interest in the workplace because of the increasing availability of high-speed communications. Video conferencing, multimedia training applications, and electronic document sharing are seen more and more as important productivity tools in the workplace.

The Multimedia PC

Personal computers fully equipped for multimedia applications are becoming more commonplace and far more competitively priced. There are two levels of multimedia PCs. A multimedia PC suitable for the home might just include a CD-ROM drive, a high-resolution color monitor, and stereo-sound capability (either 8-bit or 16-bit sound).

A more powerful multimedia PC would also include video input and output capabilities, allowing it to display and also generate full-motion video in the NTSC/PAL television video format, as well as in the computer's own display format (typically, SuperVGA on PCs and QuickDraw on the Macintosh). For example, Apple Computer's "AV" (Audio-Visual) series of computers has a a port (connection socket) for plugging in the coaxial cable from the local cable TV network, or from a VCR or a laser videodisc, allowing video from these sources to be displayed on the computer screen in a separate window. The Indy multimedia workstation from Silicon Graphics goes so far as to have a built-in video camera.

Such an advanced multimedia system would also include a digital signal processor (DSP), enabling it to record and play back CD-quality audio as well as process video data (that is, perform analog/digital conversion). Many such systems have data compression/decompression (codec) capabilities built into the hardware, allowing high-speed compression and decompression of video and audio data. Finally, such a system is "network-ready" with a built-in connection to high-speed networks such as Ethernet or ISDN. Most of the major PC and workstation vendors are delivering systems with these capabilities. [7]

We should point out, however, that a machine with the above configuration is still considerably more expensive than a standard desktop PC, costing several thousand dollars by the time you're through. The less-capable home version described above can cost as little as a two hundred dollars more than a basic desktop system.

The advanced multimedia PC has essentially the same capabilities as the set-top box of the future, except that the set-top box plugs into the TV and doesn't include the data storage capability, or at least not built-in storage capacity. It's intriguing to consider that a multimedia set-top box will cost under $500 by the end of the decade.

Multimedia in the Workplace

With multimedia becoming a basic component of desktop computers, the working world is starting to take advantage of digitized audio and video communication across networks or high-speed phone lines. Multimedia communication takes several basic forms in the workplace: video-conferencing, electronic document sharing, video- and voice-annotated electronic mail, and computer-based training.

Video Conferencing

The concept of video conferencing has come up repeatedly in this book, and that's because it's one of the few tangible, currently available technologies that could be considered part of the information highway. There have been video-conferencing products available for the PC for some time. [7] But these add-on systems are expensive, costing several thousand dollars per computer, and still have significant technical limitations. Most PC-based systems offer a video frame display rate of, at best, about 15 frames per second (and generally more like eight frames per second), while smooth full-motion video requires a display speed of about 30 frames per second. Because of the large bandwidth requirements, most PC-based video-conferencing systems display images in a small window on the screen. In addition, these systems generally provide the audio signal separately using the telephone.

These limitations are not entirely the fault of the video-conferencing vendors. The biggest limitation is the bandwidth of the current telephone system. Moderate bandwidth telephone technologies such as ISDN and Switched 56 are inadequate for full-motion video conferencing. Fiber optic cable and cable modems will change that, of course, but as we've seen, universal availability of these technologies is still years away.

But what's interesting about the advanced multimedia PC is that it has the hardware capabilities for video conferencing built in. And before long, personal computer operating systems will have built-in support for multimedia data and high-speed networking as well. Rather than a specialized and expensive add-on, video conferencing will become a basic feature of personal computers. According to the article on video computing in *BYTE*, "PC vendors may migrate up into the conferencing business by building in support for video compression and high-speed communications." [7]

Like almost everything else we've discussed in this book, video conferencing is in an early stage of development. It shows tremendous promise, however, as a tool for distance education and for holding meetings with participants all over the country or the world. The advanced multimedia PC is the beginning of a dramatic improvement in the capabilities of video conferencing. By the end of the decade, it should be a well-established and widely used technology.

Document Sharing

Parallel to the development of video conferencing is the growing interest in electronic document sharing. Electronic documents have become considerably more sophisticated than they were ten years ago. Documents today can include not only graphics, but links to other documents, voice annotations, embedded graphs or notations, and even video clips. "Documents are no longer merely an electronic analog to paper, but rather dynamic, modular, multimedia entities." writes Andy Reinhardt in *BYTE*. [8]

One of the most common activities in today's office is the preparation of documents by a group of people. Traditionally, the process goes something like this: First, someone creates the original document. It is passed to the next person for editing and revision, and then to the next, on up the hierarchy, and then back down, until finally the marked-up document comes back to the originator, who is responsible for preparing the next draft, and then the whole process starts over again until the final version is approved. This process can take days, weeks, or months, depending on the schedules and enthusiasm of those involved.

Electronic document conferencing is a way to speed up this process and make it more productive by involving all (or at least many) participants in the process simultaneously. The originator displays the master document on the screen, which is also displayed on the screens of the other conference participants. The participants can mark up and annotate the document while discussing it on a speaker phone. Electronic "whiteboards" allow multiple users to work on the same document. Many of the PC-based video-conferencing packages include this capability to simultaneously work on a document. IBM and AT&T's NCR division offer document-conferencing packages that run on local area networks and over ISDN phone lines. For more on document-conferencing products, see Andy Reinhardt's article, "Managing the New Document." [8]

Again, the advent of multimedia PCs and higher bandwidth is going to make document conferencing much easier than it is today. Unfortunately, document sharing is more complicated than video conferencing because of the incompatibility of various document formats. For example, different word processing and database programs store their documents in different formats. There are efforts underway to create standard document formats, such as the OpenDoc format promoted by Apple, WordPerfect, Novell, and others. But because there are multiple efforts by different companies, multiple standards for document sharing will probably continue to exist, just as there will be multiple standards for set-top boxes and data compression.

In spite of the complications, document sharing is likely to become an integral application of personal computers and eventually the information highway.

Electronic Mail and Multimedia

Closely related to the general multimedia document is the multimedia electronic mail message. Today's messaging is primarily text-based, because there are no basic standards for transmitting sound, video, and graphics, from one mail system to another. The additional limitation is that typical modem speeds of 14.4 kilobits per second or less simply are not adequate for sending elaborate e-mail messages with multimedia content. We discussed this limitation at length in Chapter 4, but just to add one more example, CompuServe recently announced a new single by the rock group Aerosmith, exclusively available on CompuServe. The approximately three-minute recording takes from 60 to 90 minutes to download! [9]

These limitations will gradually disappear. Multimedia PCs will make it convenient to attach an audio or video clip to an e-mail message, and broadband networks will make it affordable and practical to send the message.

Computer-Based Training

One of the most practical uses of multimedia is in computer-based training. For example, you can learn a new software application with the training video appearing simultaneously with the application being taught in a window on the computer screen. The difference between a digital training video and a training video on a VCR is that the digital training video is a computer program that can interactively respond to the input of the user and keep “in synch” with the application itself, running simultaneously on the same machine. Users can therefore learn at their own pace, with far more control over the learning process.

Training applications for mass distributed software such as a word processing program like Microsoft Word or WordPerfect can easily be distributed on CD-ROM. But CD-ROM isn’t a practical vehicle for distributing an in-house training application within a small or medium sized company. It’s a substantial investment to have applications pressed on CD-ROM, especially in small quantities, and it only makes sense for mass production and distribution to the general market.

Advanced multimedia PCs are the answer when CD-ROM isn’t practical. The training application can be broadcast over the broadband network and received by users working on multimedia PCs. Again, this technology is very much in its early stages.

Virtual Reality

Our discussion of multimedia wouldn't be complete without a brief digression into the subject of *virtual reality* (VR). While virtual reality has been oversold and overhyped in the press, it is a technology that will eventually have a significant impact on the information highway. Virtual reality is the electronic simulation of a complete audiovisual environment, which takes over the user's senses in such a way that the user perceives this simulated or virtual environment to be real. By either using goggles strapped to the head or standing or sitting within a specially designed VR chamber, the VR user is transported into the simulated environment.

Virtual reality has been oversold because much of what is billed as virtual reality in video arcades is nothing more than a spruced-up video game in a darkened room with blasting stereo sound effects. "At a storefront arcade called Virtual World in Walnut Creek, Calif.," reports *The Wall Street Journal*, "customers shell out $7 to $9 apiece for what amounts to a 10-minute video game with B-grade graphics, played in single-seat capsules decked out with stereo speakers and a dazzling array of useless buttons." [10] In spite of these criticisms, these virtual reality game arcades are very popular. Virtual World Entertainment is opening game centers around the country and in ten locations overseas. [11]

These primitive VR video games are only the beginning. The fact that they are so popular indicates that there will be demand for increasingly sophisticated video games that actually do employ virtual reality techniques. We can also expect far more elaborate uses of VR in other forms of entertainment such as theme parks from companies like Walt Disney. It is no coincidence that Disney "acquired a Long Island consulting firm owned by VR guru, Brad Ferren, who is now an executive at Disney's Imagineering unit, which dreams up new theme-park attractions." [12]

VR technology represents some of the most advanced developments in computing. In the area of display techology, VR uses miniature displays as well as sophisticated display projection techniques. High-speed digital signal processors are used in the video and audio simulations. Sophisticated three-dimensional graphic renderings make the simulations realistic.

VR is fertile ground for applications in scientific research, medicine, aviation, naval engineering, architecture, psychology, and many other fields. For example, companies that produce computer-aided-design (CAD) applications for architecture are also working on virtual-reality applications that make a building design actually come to life, complete with lighting effects for different times of day and weather conditions. Prospective home builders can take a "tour" of their future house and make desired changes before it is built. Companies can try out different office building layouts before specifying the final design.

In a special report on the "Future World," *The San Francisco Examiner* looks at the use of VR in the art world: "Beyond games and professional uses, VR is also evolving into a new expressive medium for artists. Last October, 1993, the Guggenheim Museum in New York held a groundbreaking exhibition titled 'VR: An Emerging Medium.' Multimedia artist Jenny Holzer contributed a piece inspired by a trip to Bosnia, featuring a desolate landscape full of abandoned houses; as visitors to the virtual space explored, they'd become witnesses to atrocities." [11]

There are of course dozens of other examples, and I encourage you to refer to Rheingold's *Virtual Reality* [12] for an in-depth look at virtual reality applications. But of primary interest here is how VR relates to the information highway. When you add ubiquitous broadband networks, there are some intriguing possibilities far beyond gory video games.

Indeed, the combination of broadband communications and virtual reality takes us into the realm of science fiction. Video conferencing would literally take on quite a different dimension if you had on a pair of 3-D goggles that actually put you in the room with the other conference participants. Scientists could participate in laboratory experiments taking place many miles away. Surgeons could participate in operations taking place in rural hospitals miles from their location. Students could walk in jungles full of exotic species or "virtual scuba dive" into the depths of the ocean. It's something to think about. These kinds of scenarios are not that far away.

CD-ROM: The Multimedia of Today

We've taken a peek into the future with multimedia being transmitted on broadband networks and virtual reality video conferences. But in the meantime, CD-ROM is the primary vehicle for distributing multimedia applications. As we mentioned earlier, there are a myriad of applications available on CD-ROM, ranging from elaborate video games to interactive movies to extensive reference works.

The quality of CD-ROM applications is as diverse as the applications themselves. The headline of a *Wall Street Journal* article blares: "CD-ROMs: Buggy, Boring, Slow, Frustrating." [13] The article goes on to cite a litany of complaints from CD-ROM users: Some of the applications don't work; many are infuriatingly slow. One physician reported purchasing a CD-ROM pharmaceutical drug reference program, which was so slow that it was faster to use a book.

But there have also been some big successes. Microsoft's *Encarta Multimedia Encyclopedia* has been a big hit in libraries and schools, as well as in the home. Shown in Figure 10.1, Microsoft's *Encarta* is a 29-volume encyclopedia on a single CD-ROM disk, with some 26,000 articles, 7000 photos and illustrations, and hundreds of maps, animations, video clips, and interactive charts. There are about 300,000 links between related articles. By clicking the mouse on highlighted topics, you can move from one article to the next, or open a video clip or an interactive chart. These interactive charts allow you to create customized charts and graphs by combining information from the interactive charts—a term paper writer's dream come true.

Figure 10.1 *Microsoft's Encarta Multimedia Encyclopedia.*

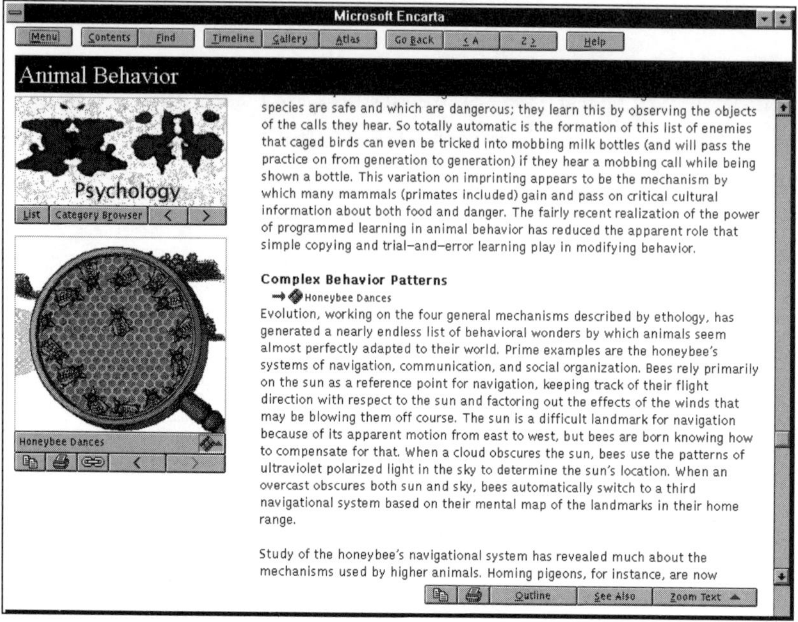

Another popular CD application is *Macbeth* from the Voyager Company, which is an interactive version of Shakespeare's play. Quoting from a description in *The Wall Street Journal*, "you can read Macbeth or Banquo the ghost, or any part you want, opposite the computer's prerecorded readings by professional actors of all the other parts. You can also click on certain words in the text to find out what they mean, or get background information." [14] There are CD-ROMs featuring classical composers, the history of rock 'n roll, museum tours, science exploration, history, literature, cookbook recipes, and of course, loads of video arcade and adventure games. One game that has received widespread praise is called *MYST*, from Broderbund Software. This an adventure game with "richly detailed 3-D landscapes," which you search for "clues to find out what has run amok on a chain of surreal islands." [14]

One of the great advantages of CDs is that they can be updated on a periodic basis. For example, reference works such as *Encarta* or *Compton's Interactive Encyclopedia* are updated periodically to include the most recent information. Registered owners can purchase an upgrade disk for a nominal fee.

A growing trend in the book publishing business is to publish a CD-ROM version along with the hardcopy version of the book. The CD-ROM expands on information provided in the book. For example, this approach was taken with *The Haldeman Diaries*, the late H.R. Haldeman's diaries during the Nixon years and particularly during the Watergate scandal. While the book is an edited version of the diaries consisting of about 1,000 pages, the CD-ROM contains all 2,200 pages of the unedited, unexpurgated diaries, as well as video clips from home movies that Haldeman made during those years, and audio commentary from Dwight Chapin, Nixon's appointment secretary. As *The Wall Street Journal* put it, the CD-ROM is a "kind of high-tech, multimedia circus for Nixon junkies." [15]

Where Is CD-ROM Heading?

CD-ROM may have finally hit its stride in the marketplace, but there are still a lot of unanswered questions and room for improvement. Of course, there will always be excellent, fair, and very bad CD-ROM applications, just like there are good and bad books. But some purely technical problems still need to be resolved. CD-ROMs are generally very slow, as pointed out earlier. Some of the performance problems will be solved by the faster microprocessors that come out every year or two. However, millions of users are stuck with their current systems and painfully slow CDs. CD-ROM drives are actually far faster than they were even a few years ago, but the computers they operate in (and certainly the hard disks that they are often compared to) have grown so fast that the CD-ROM drives will always look a little lame by comparison.

Help may be on the way. Companies are working behind closed doors to develop new ways of programming CDs to make them faster. In particular, a company based in Berkeley, California, called Rocket Science Games, Inc., claims to have developed a technology that will make CD-ROMs perform about ten times faster than they do now, and may license the technology to other CD-ROM application developers. [16] The company's main focus is on video games, but apparently the technology will be applicable to other types of CD-ROM applications as well.

CD-ROM is the predecessor to the multimedia technology that will appear on applications designed specifically for the information highway—in other words, applications designed for set-top boxes and interactive TV. Many of the programming issues are the same whether the application is to run on your PC's CD drive or to be transmitted over fiber optic cable to a set-top box connected to a television. Nevertheless, a conversion has to take place to enable CD-ROM applications to run on interactive TV.

Companies are working on developing tools for making this conversion. For example, Macromedia, a San Francisco-based multimedia application developer, and Microware Systems of Des Moines, Iowa, which develops basic operating system software for interactive TV, have teamed up to develop tools for converting CD-ROM-based applications to interactive TV. The companies claim that their conversion tools will cut the time for converting a CD-ROM application to about a month, which should help get some applications other than video on demand running on the various pilot projects that are underway. [17]Other players such as Microsoft and Oracle are likely to introduce similar tools.

On the other hand, conversion of current CD-ROM applications may not be what's needed. It's still unclear whether consumers will embrace CD-ROM over the long term. In spite of CD-ROM's growing popularity, the quality of the applications needs to improve significantly. Proponents of the "electronic book" like Michael Crichton, who I quoted at the top of the chapter, may be in for a disappointment. So far, readers seem to prefer books on paper rather than on their video screens. As the founder of Adobe Systems and one of the inventors of PostScript, John Warnock, put it, "I'm never going to read *Gone With the Wind* on a computer. To me, the power of this revolution comes not from reading a single book electronically, but having the power to access one million books." [18]

Quality and Performance Are the Keys

The information highway is the ultimate platform for multimedia. No longer will multimedia be a special feature of computing—it will be the *basis* of computing. As I mentioned above, multimedia applications on CD-ROM are only precursors of what will come. But the developers of the information highway need to learn some important lessons from the current multimedia technology. Consumers won't accept slow and amateurish applications. As broadband networks become the main transmission medium, consumers will expect fast responsiveness, crisp and colorful graphics, and bug-free operation.

The computer industry seems to have lulled itself into the illusion that it can try out inferior products on patient "early adopters," the zealous enthusiasts who will buy almost anything for the hip novelty of simply having the latest techie toy. It is remarkable how many companies, desperate to bring in some revenue, put inferior products on the market, somehow hoping that consumers and product reviewers won't notice how bad they are. This approach is not going to work on the information highway.

It was this type of strategy that essentially killed the nascent pen-based computing market. Machines like the Momenta and even the first Newton simply weren't ready to be introduced. They were ponderously slow and had other serious deficiencies, and yet, due to market pressures or other perceived urgencies, were brought to market anyway. Naturally, they were failures because they were inferior products. Momenta paid for its strategy by going bankrupt. Apple put the blame for Newton's inadequacy on John Sculley, and that's probably why he is no longer with the company. But one thing is clear: you can't fool consumers of high-technology products with inferior quality. Multimedia guru Brad Ferren's fears about virtual reality should be a warning to the entire multimedia industry: "My only hope is that we survive the embarrassing display of really awful products people are calling virtual reality, so that it doesn't set the industry back 10 or 15 years." [18] It is a warning that developers of the information highway should also take to heart.

Doing Business on the Highway

The Electronic Marketplace

> *Sure, we all knew the Net was going to become more commercial, but it still is somehow unsettling to see your formerly pastoral town filled with new high-rises, billboards, and gawking tourists.*
>
> Steve G. Steinburg, *Wired*, August, 1994

Most aspects of the information highway that we discussed in this book affect the topic of this final chapter: doing business on the information highway. The degree of control exercised by the telephone and cable companies affects the ability of small companies to gain access to the information highway. The question of universal access and other government policies will likely determine if the information highway becomes a marketplace for the privileged few or for the great majority of citizens. Obviously, the information highway will be a much more attractive and profitable vehicle for doing business if it's accessible to everyone and not only to the privileged elite. Security will probably be the decisive factor in determining the success or failure of doing business on the information highway. If there's rampant electronic fraud, businesses will drop online services like a hot rock. Multimedia will have a major impact on the way business is conducted. And eventually, people will do all kinds of business from their wireless personal communicators.

Once broadband networks proliferate, business will never be the same. The way people sell and buy products and services, and the way they are advertised, will change dramatically. As we discussed earlier, advertisers will no longer have a captive audience on a handful of TV networks. They will have to attract viewers by offering more than slick sound bites with exaggerated claims. The era of "infomercials" will emerge, in which companies attract customers by providing more detailed (and hopefully more solid) information about their products. These infomercials will have to be entertaining and interesting and will therefore open new avenues for the whole advertising industry, including the TV production studios.

From Paper to Online Catalogs

The information highway is engender ing a transition from mail-order catalogs to online shopping catalogs. The transition is already underway. There are some compelling advantages to the electronic medium as opposed to the paper mail-order catalog. The environmental benefits are reason enough to switch from paper to online catalog shopping. Think of the vast quantities of paper that will be saved when mail order catalogs are replaced with online catalogs. Substantial energy savings will also result from eliminating the printing and transportation of those catalogs. And if done correctly, online catalogs could mean the end of junk mail. That's a big "if," since one very likely scenario is that instead of your "snail mailbox" being deluged with mail-order catalogs, your electronic mail box will be flooded with junk mail. On the other hand, it is possible to create "intelligent agents" that are sharp enough to sniff out and identify electronic junk mail for deletion in a way that will never be possible with paper mail.

Electronic catalogs can offer a much greater breadth of products. There is virtually no limit to the number of "pages" in an electronic catalog. The catalog can provide far more information on a particular item than is possible in the limited space of a paper catalog. For example, let's say you're browsing through an electronic catalog and find an item that interests you. By clicking on the name of that item, a product description and list of specifications appears on the screen. Most likely, there will also be an option for viewing articles describing or reviewing the product. Catalogs like this are already being created on the Internet, through the graphics hypertext browser called Mosaic. As with much that is currently available on the Internet, such catalogs can be seen as interesting functional prototypes of what we will have in the near future on the information highway.

Shopping with Interactive Video

It seems likely that electronic marketing will take two primary paths: electronic catalogs and interactive video, and to some extent, a combination of the two. An electronic catalog with high-quality graphics and text would essentially replace the printed mail order catalog of today with the same basic characteristics, and with the additional features just described. The interactive video markets would be something more akin to the home shopping networks of today, except that they would be interactive and would give the viewer far greater control over the "home shopping process." Early demonstrations of interactive video shopping confirm this.

US West's US Avenue

For example, U.S. West's Interactive Video Enterprises (IVE) introduced its US Avenue interactive shopping service in the summer of 1994. It's essentially a menu-driven version of home shopping. The TV viewer uses the TV remote controller to select from a product directory that appears on the screen. Video clips of products start appearing on the screen and the viewer can pause and select an option to take a "closer look" at a particular product. If the "closer look" option is selected, a more detailed video of the product begins.

The viewer has the option at all times to go back to the main directory menu to select another merchandiser or product category.

The viewer also has the option to stop the video and make a purchase. U.S. West has signed up some major companies such as J.C. Penney, FTD Florists, and Nordstrom's, among others, to offer their products on US Avenue. US Avenue will appear on several cable networks around the country, Time Warner's Full Service Network, and on U.S. West's own pilot project in Omaha, Nebraska. U.S. West will obviously solicit other companies to offer their goods and services on US Avenue.

It's the Customer's Choice

It will be interesting to see what kind of response US Avenue gets in the marketplace. If the current crop of TV home shopping networks is any indication, US Avenue should be a great success. There is definitely a market for glitzy merchandising on television. On the other hand, many people would much rather browse through a catalog than watch some slick actress surrounded by ferns modeling a product to the beat of Kenny G. or sit through a dramatization attempting to convince them to buy a certain brand of instant coffee.

Online catalogs have the advantage of being more like electronic books than interactive videos. And they may turn out to be more popular. Of course, there's no reason that both forms of merchandising can't be available on the information highway.

Doing Business on the Internet

While interactive video shopping is getting its feet wet in pilot projects run by the telephone and cable companies, electronic catalog shopping and other retail services are starting to appear on the Internet. But it's a tricky business because of the strong aversion to commercialization and advertising that exists on the Internet. Nevertheless, it is possible to be successful if one adheres to some basic rules of behavior.

For example, Computer Literacy Bookshops offers its services over the Internet. Computer Literacy's network service coordinator, Robert Mudry, says that most of the store's business on the Internet is a result of word-of-mouth. "We *never ever* send unsolicited e-mail or broadcast our services on Usenet newsgroups," says Mudry. The bookstore publishes its e-mail address (info@clbooks.com) in its paper-based catalogs and the e-mail address is also published in a list of Internet booksellers that exists on a list server.

Publishing your business's e-mail address on various list servers is a good way to get publicity on Internet, since these lists are subscribed to on a voluntary basis. There are also lists that can help businesses gain publicity in other channels. For example, there is a media list that includes media companies that accept press releases by electronic mail. (To subscribe to this list, send e-mail to majordomo@world.spd.com.) Several books on the market provide directories of available list server lists (see the *Resource Guide*). Once an e-mail address is established, businesses can use a so-called "mail reflector," which automatically responds to e-mail queries.

For example, the media list mentioned above is accessible through a clever program called "majordomo" that can receive e-mail messages and respond automatically to them. Majordomo is a software program for managing lists and supplying them to subscribers based on Internet electronic mail requests. For example, to obtain the above-mentioned media publicity list, you send an e-mail message to majordomo@world.spd.com with the words "subscribe media list" as your message. The list server then automatically sends you the list, without human intervention—it could be quite a nightmare for human list managers if they had to respond to hundreds or even thousands of e-mail queries daily.

Another way to get publicity in an acceptable way is to participate in Usenet newsgroups. For example, Computer Literacy Bookshops participates in a newsgroup called misc.books.technical. According to Mudry, "we just hang out there and answer questions about books." Providing useful information without blowing your horn can be an effective way to quietly build a good reputation. Of course, this must be done carefully. There are numerous horror stories of people getting "flamed" for engaging in too blatant self-promotion. Mudry's theory boils down to this: "if you provide a valuable service, you'll get noted."

Computer Literacy Bookshops went into business on the Internet by establishing an Internet account through a service provider (Netcom, in this case). The account gives Computer Literacy Bookshops a "registered domain name" (clbooks.com), which enables it to provide full services on the Internet. It must be emphasized that most new business entrants on the Internet will require substantial technical support from their service providers or other consultants. The Internet is *not* an easy thing to figure out for people whose main line of business does not involve computing! (Even computer people find it challenging, especially if they have no prior exposure to networking.)

Computer Literacy also operates walk-in retail stores (which accept orders by telephone). Their system allows them to track the actual volume of sales resulting from the Internet. According to Mudry, many people get information on the Internet, but actually make the purchase "off-line," by telephone or mail order or at the retail store locations. For a variety of reasons, such as security concerns and basic distrust of electronic networks, people are still reluctant to make "online purchases." However, publicity gained from being on the "Net" may be just as important as actual sales, if not more so. In any case, Computer Literacy has expanded its Internet services with a World Wide Web server (http\\www.clbooks.com), and a complete online database of all the books available from the store.

Securing Internet for Business

As we've seen, the Internet in general suffers from a lack of security, but some efforts are underway to develop higher security levels within specific networks on the Internet: security that would be adequate for doing business.

One of the most notable of these efforts is an offshoot of the Smart Valley "electronic community," described in Chapter 6. This offshoot, called CommerceNet, has received funding from the federal government's Technology Reinvestment Program, as well as matching funds from the state of California and participating companies. Essentially, the goal of CommerceNet "is to make public computer networks, such as the Internet, 'industrial strength' for business use." [1] CommerceNet has attracted about 45 companies who have invested in the network and plan to use it to offer services as well as to collaborate with other companies.

The security on CommerceNet is being handled by two companies, RSA Data Security Inc. and Enterprise Integration Technologies, which are developing a "secure" version of Mosaic, the graphical browser for Internet's World Wide Web (WWW). This new version of Mosaic should make it possible to conduct Electronic Data Interchange (EDI) transactions on CommerceNet. EDI is the standard for electronic business transactions such as credit card payments and other money transfers. In fact, as this book goes to press, a new company called CyberCash, Inc. has been formed to provide a secure transaction environment on the Internet. *The Wall Street Journal* reports that CommerceNet plans to use the new company's technology, enabling users to make payments and bank transfers directly online. [2]

At this writing, CommerceNet requires the use of the World Wide Web. Each participating company has a "Web server," meaning a computer (or part of a computer) on the network that provides the company's services and also serves as the company's e-mail address. WWW is accessible through Mosaic and other special user interface programs with names like WinWeb and Cello. Mosaic is particularly popular because it is not merely a graphical user interface (GUI) but also multimedia-capable, and therefore allows communication with all features that Web servers support. (Mosaic is so far the clearly preferred interface on CommerceNet).

Using a graphics language called Hypertext Markup Language (HTML), Web servers provide full-graphic images that can be viewed by users having the appropriate WWW connection and an interface like Mosaic. Internet service providers such as those listed in the *Resource Guide* at the end of this book can provide WWW capability. Figure 11.1 shows a typical screen that might appear on a Web server.

Figure 11.1 *Catalogs on the World Wide Web.*

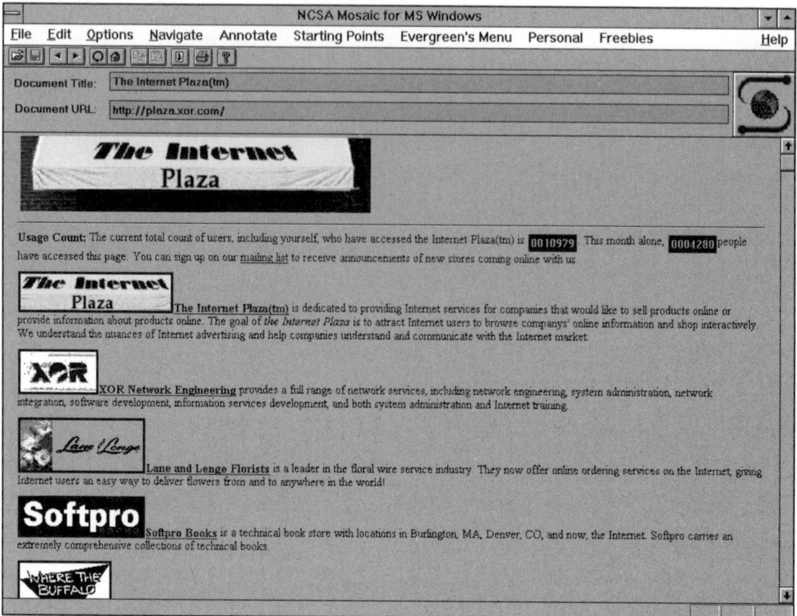

The Internet Shopping Network

Internet Shopping Network (ISN) is an example of a company doing business on CommerceNet. ISN is essentially an electronic mail-order catalog specializing in computer hardware and software, offering about 15,000 products, including complete computer systems. ISN offers some of the features that give electronic catalogs an advantage over paper mail order catalogs. For example, ISN carries the complete issues of the trade journal *Infoworld* online, with links to product reviews that appear in the journal. Customers can read *Infoworld* product reviews as part of their evaluation of available products in the ISN catalog.

ISN does not accept credit cards online. Instead, you can FAX or phone in your credit card number via a toll-free line, and then establish an account for future purchases. Computer Literacy Bookshops handles credit card payments in a similar way. Because of the Internet's inherent security problems, this approach is likely to prevail until 1995, when secure Internet credit card software becomes widespread. Once you have an account number on file with the online vendor, it is a safeway to handle credit card transactions. (ISN's e-mail address is info@internet.net or via Mosaic at URL http://shop.internet.net.)

Joining CommerceNet

ISN's vice president of marketing, Bill Rollinson, says the company got involved in CommerceNet, because it "didn't want to be the sole pioneer. We wanted to have something like CommerceNet in front of us." ISN joined CommerceNet as an "associate member" for a fee of $5000 per year. The cost of company membership on CommerceNet varies from $1250 for a basic subscription up to $50,000 per year for a full-fledged sponsorship. Basic subscribers are listed in the CommerceNet directory with links to their Web servers (the basic subscription also includes some free training in setting up a Web server).

Full sponsors are active in the direction and administration of CommerceNet. Various other financial arrangements can be made in exchange for technical expertise and other volunteer activities. Some big name companies such as Apple Computer, Hewlett-Packard, Pacific Bell, and Bank of America are among the members of CommerceNet. Enterprise Integration Technologies of Menlo Park, California, is the main technical contractor.

Business on WWW Is Just Starting toTake Off

At this writing, the flurry of business activity on the Internet revolves around World Wide Web (WWW). But according to Jayne Levin, editor of *The Internet Letter*, based in Washington D.C. [3], only about 2 million Internet users have access to WWW, while it is estimated that the total Internet user population is closer to 20 million. "Any service that requires World Wide Web is only reaching a small fraction of the Internet," says Levin, and that group mainly consists of college students and faculty, government employees, and employees at large corporations. ISN's Bill Rollinson agreed, noting that WWW usage through commercial service providers such as Netcom or PSI (see Resource Guide) "is still in its infancy."

But WWW use will undoubtedly grow at a rapid rate. Rollinson points out that ISN is not participating in WWW strictly to sell products, but also to gain experience in electronic selling and marketing in general, so that the company can easily move into the broadband networks that will begin to proliferate in the next few years.

The *Internet Letter's* Jayne Levin sees security as the main obstacle to widespread business use of Internet. "It can really be global if it's more reliable and secure."

In any event, World Wide Web is "hot." There are numerous consultants offering design services for WWW applications. For example, one business called the Internet Storefront offers a "fixed price for a combined World Wide Web and Gopher setup, including 25 documents of information and up to 10 images." This is for a price of $3500 and a monthly maintenance fee of $275. [3] In other words, as a company starting out on the Internet, you can hire a consultant like Internet Storefront to design your online catalog. (See the *Resource Guide* for more information on WWW services.)

It is also possible to advertise on World-Wide Web through online magazines such as *Global Network Navigator* (GNN), published by O'Reilly Associates (Sebastopol, California), which offers a host of books and other Internet-related services. Other commercial networks like CommerceNet are either in development or already appearing on the Internet. One such network called MecklerWeb has attracted considerable publicity.

But aside from the currently limited accessibility of World Wide Web, there are other limitations. WWW is not really designed for electronic shopping. It's a navigation, search, and retrieval tool. And Mosaic, which is is WWW's primary interface, is infuriatingly slow over the ordinary dial-up lines that dominate today's Internet markeplace. The faster dedicated lines like T1 and T3 serve installations like government labs, universities, and very large companies. Software specifically designed for merchandising over broadband networks will eventually offer stiff competition to the current tools for doing business on the Internet.

Commercial Online Services and BBSs

I won't dwell too much on commercial online services and bulletin-board systems, since we covered them extensively in Chapter 2. Both are viable options for doing business electronically. Particularly with the advent of Internet gateways available on most online services, these services may be competitive alternatives to doing business on Internet directly. Commercial online services offer better security and a more controlled environment than the Internet, but the potential audience may be considerably smaller.

Bulletin-board systems are also attractive because the business operator has complete control over the BBS. Using BBS software, businesses can set up a BBS on a desktop computer and start doing business online immediately. Businesses often use BBSs to offer customer support and other customer services. A BBS can also be used as a central repository for a group of satellite offices. For example, Citibank uses a BBS to receive audit reports from satellite offices around the world. [4]

Another advantage is that BBSs are generally cheaper to operate than an Internet or commercial service account. The disadvantage is that the maintenance and reliability of the BBS is entirely in the hands of the operator, rather than the responsibility of the service provider. Also, providing multiple phone lines into a BBS can prove very expensive. However, BBSs are generally easy to operate and maintain, compared to a wholly-owned and operated node on the Internet.

It is possible to connect a BBS to the Internet through an Internet gateway, allowing Internet users to Telnet to the BBS (connect through the Internet to the BBS using the Telnet function). For example, Computer Literacy Bookshops is developing a BBS that will be "telnetable" from the Internet. This allows an Internet user to run software under the control of the BBS, such as online catalogs designed specifically to *be* catalogs and not simply hypertext browsers (like Mosaic).

While a BBS won't give you full access to Internet services such as World Wide Web and Gopher, a BBS system is worth considering if your main purpose is to set up an e-mail address and provide direct communications with customers. There is something very attractive about the independence of a BBS.

Intelligent Electronic Shopping Software

The information highway will spawn a new type of software, specifically designed for online activities. It will be intelligent software that can learn about your habits based on how you have used the software in the past. This type of software is particularly relevant to business applications. Indeed, software developers are working on software specifically designed for electronic merchandising. The big players like Microsoft and Silicon Graphics are probably among those developers, but an interesting example is a start-up firm in San Mateo, California, called eShop.

eShop has designed a software environment for vendors and consumers to engage in electronic shopping. Electronic merchandisers use the software to design their "electronic stores." A variety of popular graphics design tools such as Adobe Illustrator or PhotoShop can be used to design the "storefronts" that appear in the eShop application. For example, a sporting goods retailer might design a storefront showing a baseball diamond, while a music retailer might design one showing a rock concert. Customers see a version of the eShop software that appears on their computer screens (and in the future, on their TV screens). eShop also includes software for operating a server, which stores the merchandiser's data.

The eShop software is designed to allow merchandisers to restock the store with different merchandise on a regular basis. The software also keeps statistics on the purchasing and shopping habits of the store's customers. If a customer regularly orders jazz CDs, for example, the software can alert the customer about new jazz releases the next time he or she "enters the store." Based on statistics kept by the software, merchandisers can see what merchandise sells well, what merchandise attracts a lot of interest, and what merchandise should be removed from the "shelves."

According to eShop's C.E.O., Matt Kursh, AT&T has licensed eShop for its PersonaLink services, which will appear on handheld communicators running Magic Cap. The eShop software is designed to be "cross-platform," so that it can run on Windows or Macintosh as well as on Magic Cap. Matt Kursh says that eShop will also be designed to run on interactive TV set-top boxes.

The eShop business strategy is to earn its revenues from service providers who use the eShop software. The merchandisers and customers pay nothing for the software. The service provider, which might be AT&T or any other telecommunications company, makes a contractual arrangement with eShop and makes the software available to its merchants and their customers. Merchants have the option to either design their "storefronts" themselves or to hire a creative design firm to do the job. Kursh says that eShop has launched a program to develop "authorized developers" of eShop applications.

eShop represents the new category of electronic merchandising software. As Kursh says, "merchandising is the art of presenting products at the right place and at the right time, and in the right way to make the customer want them." That is the goal of the eShop software. Kursh doesn't think that Mosaic and WWW are the answer for electronic shopping: "making purchases isn't done by looking at product lists. HTML (the graphics language used to design WWW applications) is designed to present hyperlinked documents. You can emulate a catalog, but it's slow. And it's not a real interactive environment, which is what we're doing with eShop." Kursh also points out that there's no reason why eShop couldn't run on the Internet on commercial servers.

The New Business Frontier

Doing business online is the new frontier. It is fraught with risks because it is so new and unproven. As I mentioned earlier, all sorts of companies are offering consulting services to help businesses get online. It's difficult to determine whether these companies know what they're doing, since there is little history to go on. With respect to the Internet, Jayne Levin's *The Internet Letter* sums up the situation as follows:

> As corporations scramble to stake a claim on the Internet, companies that offer World Wide Web services are booming. Prices and the quality of service vary widely, from several hundred dollars to several thousand dollars. Some analysts following the trend caution companies that the technology is untested for selling goods and the risks in building a Web presence could be high. [5]

Businesses need to go slow: learn from word of mouth, try to get references, talk to service providers and businesses already online.

The other aspect that is unknown is how customers will take to doing business online. An article in *The Wall Street Journal* reports that "many computer users still aren't comfortable using online services. Analysts say it will be five to ten years before online retailing dominates the software market." [6] If the analysts are right, that's a long time to wait. On the other hand, those who get involved early, establish themselves, and gain some experience, will be the ones most likely to succeed when the online marketplace takes off.

Like any other new technology, the information highway is a gamble. The PC was a gamble in the early 1980s and look what happened. It gave birth to a new generation of enormously successful companies. Bill Gates made an interesting observation about that phenomenon and how it might apply to the information highway:

> One thing that is a little bit scary is that as computer technology has moved to new generations, there has never been a case in which the leader in one generation was also the leader in the next. Microsoft, Intel, Apple, and a handful of others were the leaders in the PC generation. So, from a historical perspective, we are disqualified from leading the new generation. But we are attempting to defy the past. [7]

And so we stand poised at the threshold of the next generation of technology. No one knows how it will turn out; who will lead and who will follow; who will succeed and who will fail; and how it will change our society. Let us hope that the ultimate achievement of the information highway is to make life better and more rewarding for all human beings: To spread education and literacy, to give people the information they need to move forward, to improve communications and understanding among the peoples of the world. It's not home shopping and video on demand that makes this technology exciting. It is the opportunity to improve the well-being of all citizens through the power of information that is compelling. That is the promise of the information highway. Let us all work towards fulfilling it.

Glossary

This glossary offers brief definitions of acronyms and terminology that appear in this book and are widely used in discussions and publications relating to the information highway. Many of the cursory definitions given here are expanded upon in Chapter 4, which covers the basic technology behind the information highway, and in Chapters 2 and 3, which cover online services and the Internet, respectively.

ADSL (Asymmetrical Digital Subscriber Line) A technology based on existing twisted pair copper telephone cable that allows transmission speeds of 1.5 megabits per second for video and other broadband services.

Algorithm A set of instructions that forms the basis of a computer program similar to the idea of a recipe.

Alternative access carrier A local telephone service provider competing with the regional Bell operating company (RBOC) that services the same area.

Analog A transmission in the form of a continuous wave, "analogous" to the sound waves produced by the human voice or music. Most audio and video signals are still analog, although equivalent digital signals are the "wave of the future."

Analog/digital converter (ADC) An electronic device which converts analog signals to their digital equivalent.

ASCII (American Standard Code for Information Interchange) This code has become the standard code for representing text in binary form (*see also Byte*).

ATM (Asynchronous Transfer Mode) A transmission technology that combines features of both circuit-switched and packet-switched networks to enable transmissions speeds ranging from 155 megabits per second up to 2.4 gbits per second, making it a major contender for use in high-speed, broadband networks. However, ATM is still new.

Backbone A term for the primary transmission lines of a telephone or digital network.

Backchannel A generally low-bandwidth portion of the network reserved for responses from the subscriber back to the central information provider (for example, subscriber's menu choices would be transmitted on the backchannel back to the service provider).

Bandwidth A measurement of transmission capacity in either Hertz (cycles per second) or bits per second.

Baud A somewhat outdated term for modem speeds; equivalent to bits per second. The "baud rate" of a modem is its transmission speed in bits per second (e.g., a 2400 baud modem transmits 2400 bits per second).

BBS An ectronic bulletin board system.

Bit One unit of digital information (0 or 1); the term comes from "binary digit."

bps Bits per second; a measure of bandwidth or transmission speed.

Branch lines As the name suggests, branch lines are telephone lines that "branch off" the main "trunk lines." Lines going into a local neighborhood are branch lines.

Broadband Short for "broad bandwidth," meaning "high transmission capacity." Broadband networks enable transmission of the large volumes of data required for video and audio, as well as text.

Byte Eight bits is a byte, which is one character in the American Standard Code for Information Interchange (ASCII). ASCII includes all the letters of the alphabet, the numbers, and a variety of special characters.

CDMA (Code Division Multiple Access) An emerging digital transmission technology for cellular communications, which is supposedly 10 to 20 times faster than current analog cellular transmission techniques.

CD-ROM (Compact Disk-Read Only Memory) Currently the primary storage and distribution medium for multimedia applications on computers. CDs can hold about 600 Mb of data, making them suitable for storing audio and video data as well as text and graphics.

Cell (Cellular) The geographic area serviced by a single radio transmitter/receiver in a "cellular network." In other words, a cellular network is a network of cells, with each cell "handing off" the signal to the next cell to connect the parties of a cellular phone call.

CDPD (Cellular Digital Packet Data) A digital transmission technique that uses existing analog cellular circuits to transmit packets of data, enabling data transmission speeds of up to 19.2 kbps. CDPD uses a technique called "channel hopping" to take advantage of unused bandwidth on analog channels. CDPD is just being introduced for commercial use as this book goes to press.

Circuit switching The primary analog transmission technique used in today's telephone systems. The basic characteristic of circuit switching is that it requires an "end to end" connection between the calling and receiving parties and is therefore very inefficient for data communications.

Clipper chip A highly controversial encryption technology supported by the U.S. government.

Coaxial cable (Coax) The single copper cable wrapped in insulation that enters most homes to connect to cable TV networks. Coaxial cable is also used for many other types of communications applications, from satellite and VCR video cable to Ethernet-based local area networks.

Codec Short for coder/decoder, primarily referring to devices and software used for compressing and decompressing data, although it can also refer to the coding and decoding of encrypted data.

Common carriage This is regulatory jargon for the provision of basic telephone service on a universal basis.

Compression See Data compression.

Compression algorithm A particular set of instructions for compressing and decompressing data.

Conduit Term for the means of data transmission. For example, copper telephone cable and fiber optic cable are both types of "conduit."

Content The data that travels along the conduit. For example, electronic mail or digitized movies are "content."

Cyberspace The medium of electronic communications. When you're in cyberspace, you communicate "online" over the phone lines or over wireless radio waves.

Dark fiber Fiber optic cable that has been installed but is not in use. Many telephone companies have installed "dark fiber" alongside fiber cable that is already in operation as a means of planning ahead for the expansion of fiber optic networks. Dark fiber also refers to unused capacity of operational fiber optic cable.

Data compression Reducing the size of a given quantity of data that represents text, graphics, audio, or video, to speed up its transmission, without altering the basic content of the data. The compressed data can be reconstructed at the receiving end. Some compression techniques actually discard some of the information (lossy techniques), while others completely preserve the data (lossless). Much higher compression ratios can be realized using lossy techniques, but the quality of the preserved data deteriorates with increased compression ratios.

Decompression Reconstructing compressed data.

Digital A signal that is only either "on" or "off" represented by "0" or "1." Digital signals can be transmitted faster and are easier to work with than analog signals. Analog signals can be converted to digital equivalents, allowing digital signals to represent all kinds of information, including music and video.

DSP (Digital Signal Processor) A special purpose computer chip used for digital/analog and analog/digital conversion. It also has computational capability beyond signal conversion, so that it can be used as an auxiliary computing device.

DAC (Digital/Analog Converter) A device for converting digital signals to their analog equivalent.

DMT (Discrete Multi-Tone) A transmission technology for adapting standard copper telephone lines to digital broadband communications. *BYTE* Magazine (March, 1994) calls it "an experimental variation of ADSL." DMT provides four one-way video channels as well as two ISDN channels and an interactive "back channel," in addition to analog phone service, all on standard twisted-pair copper wire.

Downstream Data moving from a central location to the subscriber moves "downstream." Most initial bandwidth advances provide broadband capability in the downstream direction, that is, from the service provider to the office or home. Broadband capability in the upstream direction (from the home or office) is expected to come later.

e-mail Electronic mail, an electronic message containing text, graphics, even audio and video, which can be sent from one computer user to another over a computer network. Users of computer networks generally have an "e-mail address," to which you can send the e-mail message. For example, the author's email address is "nickbaran@bix.com."

Encryption Disguising information so it cannot be understood without a means of "undisguising" or decrypting the infomation.

Ethernet A popular network protocol used widely on Unix-based computer systems. Developed by Xerox, Ethernet was one of the first packet network protocols.

FCC Federal Communications Commission, charged with establishing regulatory policy for all forms of telecommunication in the United States, and therefore instrumental in determining the future of the information highway.

FDDI (Fiber Distributed Data Interface) A high-speed fiber optic based network technology primarily intended for local area networks.

Fiber in the loop Telecommunications jargon for fiber optic cable installed in the local telephone loop that services a neighborhood.

Fiber optic cable Glass fiber cable that sends signals by means of light pulses, allowing much faster transmission speeds than have been possible using copper cable.

Fiber to the curb Telecommunications jargon for fiber optic cable that's been installed up to the curb in front of the house. The final distance into the house is still copper cable in "fiber to the curb" installations. The idea here is that high-speed data can be transmitted into the neighborhood and then distributed using lower bandwidth cable such as coaxial.

Firewall Secure networks that can communicate with the Internet but are tightly controlled to prevent unauthorized access.

Flame An abusive or angry message on an online network.

FreeNet A community-sponsored network on the Internet, allowing citizens free access to the Internet.

Frequency The number of times per second a signal travels a complete wave length, measured in cycles per second or Hertz.

Full-motion video A minimum of 30 frames per second is considered full-motion video. The digital storage and transmission of full-motion video requires enormous storage capacity and high bandwidth, thus representing one of the major technical challenges of the information highway.

gbps Billions of bits per second.

GHz Billions of cycles per second (gigahertz).

Gigabyte One billion bytes.

Head end The central location from which cable TV networks broadcast to their subscribers. The cable head end is equipped with satellite dishes and radio transmitters that pick up the programs to be delivered to the network subscribers. Many cable head ends are switching to fiber optic cable for both receiving and delivering programming.

Hertz (Hz) Cycles per second, which is the unit of measurement of frequency.

HDTV (High-Definition TV) Advanced television technology that provides from two to four times the picture quality of standard television. Still very expensive and hampered by conflicting international standards, HDTV has been slow to emerge as a major force in the marketplace. Nevertheless, HDTV is expected to become very popular in the next few years and will probably be a major platform for interactive video services (*see also Platform*).

Hybrid fiber/coax Telecommunications jargon for a network consisting of a combination of fiber and coaxial cable. Fiber-to-the- curb systems are hybrid fiber/coax networks.

Hz (Hertz) Cycles per second.

Interactive Live, two-way communications; the ability to immediately send and receive responses on a computer or on a network.

Interexchange carriers A fancy term for long distance telephone companies.

ISDN (Integrated Services Digital Network) A digital transmission technology that operates on standard copper telephone cable, providing a standard bandwidth of 64 kbps and with options for bandwidth up to 1.5 mbits per second. Available through most major telephone companies, ISDN is popular in Europe and Japan but has been slow to take off in the U.S.

JPEG compression Joint Photographic Experts Group compression algorithm for still images.

kbps Thousands of bits per second.

KHz Thousands of cycles per second (kilohertz).

Kilobyte One thousand bytes.

LAN Local area network.

Local exchange carriers A fancy term for local phone companies.

mbps Millions of bits per second.

Megabits Millions of bits.

Megabyte One million bytes.

MHz Millions of cycles per second (megahertz).

MPEG compression Motion Pictures Experts Group compression algorithm for motion-picture images (video), which is likely to become the standard compression scheme used on the information highway.

Multimedia The combination of audio, video, text, and graphics in computer applications.

Network protocol (*see also Protocol*).

Node Term used for a computer or other device (e.g., a laser printer) that is part of a network. Information on the network travels from one node to another.

Online service Generally a centralized computer system that provides commercial electronic messaging and conferencing services to a network of subscribers (e.g., Compuserve, America On-Line).

Operating system The software that controls the basic functions of the computer (e.g., MS-DOS, Macintosh Finder). Set-top boxes also require an operating system.

Packet networks The idea of sending data in packets rather than in a continuous stream was developed for the ARPAnet project in the 1970s. It allowed data to be divided into small packets, each containing a destination address and sequencing codes so that the packets could reassembled at the receiving end, as well as error correction codes so that packets could be retransmitted if necessary. The concept of packets led to the development of "packet switching" as the preferred method for transmitting data as opposed to circuit switching used for voice transmission. Packet switching is the basic technology used in computer networks today.

Parallel processing A computer system that has multiple microprocessors working in parallel. Conventional desktop computers have a single central processing unit (CPU). Parallel processing systems are likely to be used for the video servers of the information highway.

PCS (Personal Communications Services) Services that will appear over the next few years in the wireless and cellular communications market. Companies are competing for a limited range of frequencies being auctioned off by the FCC for the purpose of PCS.

Personal communicator A handheld computing and communications device such as the Motorola Envoy. Personal digital assistants such as Apple's Newton are also evolving into personal communicators.

Pipes Telecommunications jargon for the means of transmitting data such as fiber optic cable, coaxial cable, radio waves. (*see also Conduit*).

Platform A particular computer or operating system on which applications run. For example, the Macintosh is a platform, as is MS-DOS. Unfortunately, there may be different and incompatible platforms on the information highway.

POTS (Plain Old Telephone System) Jargon for the current analog, copper-based telephone system.

Protocol An agreed upon set of instructions or commands that form a basis for communications.

RBOC Regional Bell Operating Companies or "baby Bells," resulting from the court-mandated breakup of AT&T in 1984.

Real-time If something takes place in real-time, it means that it is "live." There is no delay due to programming or scheduling. For example, when you "chat" on an online service with other users, exchanging messages that appear on your screen as they are entered from participants' keyboards, you are working in real-time. When you check your e-mail messages from yesterday, your dealing with stored information rather than with real-time communications.

Server A computer system that "serves" a distributed network of other computers by delivering information and serving as a central repository. For example, a "video server" is a computer system designed to deliver video programming to a network of connected computers (or set-top boxes).

Set-top box or converter The box that will sit on top of your television set and transmit and process the digital signals to and from the information highway. It will have the processing power of a modern desktop computer, as well as functions for analog/digital conversion, graphics, data encryption, and data compression/decompression. Basically, the set-top box converts your TV into a full-fledged multimedia computer system.

SONET (Synchronous Optical Network) A standard fiber optic transmission technology.

TCP/IP (Transport Control Protocol/Internetworking Protocol) The networking protocol that has become standard on the Internet, which primarily uses Unix-based computers (*see also Unix*).

Telco Jargon for "telephone company."

TDMA (Time Division Multiple Access) Like its cousin CDMA TDMA is an emerging form of digital wireless communications, which may be 10 to 20 faster than current analog transmission techniques.

Token Ring A packet network protocol that emerged about the same time as Ethernet and is popular on IBM-based computer networks.

Topology The layout of telephone cable. The "trunk and branch topology" of modern telephone systems means that long distances are connected by "trunks" (as in tree trunks), with local access provided by branches that connect to the trunks.

Trunk lines Long distance telephone lines (*see also Topology*).

Twisted-pair Current copper phone wire into most residences is so-called "twisted pair" wiring (two copper wires twisted together), in contrast to coaxial cable which is a single copper cable.

Unix A computer operating system developed in the early 1970s which is still the most popular operating system in universities and the federal government, and thus is the basic operating system used in the Internet networks.

Upstream The channel from the network subscriber back to the central server (*see also Downstream*).

User interface The software that allows the user of a computer system to execute commands or make choices is called the user interface. Microsoft Windows and the Macintosh Finder are graphical user interfaces (GUIs), with icons and menus that the user can select with a pointing device or a mouse. The user interfaces on the information highway are likely to be GUIs.

Video dial tone The "broadband" equivalent of the audio dialtone of today's telephone; the concept of an ever-present, always available signal that enables the user to connect to broadband services such as video programming, with the same ease associated with picking up a telephone and making a call.

Video server See Server.

VOD (Video On Demand) The ability to watch a video program of your choosing at any time of day simply by issuing a command or selecting a menu item on your TV screen. The video "content" could be anything from CNN news to first-run movies, waiting to be instantaneously transmitted from the video server.

WAN Wide area network; networks that operate over long distances as opposed to within a building or campus, which use a local area network. The information highway is essentially a collection of wide area networks.

Wireless Communications by radio waves are wireless communications (e.g. pagers, satellite communications, cellular telephones).

Wireline Communications involving wire or cable; primarily used when discussing wireless communications to distinguish between the wireless and wireline.

References

Chapter 1

1. Ray Valdes, "The Internet: Here Today," *Dr. Dobb's Developer Update*, Volume 1, Number 6, August, 1994
2. Summary Statement, Blacksburg Electronic Village, Blacksburg, VA, January 1, 1994

Chapter 2

1. John Levine, *Modems for Dummies*, IDG Books
2. Daniel Dern, *The Internet Guide for New Users*, McGraw-Hill, 1994, pps. 451-2

Chapter 3

1. Mary Luc Carnevale, "World-Wide Web," *The Wall Street Journal*, special Technology insert, November 15, 1993
2. Robert Kahn, "Networks for Advanced Computing," *Scientific American*, October, 1987
3. Daniel P. Dern, *The Internet Guide for New Users*, McGraw-Hill, 1994
4. Mary Luc Carnevale, op. cit.
5. Paul Wallich, "Wire Pirates," *Scientific American*, March, 1994
6. *The Wall Street Journal*, March 8, 1994
7. *The Wall Street Journal*, January 17, 1994
8. *The Internet Business Journal* (Ottawa, Ontario, Canada) Telephone: 613-747-6106
9. The National Public Telecomputing Network
P.O. Box 1987
Cleveland, OH 44106

Chapter 4

1. Robert Kahn, "Networks for Advanced Computing," *Scientific American*, October, 1987
2. Vinton Cerf, "Networks," *Scientific American*, September, 1991
3. Nicholas Negroponte, "Products and Services for Computer Networks," *Scientific American*, September 1991
4. Mark Clarkson, "All-Terrain Networking," *BYTE*, August, 1993
5. "Telecommunications Systems," *Encyclopaedia Britannica*, Volume 28, Chicago, 1991
6. Andy Reinhardt, "Building the Data Highway," *BYTE*, March 1994
7. Gary Stix, "Domesticating Cyberspace," *Scientific American*, August, 1993
8. *The Wall Street Journal*, February 18, 1994
9. *Fiber Optic Product News*, May, 1993
10. *The Wall Street Journal*, special insert on wireles communications, February 11, 1994
11. *The Wall Street Journal*, February 22, 1994
12. Gary Stix, "Aging Airways," *Scientific American*, May, 1994

Notes:

The September 1991 special issue of *Scientific American*, "Communications, Computers, and Networks" is highly recommended if you want to get the views of some of the leading scientists who are developing this technology.

Andy Reinhardt's article in *BYTE* is an excellent, but fairly technical overview of some of the primary technical and political issues regarding the information highway.

For a unique perspective on the Time Warner Orlando project, see Ken Auletta's article, "The Magic Box," in the April 11, 1994 issue of *The New Yorker*.

Chapter 5

1. *The Wall Street Journal*, February 9, 1994
2. *Computer World*, December 6, 1993
3. Mead Data Central press information (800-253-5624)
4. *The Wall Street Journal*, February 21, 1994

5. *The Wall Street Journal*, March 8, 1994
6. *Newsbytes*, March 30, 1994
7. *The Wall Street Journal*, April 8, 1994
8. *PR Newswire*, March 3, 1994 (800-832-5522)
9. *Newsbytes*, March 11, 1994 (on-line news service)
10. *The Wall Street Journal*, February 18, 1994
11. *The Wall Street Journal*, January 25, 1994
12. *Newsbytes*, April 20, 1994
13. *Newsbytes*, May 12, 1994
14. *The Wall Street Journal*, April 7, 1994
15. *The Wall Street Journal*, May 19, 1994
16. *PR Newswire*, May 3, 1994 (comments of C. Michael Armstrong, chairman of GM Hughes Electronic Corp., which manufactures satellite systems and commissioned the cited study)
17. Smart Valley Corporation press materials, February, 1994
18. *Information Week*, August 16, 1993
19. *The Wall Street Journal*, May 9, 1994
20. *The Wall Street Journal*, May 4, 1994
21. *The Wall Street Journal*, May 13, 1994
22. *The Wall Street Journal*, March 21, 1994. Special Insert on Entertainment and Technology

Chapter 6

1. *Congressional Quarterly*, Special Report, "The Information Arena," May 14 1994, Supplement to No. 19, Washington D.C.
2. *Newsbytes*, May 19, 1994
3. *The Wall Street Journal*, May 23, 1994
4. As of this writing, the two bills before the Senate and House which will determine the degree of competition and provisions for universal access are S 1822, sponsored by Senators Hollings and Danforth, and H 3626, sponsored by Representatives Brooks and Dingell. Another bill that will affect telecommunications policy is H 3636, sponsored by Representatives Markey and Fields. For a detailed summary of these bills, see the *Congressional Quarterly* Special report.

5. The FCC ruled in 1992 that "local exchange carriers" could provide video dialtone service.
6. *Phoenix Gazette*, May 14, 1994; also *USA Today*, May 14, 1994
7. The Electronic Frontier Foundation, "The Open Platform," Washington D.C.
   See also Electronic Frontier Foundation's newsletter, "Networks and Policy," Vol. 1, Issue 1, Washington D.C. (email address is eff@eff.org)
8. *Wall Street Journal*, April 4, 1994
9. *BYTE* Magazine, "Building the Data Highway," March, 1994
10. Information Infrastructure Task Force, "The National Information Infrastructure: Agenda for Action," September 15, 1993, Washington D.C.; available from the National Telecommunications and Information Administration (NTIA), Washington D.C. (email address is nii@ntia.doc.gov)
11. Taxpayer Assets Project, Information Policy Note, "Comments on the Clinton Administration 'Vision Statement' for the NII," September 14, 1993, Washington D.C. (email address is tap@essential.org); see also *The Wall Street Journal*, "Gore's Data Highway: Another Entitlement," January 31, 1994; and *Newsweek*, "Is the Devil in the Details?" January 24, 1994
12. Ken Auletta, "Under the Wire," *The New Yorker*, January 17, 1994
13. Cross Industry Working Team (XIWT), press release, December 13, 1993 (main contact is Corporation for National Research Initiatives (CNRI), Washington D.C.)
14. *Newsbytes*, May 25, 1994
15. *The New York Times*, November 24, 1993
16. *The Wall Street Journal*, May 27, 1994
17. *The Wall Street Journal*, April 9, 1994
18. *The New York Times*, April 19, 1994
19. John Seabrook, "My First Flame," *The New Yorker*, June 6, 1994
20. *The Wall Street Journal*, April 22, 1994
21. *The Wall Street Journal*, May 27, 1994
22. *Newsbytes*, April 21, 1994
23. Anne W. Branscomb, "Common Law for the Electronic Frontier," Scientific American, September 1991 (We strongly recom-

mend this issue for an excellent overview of both the technical and social issues in telecommunications and networks.)

24. *Publisher's Weekly*, April 18, 1994
25. *The Wall Street Journal*, December 17, 1993

Chapter 7

1. *The Wall Street Journal*, special technology supplement, June 27, 1994
2. Alan Kay, "Computers, Networks, and Education," *Scientific American*, September, 1991
3. Smart 2000 Conferencing System, Smart Technologies, Calgary, Alberta, Canada; telephone: 403-233-9333
4. TeleEducation NB Annual Report, 1994, Fredericton, New Brunswick, Canada
5. *Newsbytes*, June 28, 1994
6. *Big Sky Telegraph*, University of Montana, Western Montana College, Dillon, Montana (e:mail franko@bigsky.dillon.mt.us)
7. For more information on satellite courses, contact U.S. Distance Learning Association, Box 5129, San Ramon, CA 94583, Tel: 510-606-5150
8. Society for Applied Learning Technology, 50 Culpeper Street, Warrenton, VA 22186 Tel: 703-347-0055
9. *The Wall Street Journal*, special technology supplement, November 15, 1993
10. PBS Learning Link, 1320 Braddock Place, Alexandria, VA 22314, Tel: 703-739-8464 (e-mail: pheeter@ll.pbs.org)
11. PBS Learning Link, Content Summary Guide, Alexandria, VA
12. *Bay Area Computer Currents*, February 8, 1994
13. Newbytes, January 11, 1994
14. *ED, Education at a Distance* (Journal of the USDLA), January, 1994, Volume 8, #1
15. *Spokesman-Review* (Spokane, WA), June 27, 1994
16. *Newsbytes*, May 12, 1994
17. *Newsbytes*, June 6, 1994
18. "Libraries," *Encyclopaedia Britannica*, Volume 28, Chicago, 1991
19. Nicholson Baker, "Discards," *The New Yorker*, April 4, 1994
20. National Public Radio, June 27, 1994

Chapter 8

1. Bruce Schneier, *Applied Cryptography*, John Wiley & Sons, New York, 1994
2. Paul Wallich, "Wire Pirates," *Scientific American* , March, 1994
3. William J. Mitchell, "When Is Seeing Believing?" *Scientific American*, February, 1994
4. *Newsbytes*, July 6, 1994
5. Special Report on Invasion of Privacy, *Boston Globe*, September 5 to September 8, 1993 (This report appeared in the *Spokesman-Review*, Spokane, Washington, on Jan. 30, 1994, and may have appeared in other newspapers.)
6. *Spokesman Review* (Spokane, WA), February 25, 1994
7. *Scientific American*, March, 1994 op. cit.
8. Winn Schwartau, *Information Warfare: Chaos on the Electronic Superhighway*, Thunder's Mouth Press, New York, 1994
9. Shaffer and Simon, *Network Security*, Academic Press (Harcourt Brace), Cambridge, MA, 1994
10. *Scientific American*, March, 1994 op. cit.
11. *The Wall Street Journal*, March 22, 1994
12. *Fortune*, May 16, 1994
13. *The Wall Street Journal*, June 3, 1994
14. Paulina Borsook, "Highway Safety: The Key Is Encryption," *BYTE*, March, 1994 (sidebar to the feature story entitled "Building the Data Highway")

Chapter 9

1. Links, Diepstraten, Hayes, "Universal Wireless LANs," *BYTE*, May, 1994
2. Andrew Seybold, *Using Wireless Communications in Business*, Van Nostrand Reinhold, New York, 1994
3. *The Wall Street Journal*, special insert on wireless communications, February 11, 1994
4. Harvey and Santalesa, "Wireless Gets Real," *BYTE*, May, 1994
5. *Newsbytes*, March 1, 1994
6. *Newsbytes*, July 28, 1994
7. *The Wall Street Journal*, March 1, 1994

8. *The Wall Street Journal*, June 30,1994
9. Media Advisory, AirTouch Communications, June, 1994
10. *The Wall Street Journal*, July 22, 1994
11. *The Wall Street Journal*, July 26, 1994
12. *The Wall Street Journal*, August 1, 1994
13. Peter Wayner, "Agents Away," *BYTE*, May, 1994

Chapter 10

1. *The Wall Street Journal*, June 1, 1994
2. *San Francisco Examiner* "Future World" supplement, July 17, 1994
3. Bill Gates' speech to the Commonwealth Club, San Francisco, October, 21, 1993
4. *The Wall Street Journal*, March 21, 1994
5. Veronis, Suhler & Assoc. *Communications Industry Forecast*, New York, July 1994
6. *San Francisco Examiner*, op. cit.
7. Andy Reinhardt, "Video Conquers the Desktop," *BYTE*, September, 1993
8. Andy Reinhardt, "Managing the New Document," *BYTE*, August, 1994
9. Spokesman-Review (Spokane, WA), June 20, 1994
10. *The Wall Street Journal*, Special "Entertainment and Technology Supplement," March 21, 1994
11. *San Francisco Examiner*, op. cit.
12. Rheingold, Howard, *Virtual Reality*, Summit, New York, 1991
13. *The Wall Street Journal*, July 6, 1994
14. *The Wall Street Journal*, Special "Entertainment and Technology Supplement," March 21, 1994
15. *The Wall Street Journal*, May 23, 1994
16. *The Wall Street Journal*, July 6, 1994 (op. cit)
17. *The Wall Street Journal*, August 1, 1994
18. *The Wall Street Journal*, Special "Entertainment and Technology Supplement," March 21, 1994

Chapter 11

1. CommerceNet press release, Smart Valley, Inc., November 24, 1993, Menlo Park, California
2. *The Wall Street Journal*, September 13, 1994
3. *The Internet Letter*, Washington D.C., e:mail: netweek@access.digex.net, Netweek, Inc., Telephone: 202-638-6020
4. Nicholas Baran, "Businesses Turn to BBSs," *BYTE*, September, 1994
5. *The Internet Letter*, op. cit., July 1, 1994
6. *The Wall Street Journal*, January 17, 1994
7. Bill Gates, speech to the Commonwealth Club, San Francisco, California, October 21, 1993

Resource Guide

This resource guide presents some of the BBS systems and on-line services mentioned in the book and other services that are worth checking out. Obviously, the list is just a sampling of the available services. Some reference books with more comprehensive listings are also provided. Note that if no "modem number" is provided, it is necessary to call the voice number and get the local modem access number. Many services provide local phone connections, depending on where you live.

Bulletin Board Systems

Audiophile Network:
Modem: 818-988-0452
This BBS will be music to your ears if you are interested in audo equipment and state-of-the-art music systems.

Aviation Total Information Systems:
Voice: 703-242-0161; Modem: 703-242-3520 or 703-242-3534

CompuFarm BBS:
Modem: 403-556-4243
Farm and livestock, agricultural information.

Exec-PC:
Voice : 414-789-4200; Modem: 414-789-4210
The November15, 1994 *Wall Street Journal* says this is "the largest BBS in the country, with focus on business-oriented discussions and software."

Federal Communications Commission (FCC) Public Access Link:
Voice: 301-725-1585 Modem: 301-725-1072

FedWorld:
Modem: 703-321-8020
If you're interested in getting the latest information that the U.S. federal government puts out, you'll need to access this BBS. This

BBS is also a gateway to more than 100 other government-agency bulletin boards.

Government Printing Office BBS (GPO Access):
Voice: 202-512-1530; Modem: 202-512-1387
Provides online access to federal documents such as the *Congressional Record* and the *Federal Register*, with more government information going online all the time. Supports Wide Area Information Server (WAIS) search and retrieval software for Internet users.

Greenpeace Environet:
Modem: 415-512-9120
If you are concerned about protecting the environment, this BBS will keep you informed about the latest issues and trends.

HerpNet:
Voice: 215-464-3561; Modem Number: 215-464-3562
BBS on reptiles and herpetology.

HouseNet:
Modem: 410-745-2037
This BBS provides useful information on every household related topic you can think of from repairing your roof to adding a security door.

Legal Ease BBS:
Modem: 509-326-3238

Movies-by-Modem:
Voice: 216-861-0467; Modem: 216-694-5736

NASA Space Link:
Voice: 205-544-6360 Modem: 205-895-0028

National Genealogical Society:
Voice: 703-525-0050; Modem: 703-528-2612
The place to go for information on genealogy; tracking your ancestry.

On-line Bookstore:
Voice: 800-233-0233; Modem: 215-657-6130

People's Electronic Exchange:
Modem: 908-685-0948
This is the BBS to check when you are looking for a new job.

Small Business Administration BBS:
Voice 800-827-5722; Modem: 800-859-INFO (2400 bps), 800-692-INFO (9600)

Software Creations:
Modem: 508-368-7036
Software Creations was voted the best BBS in the country by readers of the leading online magazine, *Boardwatch*. This BBS is the clearinghouse for great game software, shareware, freeware, graphics files, and much more.

Superdemoceracy Foundation BBS:
Voice: 305-370-7850; Modem: 305-370-9376
Discuss electronic democracy and other issues related to democracy.

Trader's Connection (computerized classified ads):
Voice: 800-753-4223 (call for local access modem numbers)
Modem (central modem number, where you can find local access numbers and also get a "guided tour"of the system): 317-359-5199

U.S. Census Bureau:
Voice: 301-763-7662; Modem: 301-763-4574

Windows Online
Modem: 510-736-8343
This BBS offers more than 12,000 files of Windows software for downloading.

Online Services and Databases

The numbers provided here are voice numbers, since these services all have local telephone access. Services such as CompuServe and America Online also offer special deals for new customers in computer magazine advertisements. Also, many computer retail outlets sell start-up packages for the big online services, which provide the software as well as local phone access numbers.

America Online: 800-827-6364
CompuServe: 800-848-8199
BIX: 800-695-4775
Delphi (Internet access): 800-695-4005

Dow Jones News/Retrieval: 800-522-3567

GEnie: 800-638-9636

MCI Mail: 800-444-6245

NewsNet: 800-345-1301 Online database with full text of 600 newspapers, magazines, and other publications.

NEXIS/LEXIS (Mead Data Central): 800-253-5624

Performance Systems International (Internet access): 703-620-6651

Prodigy: 800-776-3449

BBS Information

BBS Software Providers

Galacticomm, Inc. (IBM PC-compatible)
Fort Lauterdale, FL
305-583-5990

Spider Island (Telefinder for Macintosh)
Irvine, CA
714-669-9260

Mustang Software (IBM PC-compatible)
Bakersfield, CA
805-873-2500

BBS-Related Publications

ModemUSA, Second Edition
Allium Press
P.O. Box 5752-55
Takoma Park, MD 20912

Provides listings of BBSs

Boardwatch
8500 Lo. Bowles Ave.
Suite 210
Littleton, CO 80123
800-933-6038

Provides listings of BBSs as well as BBS software for setting up your own BBS

Online Access
900 N. Franklin, Suite #310
Chicago, IL 60610
312-573-1700

Rutten, Bayers, Maloni, *Netguide, Your Map to the Services, Information, and Entertainment on the Electronic Highway*, Random House, 1994

This book has been called the "TV Guide to Cyberspace," and that's a fairly accurate description. It has comprehensive information on Internet, BBSs, and on-line services.

Rittner, *The Whole Earth Online Almanac*, Prentice Hall, 1994

Books about the Internet

1. Daniel P. Dern, *The Internet Guide for New Users*, McGraw-Hill, 1993
2. Ed Krol, *The Whole Internet User's Guide and Catalog*, Second Edition, O'Reilly & Associates, 1994
3. Lambert & Howe, *Internet Basics*, Random House, 1993
4. Rutten, Bayers, Maloni, *Netguide, Your Map to the Services, Information, and Entertainment on the Electronic Highway*, Random House, 1994
5. Susan Estrada, *Connecting to the Interent*, O'Reilly & Associates, 1994
6. Cheswick and Bellovin, *Firewalls and Internet Security*, Addison-Wesley, 1994
7. John Levine and Carol Baroudi, *The Internet for Dummies*, IDG Books, 1993
8. Harley Hahn and Rick Stout, *The Internet Complete Reference*, Osborne McGraw-Hill, 1994
9. Virginia Shea, *Netiquette*, Albion Books, 1994
10. Harley Hahn and Rick Stout, *The Internet Yellow Pages*, Osborne McGraw-Hill, 1994
11. Michael Fraase, *The PC Internet Tour Guide*, Ventana Press, 1994
12. Paul Gilster, *The Internet Navigator*, John Wiley & Sons, 1994
13. Tracy LaQuey, *The Internet Companion*, Addison-Wesley, 1994
14. Pat Vincent, *Free $tuff from the Internet*, Coriolis Group Books, 1994
15. Carl Malamud, *Exploring the Internet: A Technical Travelogue*, Prentice-Hall, 1992
16. Joshua Eddings, *How the Internet Works*, Ziff-Davis Press, 1994

17. Greg Notess, *Internet Access Providers: An International Resource Directory*, meckler, 1994
18. Eric Braun, *The Internet Directory*, Fawcett Columbine, 1994
19. Mary Cronin, *Doing Business on the Internet*, Van Nostrand Reinhold, 1994
20. Brent Heslop & David Angell, *The Instant Internet Guide*, Addison-Wesley, 1994
21. Paul Gilster, *Finding It on the Internet*, John Wiley & Sons, 1994
22. Bryan Pfaffenberger, *Internet in Plain English*, MIS Press, 1994
23. David Peal, *Access the Internet*, Sybex, 1994
24. Sharon Fisher and Rob Tidrow, *Riding the Internet Highway*, New Riders Publishing, 1994
25. Adam Engst, Corwin Low, and Michael Simon, *Internet Starter Kit for Windows*, Hayden, 1994
26. David Sachs and Henry Stair, *Hands-On Internet*, Prentice Hall, 1994
27. Mark Veljkov and George Hartnell, *Pocket Guides to the Internet*, Volumes 1-4, Mecklermedia, 1994
28. *The Internet Resource*, Que Publishing, 1994

Information about FreeNets

National Public Telecomputing Network
Cleveland, OH
216-247-5800
e-mail: info@nptn.org

General Internet Information

International Internet Association
Washington, DC
800-669-4780
Commercial Internet Access Providers

The following is a sampling of Internet providers taken from a *PC Week* special report:

Company	Service Area	Telephone
Alternet	U.S. and International	800-488-6383
ANS	U.S. and International	313-663-7610
BARRNet	Northern and central Calif.	415-723-7520
CERFnet	Western U.S. and International	619-455-3900 or 800-876-2373
CICnet	Midwestern U.S.	313-998-6102
COSupernet	Colorado	303-273-3471
CONCERT	North Carolina	919-248-1404
CSUnet	California	310-985-9661
Interaccess	Chicago	708-671-0111
International Connections Manager	International	703-904-2230
INet	Indiana	812-855-4240
JVNCnet	U.S. and International	800-358-4437
Los Nettos	Los Angeles	310-822-1511
MichNet/Merit	Michigan	313-764-9430
MIDnet	Middle U.S.	402-472-5032
MRnet	Minnesota	612-342-2570
MSEN	Michigan	313-998-4562
NEARnet	Northeastern U.S.	617-873-8730
NETCOM	California	408-554-8649
netIllinois	Illinois	309-677-3100
NevadaNet	Nevada	702-784-6133
NorthwestNet	Pacific Northwest	206-562-3000
NYSERnet	New York	315-453-2912
OARnet	Ohio	614-292-8100
PACCOM	Hawaii	808-946-3499
PREPnet	Pennsylvania	412-268-7870
PCSnet	Eastern U.S.	412-268-4960
PSInet	U.S. and International	800-827-7482 or 703-620-6651

(continued)

Company	***Service Area***	***Telephone***
SDSCnet	San Diego	619-534-5043
Sesquinet	Texas	713-527-4988
SprintLink	U.S. and International	703-904-2230
SURAnet	Southeastern U.S.	301-982-4600
THEnet	Texas	512-471-3241
VERnet	Virginia	804-924-0616
WELL	U.S. and International	415-332-4335
Westnet	Western U.S.	303-262-8874
WiscNet	Wisconsin	608-262-8874
Wordl dot Net	Pacific Northwest	206-576-7147
WVNET	West Virginia	304-293-5192

Index

D

J

K

L

M

N